Trust Training:

A Field Manual for Confident Trust in God
Before, During and After Life's Battles

By Dionne Carpenter

Blessings on your head ~
Dionne Carpenter

Wild Socks Press
San Diego, CA

Published by Wild Socks Press
San Diego, CA

In association with
Brilliant Printers Pvt. Ltd. – India
#18 & 19, L G Halli, R M V II Stage
Bangalore – 560 094, INDIA

ISBN: 978-0-615-24559-1

Design and layout by Melanie Myers Design
design@melaniemyers.net

Requests for information should be directed to Dionne Carpenter at

Wild Socks Press
www.wildsockspress.com
dionne@wildsockspress.com

ACKNOWLEDGEMENTS & DEDICATION

I didn't start writing until a few years ago. Before then I had no answers – only questions and angst. Trust training helped me piece things together. Eventually the principles I learned fit together into a full-blown book outline. I even wrote a few chapters. But the words wouldn't come yet, and my dream book sat on the shelf for four years.

Then Bonita Valley Baptist Church invited Jim to become her senior pastor and we moved here to San Diego. Little did we know how much we would come to love and need this amazing church family.

In August, 2006, I underwent routine out-patient surgery to remove my gall bladder. It went terribly wrong and I almost died. But an odd thing happened. My hospital stay was a final exam of sorts of my own trust training. I did what God had trained me to do. And it worked!

I came home fired up to share what I'd learned. Within weeks after leaving ICU, I started the first *Trust Training* Bible study, using the chapters I had already written. The ladies liked what they saw, and encouraged me to finish the book, which I did in between two more surgeries.

For the past two years they have journeyed with me through two versions of this Bible study, helping me to hone the ideas and make them more user-friendly, so that, although my outline stayed the same, the book is far richer because of what we learned together.

This book is gratefully dedicated –

To Angela, Ann, Danielle, Debbie, Jennifer, Jerleen, Julie, Karen N., Karen S., Lois, Lynn, Michelle, Pat B., Pat T., Paula, Rhonda, Susan, and Treva – the caring and courageous women in the *Trust Training* Bible studies;

To Jim, the love of my life, whose support gave me a safe place to wrestle with God until I finally saw that God was maybe a perfect version of him;

To the women who generously shared their stories;

To Jim, Debbie Vail, Karen Northrup, and Barbara Chenault, chief among many who proofread countless revisions of this book and gave invaluable feedback;

To the people of Bonita Valley Baptist Church who supported us in a hundred big and little ways, and who prayed me back to health;

But, most of all, to my Abba Father, who kept my incision from healing for more than nine months, giving me precious time to write the rest of the book I had carried in my heart for so long, and who gave me exactly enough pain to keep the writing real.

TABLE OF CONTENTS

PART ONE:

Introduction

WAIT! BEFORE YOU START READING...

This book explores Bible stories that may be unfamiliar to some. To bring everyone up to speed in each chapter, we've provided a short pre-study exercise to read the relevant Bible story and nail down a few main ideas. You'll find it at the end of the chapter, as *Part 1* on the page entitled *"FACE TIME WITH MY TRAINER."*

Although it's tempting to read the chapter first, you'll get a lot more out of it and it will make more sense if you've done that bit of homework first. *Part 2* is intended to help you process the chapter itself and will be easier to complete afterwards.

Oh, and double your fun by going through this Bible Study with a friend or two!

CHAPTER 1

Trust Training

He trains my hands for battle…
Psalm 18:34

I can remember rattling off Proverbs 3:5, 6 to Mrs. Hill, my third grade Sunday school teacher, *"Trust in the Lord with all your heart; and lean not on your own understanding; in all your ways acknowledge Him, and He will make your paths straight."*

It's easy to remember. People often throw in those verses when they give advice.

You've got a problem, a worry, a fear, a dilemma, a decision to make? What should you do?

Simple.

Trust God.

Maybe not so simple.

Given half a chance, most children find it easy to trust. I know I did. I couldn't have asked for a better beginning. From the day my folks brought me home from the hospital and proudly showed me off to the other seminary students at Bible College, I thrived under their loving protection. My brother learned to walk on an ocean liner that carried us overseas to the mission field. We had a great heritage, the branches on both sides of our family tree generously sprinkled with missionaries, church planters, and passionate lay leaders.

Surrounded by love in a stable home, attending healthy, Bible-believing churches, with Christians on all sides, you might think it would have been easy to trust God.

Within two years after graduating from Mrs. Hill's class the bottom fell out of my world. A close family member began to molest me, a nightmare that went on for six excruciating years. I felt so ashamed. I thought it disqualified me beyond any hope of cleansing or redemption. I was utterly alone and afraid, so I kept the secret. When I finally worked up the courage to tell someone, it did not go well. My family members closed ranks, blamed everything on me, and pretended that nothing had happened. I gutted it out alone for two more years, eluded my tormenter as best I could, and fled away to college. I left home, pretty much forever.

Something breaks inside your spirit when the worst thing you can imagine actually happens to you. It kicks open a door in your mind leaving you vulnerable to every fear and insecurity. You have no defense against your fears, and no way of reassuring yourself, "Oh, don't be silly. That could never happen." You stop taking anything for granted. You stop trusting.

Even if the respectable Christian family I thought I could trust had rallied around me, it would have been difficult to learn how to trust again. When they turned against me, it became that much harder to fight my way back to a simple childlike trust.

Either way, I found it impossible to trust God. Why had He allowed it to happen to me? I thought He was angry and distant, like my dad. I assumed that He condemned me, too. God seemed too powerful to trust. How could I be sure He wouldn't betray me?

By high school, my heart grew hard and callous. After hearing hundreds of evangelistic sermons over the course of my young lifetime, I stopped going forward when I heard an altar invitation. Instead, I sat in the back row and evaluated the speaker's technique.

Every once in a while when I worried about my stony heart, I prayed what turned out to be a powerful prayer, "God, my heart is dead. I can't change it. If You really exist somewhere out there, please break through to me and give me a heart of flesh to follow You."

Even though I kept going to church, married a wonderful preacher, and remained active in church ministry, I locked away my deeply wounded heart. I worshiped God, but held Him at a distance.

I write about trust because God answered my high school prayer. For thirty years He patiently helped me mend bits and pieces of my shattered heart and gently coaxed me back to Himself. I am a trophy of His grace.

He worked through godly counselors and significant experiences along the way. He worked through my wonderful husband who showed me unconditional love and gave me a better model of what God might be like – patient, kind, and understanding.

When my heart was whole, God introduced Himself to me all over again, and like a newfound soul mate invited me to get to know Him as friend. As I became more comfortable in His presence He taught me how to trust Him. Praise God, He helped me to feel safe in His presence.

Well, that's my story. Now let's stop a minute and think about your story. Some of you have identified with my trauma because you've also had some pretty hard hits in your life. The details may be different, but you know all about that yearning for safety and protection. Some of you can't relate at all. You had a great childhood that seamlessly ushered you into an adult trust in God.

The rest of you are somewhere in the middle. Even if you've been a Christian for awhile, you've tripped over some bumps in the road. Maybe you prayed for something and God didn't answer the way you expected. Your disappointment has raised a barrier between you and God. Maybe you grew up in a church that emphasized God's wrath and obeying lots of rules. Maybe your church didn't talk much about having a personal relationship with God. Maybe people betrayed your trust and you have protected your heart to avoid more pain. You didn't notice that, in your zeal not to get hurt, you were also shutting out God.

Whatever your situation, it's my observation that trust in God does not grow unless we work at it. It is far easier to drift away from trusting God than to drift into deeper trust in God.

If you think about it, the command to trust God with all our hearts is one of the most challenging tasks of the Christian life. People like me who have had some traumatic experiences find it hard to wade through our emotional baggage and learn to trust God. You might think that people with happy, untroubled lives find it easier, and some do. But those with easy lives often merely skim the surface in their understanding of how to trust God.

That familiar Proverb tells us to *"trust in the Lord <u>with all our hearts</u>."* The heart is the arena where trust happens. Most other commands in the Bible can be done as an act of faith or even as ritual, without regard to how we feel at a particular moment. We can put money in the offering plate or bite into a communion wafer whether we feel close to God or far away. We can memorize Bible verses and the *Four Spiritual Laws®* and fill our heads with Bible facts even if we've bolted the door of our heart against the unpredictable presence of the Holy One.

But God wants our hearts. Listen to the grief in His voice, *"These people honor Me with their lips, but their hearts are far from Me"* (Mt. 15:8). He longs to save us to the uttermost, not just redeeming our head with its logical left-brained, methodical pursuit of truth, but also our messy right-brained subconscious mind, full of its grab bag of contradictory and fluctuating feelings and emotions. He wants us, PMS, bad hair days and all!

He wants us to feel safe with Him. He wants us to move beyond duty into delight. **He wants us to learn to trust Him the same way we learn to trust any other person in our lives – by getting to know Him and by finding Him to be reliable in tough times.**

In this book I'll explore some of the questions that baffled me, and share what helped turn on the light for me. If you look at the table of contents you'll notice a few introductory chapters and then a grid of chapters under the headings *Before, During* and *After.* In the first five chapters I'll explore these basic questions.

- What is trust and how exactly do we trust God?
- Why don't we learn to trust just by memorizing a few verses, listening to sermons or reading books?
- What's the difference between faith and trust?
- What's the difference between passive and active trust?
- How can the crises we face make it both harder and easier to trust God?
- What's God doing up there while we're having trouble trusting Him?

Then we will look at how to make good use of those big and little scary situations that come up in our lives. We'll learn how to turn them into training exercises.

I've noticed that we all juggle two types of trust dilemmas. We always have "the small moment," the trust issue for today, the daily choice to trust God. We'll talk about what we can do anytime or anywhere to bring ourselves into a trust connection with God.

We also have "big trust challenges." These are ongoing situations that may take some time to navigate. They ebb and flow and usually have some kind of beginning, middle and end. They take many forms, like maybe a stressful job situation, a family conflict, some persistent bad habits or the struggle to recover from a devastating loss. They can be worries like "How will we pay for college?" or "How can we prepare for retirement?" We'll talk about how to approach these situations as a whole, and how to handle the various trust issues that come up as each phase unfolds.

I'm guessing that this study caught your eye because you also find it frustrating and confusing to trust God. Together we can figure out this problem. The rewards are huge. It's good to be able to rattle off a Bible verse. But together, let's move beyond quoting Bible verses and discover the deep satisfaction that comes from trusting God.

Let's start by talking about the title of this study.

WHAT EXACTLY IS TRUST TRAINING?

I learned this model of evaluating trust situations (or *trust battles* as I came to think of them) about eight years ago. God had healed many of the wounds of my childhood and I started fresh, armed with a lifetime of experience and hundreds of sermons, Bible studies and personal observations. But I had no clue how to trust God in a particular situation. I knew one new thing: God is trustworthy. He is my Refuge and my Rock. He became for me the God who is safe.

About that time, I hit an unusually rough patch when I started a new job. Usually I settle in quickly but this job threw me for a loop. One thing after another went wrong, such as confusing task procedures, co-worker issues, and a short-term financial shortfall. My hormones got out of whack. Oh, and with impeccable timing, my mother sent me an upsetting letter.

I stumbled around for awhile dealing with each crisis. I'd pray like crazy – all the while feeling guilty about my churned up emotions. I'd beat myself up for my lack of trust in God. Eventually, I'd figure out a way to muddle through, only to tumble headlong into another problem. These back-to-back crises went on for about two months.

What bothered me the most during those two months was that I found it impossible to live up to my idea of what it meant to trust God. Although I didn't realize it at the time, I had a pretty narrow view of what this trusting business might look like. It was as if I had two choices when problems came my way – either trust God or do something. I saw trust in God only as an attitude of patient, calm, and mostly passive waiting.

Back then my unconscious image of trust probably came right out of those medieval paintings of the saints or the Madonna sitting quietly, with hands folded, gazing sweetly toward heaven, calmly waiting for God. Can you just picture the hint of a halo?

However, I was in the middle of so much turmoil at my new job that I couldn't figure out how to pull off that type of trust. I had no time to sit, either figuratively or literally. I desperately needed answers and strategies – right then – to solve my problems. Even so, I longed to trust God in the middle of all that chaos and uncertainty. I just didn't know how.

Finally, I went to the Lord to complain.

"Enough is enough. I'm sick of fumbling around. Please show me a better way to face these problems. Now that I know You can be trusted, show me how exactly to trust You."

God answered my cry for help by leading me to Psalm 18. Probably more than any other Bible character, David understood the nuances of God's trustworthiness and how to live by the light of that great truth. As I studied Psalm 18, to my surprise David sketches two main ways to approach trust in God. Both ways truly honor God and work just fine. The first way fit pretty well with my preconceived idea of the passive trust illustrated so beautifully in those Madonna paintings. I had never noticed the second.

David starts the Psalm with a glorious song to God, piling up word pictures that describe God's trustworthiness.

> *I love you, O LORD, my strength. The LORD is my rock, my fortress and my deliverer; my God is my rock, in whom I take refuge. He is my shield and the horn of my salvation, my stronghold. I call to the LORD, who is worthy of praise, and I am saved from my enemies.*

Because David trusted God, when he got into trouble, into situations he was helpless to change, he cried out to God for help. Verses 4 – 19 describe the thrilling story. I won't quote the whole passage. You can get the general idea from these excerpts:

> *The cords of death entangled me; the torrents of destruction overwhelmed me. In my distress I called to the LORD; I cried to my God for help. From his temple he heard my voice; my cry came before him, into his ears. He parted the heavens and came down. The LORD thundered from heaven; the voice of the Most High resounded.*
>
> *He shot his arrows and scattered the enemies, great bolts of lightning and routed them. He reached down from on high and took hold of me; he drew me out of deep waters. He rescued me from my powerful enemy, from my foes, who were too strong for me. They confronted me in the day of my disaster, but the LORD was my support. He brought me out into a spacious place; he rescued me because he delighted in me.*

Did you notice that David actually did only one thing in this whole passage? He cried out to God for help. Nothing else. Then he waited. In that sense, these verses dovetailed with my impression of what it means to trust God. Sometimes all we can do is to sit quietly and pray while God does all the work. That's when trust focuses solely on how patiently we put ourselves into God's hands, waiting for Him to act.

God answered David's prayer in a dramatic way. Wouldn't you like God to do that for you the next time you get into a jam? I'd love to see God *part the heavens* and come down. Come to think of it, He's done exactly that, more than once. I've faced a few "days of disaster," as David phrased it, terrifying days when I prayed with desperation. And God rescued me.

Think back for a minute over your life story. Maybe it was the time you got some bills you couldn't pay and you cried out to God. Maybe someone you loved lay in a hospital bed. The doctors couldn't do anything more. You threw yourself on God's mercy and He heard your prayer. Maybe you faced enemies far stronger than yourself. You cried out to God and He saved you when everything seemed hopeless.

God hears your cry and mine because that's the kind of God He is. He helps us when we get into trouble. Stranger still, He even helps us when our troubles are our own darn fault, caused by our stubborn disobedience. He always tunes His ear to catch the cry for help. Psalm 46:1 puts it this way. *"God is our Refuge and strength, an ever-present help in trouble."* He is willing to help us whenever we get into trouble – every time. God cannot change His nature. He is the great Refuge for the believer.

Sadly, after awhile many of us begin to take God for granted. When the crisis ends, we go back to living our lives and we depend on our own resources to deal with "the little stuff." Since we know God will help us out of a jam, we begin to reserve trust in God for emergency situations. Trusting God becomes like our emergency stash of candles and flashlights that we keep on hand in case the power goes out. We think of prayer as a 9-1-1 hotline to God. We assume that trust means we cry out for help only after our best efforts fail to pull us out of the mess and we need outside help.

God does rescue us when we get into trouble, if we call out to Him. The word picture of Refuge brings to mind a castle or safe haven. When we run for shelter, the Lord of the castle protects us and then fights our battle for us.

But in Psalm 18, David didn't stop there with that passive kind of trust. He pursued an intimate relationship with God that went beyond defining God as his Rescuer. As he learned more of God's ways and lived an obedient lifestyle, he discovered God the Trainer. Listen to these excerpts from Psalm 18:29 – 40.

> *With your help I can advance against a troop; with my God I can scale a wall.*
>
> *As for God, his way is perfect; the word of the LORD is flawless. He is a shield for all who take refuge in him. For who is God besides the LORD? And who is the Rock except our God?*
>
> *It is God who arms me with strength and makes my way perfect. He makes my feet like the feet of a deer; he enables me to stand on the heights. **He trains my hands for battle**; my arms can bend a bow of bronze. You give me your shield of victory, and your right hand sustains me;*
>
> *You stoop down to make me great. You broaden the path beneath me, so that my ankles do not turn. [My highlight]*

I already knew that the word picture of the Refuge and the Rock speaks of God's trustworthiness. But I had never seen such active trust, trust that climbs walls, shoots arrows and learns to use God's shield, that charges against the enemy and runs up to the mountaintops. This was far more active than my notion about sitting in the chair with my hands folded and letting God do all the work.

Immediately, I asked God to "train my hands for battle." I wanted to learn this more active trust. I wanted to do more than sit (or cower) behind the walls of the Refuge. I wanted the Lord of the castle to train me for battle.

God kindly took me on as a student. We got right to work tackling the problems at my job. It was as if God put on work clothes and joined me at my workplace. I began to see all my problems in a new two-dimensional light: as a particular puzzle to be solved, and also as a training exercise to learn how to trust God. Each new crisis brought another trust lesson.

TRUST TRAINING

Viewing all my problems and difficult circumstances through two dimensions:
- As a particular problem to be solved or handled, and
- As a training exercise, wisely given by God to help me learn how to trust Him

---

I learned that while my mental image of sitting in the chair works well to help us to trust God in some situations, trust doesn't always look like that. Active trust works better in situations where we have options for how to handle things and, most importantly, where we already have even a little bit of ability, resource or skill.

Think about David. He knew a thing or two about using swords and bows. As a mere boy he had faced and killed the giant, Goliath. Certainly, he mastered other battle skills because he became one of Israel's best warriors. That's why it's so interesting that, here, when he talks about learning to trust God as his Refuge, he uses the analogy of weapons and warfare. It wasn't that he needed to learn how to bend an actual bronze bow or how to use his own shield. But he did need to learn the trust lessons that would enable him to rely on God's weapons and God's strength instead of merely his own.

When I applied these verses to my job situation, I saw how much I had been trusting in my own abilities and job experience. Those challenging days gave me the ideal opportunity to learn how to rely on God's strength and His guidance at work. He showed me that I didn't have two choices: either trust God OR do something. Instead, I could trust Him BY doing something that expressed trust. He especially showed me what to do with my churned up feelings. Even after things settled down into a routine, I still saw God as my supervisor and relied on Him for daily grace to do each day's tasks.

The scary times of our lives give us the chance to learn how to express both passive and active trust. I noticed several kinds of crises. The first kind tends to happen quickly and end just as suddenly. We find ourselves in a situation where we can't do anything. For instance, if I saw my son swerving on the road as he drove up the hill toward home on a stormy night, I would be helpless to do anything other than to cry out to God to save him. That's passive trust.

We never outgrow our need for passive trust in God, especially regarding our salvation. But most of the time we don't feel totally helpless. We think we can handle the "little stuff." That's the arena for learning active trust. This kind of trust covers most of our real lives, our relationships, and our daily struggle to meet life's challenges. Most of us bring some level of competency to these challenges even though we run into trouble from time to time. But we desperately need to learn how to rely on God instead of relying mainly on something else.

Our trust battles can help us to discover a great truth: that everything we need to face any challenge, crisis, stress, or normal day can be found in God. And since we learn to trust God in community, I have included short stories throughout this book of regular women who have learned how to trust God before, during and after life's battles.

David fought many battles using the skills God taught him. He concluded Psalm 18 by praising God for giving him great victories. He accomplished far more working with God the Refuge than he would have by trying to handle things on his own. And he rightly gave the glory to God. That's what I long for, both for you and for me. May God train us to trust Him.

SUMMARY OF THE BIG IDEA
Two Models for Trusting God

	PASSIVE TRUST See Psalm 18:4-19	ACTIVE TRUST See Psalm 18:29-36
God's Role	Rescuer	Trainer and Rescuer
What God does	He delivers us **out of** a difficult situation.	He uses the crisis as a training opportunity and guides us **through** it.
Time Frame	Tends to be quick and/or to have one main phase.	Tends to take more time and usually goes through several phases.
Because...	We have no control over the situation other than to ask God for help.	We can choose from a variety of options as we evaluate and deal with each phase of the situation.
What we do	Mainly run to God for help and expect Him to help.	We display trust in lots of ways, including prayer. In this book we'll explore what to do.
Examples of this kind of trust	Paul and Silas in jail; Daniel in the lion's den; Everyone who accepts Jesus as Savior.	Israelites marching around Jericho; David fighting Goliath; Nehemiah rebuilding the walls of Jerusalem.
Typical Results	Our trust glorifies God. We get new testimonies of times God rescued us. Sometimes passive trust can result in some confusion if God didn't answer the way we wished.	Our trust glorifies God. Our relationship with God deepens because we go through hard times together with Him. We see God at work and, hopefully, how to trust Him better. We also pick up testimonies along the way.

FACE TIME WITH MY TRAINER

PART 1: Answer these Bible study questions BEFORE reading the chapter

Read Psalm 18:4 – 19 and answer the following questions.
What is the only thing that David does in this entire passage (verse 6)?

What does God do on David's behalf (see vv. 7 – 19)?

Read Psalm 18:29 – 40 to answer these questions.
In this passage list the things that David does.

What does God do?

PART 2: Questions & Reflection

1. In this chapter we explored several mental pictures of what it might look like to trust God. How would you describe the mental picture that you have now, or have had in the past?

2. What are some reasons why the command to trust God with all our hearts is one of the most challenging tasks of the Christian life? Why is it harder to truly trust God than merely go through the motions of "doing church?"

3. As you begin studying this book, what questions about trusting God would you like answered? (They may or may not be the same ones I had.) What would you consider to be your biggest challenge as you think about developing more trust in God?

4. Describe how you would explain to someone else the difference between passive and active trust. Think about what's going on in your life right now. Where could you begin now to practice some active trust in God?

5. How does that make you feel to read that God would be willing and happy to train you to trust Him? Would you like Him to "train your hands for battle?" If so, why not pray right now and ask Him?

6. What did you find to be the most encouraging or intriguing idea in this chapter?

Mary's Story

After my husband and I had been married for three years, we decided that we would like to try to have children of our own. I already had two children from a previous marriage and they were 13 and 14 years of age. As soon as I found out I was pregnant, I started to get really stricken with morning sickness, which I had all day long. By my third month of pregnancy, I had lost 25 pounds. The doctors put me on bed rest and gave me an IV of vitamins and nutrients twice a week.

Sadly, I was seeing Navy doctors and because my health was an issue, they suggested I have an abortion. I continued to lose weight. My ribs were sticking out, I couldn't stop throwing up, my skin had turned gray, there were big dark black circles under my eyes, I was bedridden, being fed from the IV's and I was plain miserable. I refused to have an abortion, and my husband and I prayed constantly about what we were supposed to do. The only thing that comforted me was my husband telling me that in the Bible, it says that God knew us in our mother's womb.

At the four-month point, the doctors told me that I was going to die if I did not abort the baby. I refused, saying to them, that God's will be done. I had to sign paperwork refusing the abortion stating that I knew I might die if I didn't go through with the abortion.

The doctors did all they could to try and comfort me. But at this point they had decided to do an ultrasound to really look at the baby. My baby's kidney had swollen to that of a one-year old child. They told me the baby was going to die. I cried, prayed, and cried some more. I begged the doctors to do something. They suggested surgery through my stomach and into the unborn baby to fix the kidney or possibly to remove that one kidney.

I was devastated. I was still just as sick, and now I had a sick baby inside of me. My husband and I prayed and he told me that whatever I decided, he would stick by me. I told him that under no circumstance would I murder a baby. I would have to trust God to pull us through this, no matter what.

That night before bed, I prayed to God that He would show me the way somehow, to let me know what I could do. In my dreams, God revealed to me that I would give birth to a beautiful girl and the reason she would live is because I had taken medicine for the kidney disorder.

The next morning I called my doctor and told him of my dream. He said that he would have to talk it over with the rest of the staff. Two days later, he gave me a low dose of the medicine used for kidney malfunction. Every week I had an ultra sound done and little by little, her little kidney shrank back to normal size. The low dosage I took filtered down to her and when she was born, I gave her to God. I held her up in the delivery room and said, "She is yours and I will teach her all about you and your glorious ways, Lord. Thank you for saving her and giving her to us."

Today, she is six years old, has no kidney disorders or any medical problems whatsoever, and she is a blessing from God. If you ask her what she is, she will say, "I am a present from God given to my mommy and daddy."

Not every time is God's will our own, for only He knows what is best for us and for His plans for us. I thank God every day for my blessings and especially for her.

CHAPTER 2

What is Trust?

O LORD Almighty,
blessed is the man [or woman] who trusts in You.
Psalm 84:12

One of the biggest hurdles I faced when learning to trust God was that, for the longest time, I confused 'faith' and 'trust.' I had a lot of company. Many Christians confuse the two or think that they are identical. I would ask people how to trust God, and they would honestly think they answered my question, but usually they gave me advice instead on how to build faith. I couldn't figure out why I still felt frustrated after following their advice to the letter.

Has that happened to you as well?

Don't get me wrong, their advice helped. Sort of. Of course, we should have faith. And the more I worked at building faith, the more little bits of trust would emerge. But for years I walked around with an itch in my spirit that I couldn't scratch.

So before we start talking about trust training, let's clear up the confusion about the difference between faith and trust. Once we sort this out, it will simplify the task of cultivating both of them. In this chapter we will examine faith and trust, and then explore how they interact by looking at a story.

We tend to confuse faith and trust because they resemble each other and they work so closely together. Faith and trust are two of the most basic tools for any Christian who wants to grow in Christ.

FAITH

Let's talk about faith first. Webster's dictionary defines faith as "a confident belief in the truth or trustworthiness of a person, idea or thing." The Hebrew word for faith is *aman* – "to regard as true, to realize, to believe." Notice that both definitions talk about truth and belief.

The Hebrew word, *aman*, implies the idea of receiving a message from someone – a statement, a warning, a promise or a command. We *"aman"* by believing the message to be true. For example, let's say that we live in Florida and hear a report from the National Weather Service about a hurricane heading for our coastline. We would *aman* by accepting

19

that news as truth. We would believe it even if we poked our head out the window and saw only sunny skies.

The Hebrew concept of faith makes the practical assumption that, if people truly believe a message, they will act on it in some way. Whatever people do simply because they believe the message becomes an *amunah* – an act of faith. James said that faith without works is dead (James 2:26). As Florida residents, if we really believe the weather service warning, we'll show it by taking action, maybe by boarding up our windows or heading for higher ground.

The Bible tells many stories of people who heard a message from God and took some kind of action as a result. Abraham headed for the Promised Land. Noah built an ark. Rahab dangled a red cord out the window of her Jericho home. All through the Old Testament, people chose to believe God's promise that someday He would send a Messiah, who would save them from their sins. And then Jesus came as the Messiah. Ever since, people like you and me become Christians by putting our faith in Jesus instead of relying on our own good works to make us right with God.

People make the mistake of thinking that faith only applies to religion, but every functioning member of society exercises tons of faith throughout the day. Even atheists. Remember that faith believes in the truth or trustworthiness of a person, idea or thing – not limited to religious matters.

Faith jumps the gap between what we can verify with our senses and what we need to assume to be true in order to eat and work and live our normal lives. Let's see how this works at the grocery store. Let's say we pick up a can of chicken and rice soup. We can't see what's inside the can. Furthermore, we have no way of knowing where that chicken hatched, the conditions under which it was prepared or shipped, the sanitary conditions of the rice fields or the carrot farms, or how long it sat in a warehouse before we noticed it on that grocery shelf. The only clues we have to go by are the brand label on the can, the government sticker describing the ingredients and our previous experience with that brand of soup and with that grocer.

We buy food (an act of faith) at markets that seem clean and reliable. We could never eat anything at all unless we regularly jumped the gap between all the things we can verify with our own eyes and all the factors that make that food – in fact – safe enough to eat.

We couldn't possibly certify the truth or trustworthiness of every tomato or aspirin or washing machine repairman that comes our way. We evaluate things in a general way, not a specific one. Normally, when I'm home alone I don't let strangers in, but I will unlock the door to let in the stranger with the nametag from the repair company I called. That's an act of faith.

Any kind of faith is only as good as its object. Sincerity doesn't matter much. In a typical day, we do most of our acts of faith without any fanfare or emotion. Think back to the last time you drove down a busy, undivided road. Any one of those cars coming at you from the opposite direction could have slammed into you. How much emotion do you invest when you put your faith in the driving ability of every single driver on the road? Your emotion didn't matter; neither did your sincerity, only the actual reliability of the objects of your faith – the drivers.

I said before that faith and trust are the most basic tools for Christians. Faith is a stand-alone tool, like a knife. If we found ourselves stranded on a desert island with nothing but our pocket knife, we would probably survive pretty well (assuming we found water). We could use our knife to build shelter, capture and prepare food, fix stuff and protect ourselves from predators.

Likewise, **faith is the most crucial stand-alone tool for Christians.** Romans 1:17 puts it this way. *"For in the gospel a righteousness from God is revealed, a righteousness that is by faith from first to last, just as it is written: 'The righteous will live by faith.'"* We become Christians by exercising faith (Rom. 3:28). We live the Christian life by faith, not by sight (II Cor. 5:7), and we overcome Satan and the world by faith (Eph. 6:16; I John 5:4). In fact, Paul went so far as to say that whatever does not come from faith is sin (Rom. 14:23).

Most of what we receive and do as Christians uses faith alone, with or without much emotion. We receive the message in the Bible, choose to believe it, and act accordingly. We act as if God will keep His promises. We avoid doing things the Bible warns against. We obey commands by adopting an obedient lifestyle and we view life from the Bible's point of view.

TRUST

Now, let's shift our attention to trust. Webster's dictionary gives us two definitions:

1. Firm reliance on the integrity, ability or character of a person or thing
2. Reliance on something in the future; hope

While we're at it, let's look at two Hebrew words commonly translated as trust.

Hasa   Seek refuge, flee for protection, put trust in, confide, hope in
Batah   Trust in, feel safe, rely on, be confident, be careless or complacent

While faith refers to believing the truth about something, trust means to rely on or to put our hope in something. Trust deals with the uncertainties of life, how we manage risk or danger. It determines who or what we run to when we feel afraid or nervous. Here's the difference. We put our faith in people or things we believe to be true. But we trust people or things we believe to be safe.

While faith centers mainly in our mind and our will, trust goes deeper than our conscious mind and will to center mainly in our emotions and our subconscious. In our heart. That's why we instinctively trust some people on sight and instinctively distrust others before they do anything either good or bad.

Remember that repairman we mentioned? I might exercise faith by letting him come in after checking his nametag. But whether or not I trust him will depend on many, mostly unconscious factors. Does he remind me of other safe people or other dangerous people?

Does this experience remind me of other safe situations or past dangerous ones? Does he do things that set me at ease or does his body language, his tone of voice or his behavior set off alarm bells?

How much initial trust we give to people when we first meet them will depend largely on our past life experiences. People without much significant trauma will tend to trust new people from the start. Those with more painful experiences might dole out trust in tiny doses. After we get to know people we fine-tune how much we trust them based on our experience with them. **In general, we tend to trust people who prove themselves reliable even under difficult conditions.**

Let me give an example. Have you ever noticed how this works when people start a new Bible study group? Usually, for the first few weeks, we all share little prayer requests that don't reveal much about ourselves. Then some brave soul will send up a little trial balloon and share a request that hits closer to home. The trust level in the group will go up if people show kindness and sensitivity, or go down if someone stomped on the feelings of whoever shared. Trust can't be forced but it flowers under the right conditions.

We can't avoid some element of risk in a trust relationship. We might have many acquaintances who don't know us well so we risk nothing with them. But for acquaintance-ship to mature into deep friendship, into trust, we have to let down our guard and let our friend see us for who we really are. We will come to trust the friend who listens to what we say and how we feel, who reacts kindly, who keeps our secrets, who watches our back, and who always acts in our best interest. That kind of friendship only develops over time and it grows by accumulating many little shared experiences.

Now, how does this relate to trusting God? Remember all that well-intentioned advice that didn't scratch where I itched? Many Christians think we build trust in God by studying the Bible, memorizing promises and choosing to believe. Good advice. But from what we've discussed in this chapter, that sounds more like faith, doesn't it?

If faith is a stand-alone tool like a knife, trust is a two-part tool, like a pair of scissors, with two blades – faith and trust – that work together. You can exercise faith without trusting, but you cannot trust someone without also exercising faith. Let's see how this works in that Bible study I mentioned. Faith kicks in when we find out about the Bible study. That's the message: *Please come to this worthwhile Bible Study.* That leads to our *amunah* act of faith – when we show up for the study. The trust part gradually kicks in as we get to know the people better, share the experience of the Bible study with them, and begin to share our deeper self with them. Now, we'll only do that if we start to feel safe with those people. Some folks could attend for years without ever letting down their guard.

This same two-pronged approach applies to building trust in God. Since we can't see or hear God with our eyes or ears, our only option to begin a relationship with Him is by exercising faith. We can read the Bible, and choose to believe it. By an act of faith we accept Christ as our Savior and learn the basics of the Christian life. We learn to walk by faith not by sight.

Trust goes further. We build trust in God, not merely by affirming truths about Him, but by pursuing a personal relationship with Him. We take the risk of opening the door and letting God in to our real life to help us face things together, as if He were a friend of ours. Look at it this way. Faith claims the promise that God will keep us safe on a dangerous night. Trust has gotten to know the Almighty as friend and so sleeps like a baby.

This may sound like heresy, but we can't force ourselves to trust God, any more than we could grit our teeth and force ourselves to feel safe in that Bible study. However, we can choose to run to God when we get scared. That's what the *hasa* kind of trust is all about. When we run to Him and let down our guard we will discover that, like a good friend, He listens, He treats us kindly, He keeps our secrets, He watches our back, and He always acts in our best interests. Over time we develop that deep inner assurance of God's reliability.

This can be a scary process and our trust will develop by fits and starts because God doesn't act exactly like other people we know. Often, we'll misunderstand the things God does. That's why many Christians don't trust God even though they believe in Him.

In this book we'll show how to cultivate both faith and trust so we can get to know God in a more personal way and learn how to trust Him. You will notice that we emphasize stories – stories from the Bible, stories of people like you and me, and your story. If you allow God to enter your life story, you will begin to trust Him. After awhile, your shaky trust will mature into confident hope as God becomes your trusted friend.

EXHIBIT A: A STORY OF FAITH WITHOUT TRUST

Has it been a new thought to you to make such a distinction between faith and trust? Even after going through these definitions and examples, maybe it seems like I'm trying to split hairs. Most people see so much overlap between these two ideas that it's impossible to separate where faith leaves off and trust kicks in.

Well, relax; I think that's normal and healthy. It reminds me of the human brain. Normal people have a thick cable of nerve cells that connect the left and right side of the brain called the corpus callosum. Because normal people have such a strong bridge between the two sides of their brain it used to be impossible to nail down exactly how each side works.

On rare occasions, though, a serious brain injury or a huge emotional trauma breaks that bridge of the corpus callosum. Some babies are born without that bridge part. Years ago, it dawned on a few brain researchers to study these unusual people. Scientists learned a great deal from them about what each side of the brain does. The atypical cases helped to clarify the way things worked in normal brains.

In a weird way, my life story has been similar regarding the distinction between faith and trust. Severe early trauma profoundly damaged my ability to trust. When I talked about people who can have faith in God but find it hard to trust Him, for many years I was Exhibit A. So, speaking of stories, allow me to share a little more of mine.

No matter how bad things got, God consistently gave me grace to have faith in Him. Even though I felt all muddled up inside and even though I constantly assumed that whatever I did was not good enough, at every major crossroad He helped me to choose the path of faith. A year after leaving home for college, God touched my stony heart. I chose to rededicate my life to Christ. In spite of what had happened in my childhood, I wanted Jesus to be Lord of my life. I embraced a lifestyle of Christian service as part of the package when Jim asked me to marry him, knowing that he was called to ministry. So, because of Jim, and also because God honored the prayers of my grandmother, He kept me connected to the church throughout my entire recovery.

Even so, I had enormous difficulty with the whole idea of having a personal relationship with God. I was a true Christian who was afraid of God. I found my private quiet times of prayer and Bible study terribly frustrating. It killed me to confess the same dreary little list of sins day after day. When I studied the Bible I rarely encountered the Lord. It usually stayed at the level of head knowledge and creating three-point outlines and discovering the right answer. I hardly ever found comfort or compassion because I couldn't wrap my brain around the idea that God would want to comfort me. I felt profoundly unacceptable in His sight.

It wasn't until I went into counseling, at age thirty, that I realized how deeply I distrusted God. Although counseling helped me to shed many of the dysfunctional messages from my childhood, I still couldn't make headway regarding my personal, emotional relationship with God. I began to second-guess everything about my walk with God, such as it was.

About then, seemingly out of the blue, I got the idea to study the Book of Joshua to look for principles about how to exercise faith. All of a sudden, just for the time I did that study, the Bible came alive to me. I discovered many of the insights about faith that I shared in this chapter. I saw that faith is like a muscle that becomes stronger every time we stretch it and use it.

I had assumed that I didn't have faith or that my faith was too small. So the idea that everybody exercises tons of faith all day long gave me huge encouragement. It strengthened my resolve and gave me something concrete to do.

I swore to myself, "I'll be darned if I put faith in nameless drivers on the road, and in the complete strangers who put food on the shelves at the grocery store, and not put my faith in God, who deserves it so much more than they do!"

Back then, it was too much of a leap for me to consider how to trust God. But I learned to ask a great question: **How can I exercise faith in this situation?** When things got scary, when I encountered what I now refer to as trust battles, I would ask God for a Bible verse to stand on for that situation. I'd ask Him to show me something practical to do as an act of faith. And I'd do it.

I remember back then, my friend Martha asked me, "How do you see yourself? What do you want God to do for you?" I told her I identified with that leper (in Matthew 8) who came to Jesus and said, *"If You are willing, You can make me clean."* I also asked Him to redeem the years that the locusts had eaten, standing on Joel 2:25. From Psalm 1, I chose to believe that God was fulfilling His promises in my life even though I didn't see it at all.

I found faith to be a reliable stand-alone tool at a time when I couldn't figure out how to trust God. My exercises of faith were usually dry, pragmatic, and unemotional. They skirted the edges, avoiding the wounded parts of my life I didn't know how to handle, and helped me to exercise faith as I could. During those years, prayer was usually a struggle. But when a crisis would come up in our family or at church, all my fears about God would vanish and I would pray with confidence and faith. I instinctively knew what to do.

God eventually won my trust, one exercise of faith at a time. One answered prayer on top of another answered prayer. One long waiting time that ended well after another. Line by line. Brick by brick. Looking back, I see a few times when I really did trust God, although I wouldn't have labeled it as such at the time. The last barriers began to fall when I was introduced to something called *listening prayer*, and for the first time I began to relate to God in a much more personal way. By then my healing process had prepared me for intimacy with God. (By the way, we'll talk more about listening prayer later on.)

In one fell swoop, the long-deferred trust blessings from all those acts of faith cascaded into my heart. I suddenly saw that, even though I had let God into my life like that washing machine repair man, only to sit there in distrust while I watched Him work in my life, He had always been worthy of my trust. He had never let me down.

My prayer life changed dramatically as trust rushed in to join my faith. Since trust has been such a recent addition to my life, I've noticed some sharp contrasts between trust-filled prayer and the kind of prayer that keeps God at a distance. Maybe this diagram will highlight the difference.

PRAYER THAT LACKS TRUST	TRUST-FILLED PRAYER
Guarded, defensive and tentative	Self-disclosing, confident and open
Approaches God seriously only when some current danger overcomes a reluctance about being near God	Approaches God often, no matter what's going on, just for the pleasure of being in His company
Shame-based, worried about unworthiness	Love-based, secure in a covenant relationship
More formal, impersonal and rigid	More informal, personal and flexible
Emphasizes the "proper" prayer format	Emphasizes the personal relationship

I hope my story has helped you see some differences between faith and trust, and in the process, helped you to define each more precisely. And I hope that you already have such a great relationship with God that a thick corpus callosum bridge robustly intertwines your faith and your trust.

If not, I especially welcome you as a reader. Most of us are wounded in some way. Even if we can't see God at work in our lives, He's still there behind the scenes, like He was in my life, stirring the heart of my grandmother to pray, giving me Jim, and whispering in my ear, "Hey, how about studying Joshua?" Answering prayer after prayer in His silently faithful way.

Think back over your life. Even if you're as broken as I was, if you belong to Him, God has been at work in your life and He continues to repair your damaged parts to create new habits, new joy and a whole new person. That's the kind of God He is.

Some of you trust God pretty well but need more practice exercising faith. This book will give you lots of suggestions of ways to do just that. If, like me, your ability to trust God has been damaged, I hope that this chapter has given you some ideas for how to scratch that itch in your soul. Although exercising faith in God doesn't directly or automatically build trust, it's the best foundation to lay, because it builds our house on the solid Rock.

Realizing that faith and trust are ultimately connected may encourage you to do what you can, even if you can't do much. Who knows, you might find the courage to send up a little trial balloon of your own, and see for yourself how God responds.

SUMMARY OF THE BIG IDEA
How Faith and Trust Work Together

	FAITH	TRUST
Definition	Belief in the truth or trustworthiness of a person, idea or thing. Faith jumps the gap between what we know and what we must assume to be true in order to take action.	Firm reliance on the integrity, ability or character of a person or thing; To seek refuge, flee for protection, put trust in, confide, hope in; Feel safe, be confident
Role in the Christian life	Provides the most **basic essentials** of the Christian life: • Salvation • Power for living • Victory over Satan and the world	Provides the **blessings** of the Christian Life: • Peace and security • Confidence • Joy
Centered where?	Mainly in the mind and the will	Includes mind and will but centers more in the heart, the subconscious and the emotions
How we build it	• Read and study the Bible • Choose to believe what we read • Act on what we believe	• Pursue a relationship with God; • Take a risk to let God into our deep heart • Run to God for help to handle situations

FACE TIME WITH MY TRAINER

PART 1: Answer these Bible study questions BEFORE reading the chapter

In each of the following passages, look for two things:
1. What message did this person receive from God?
2. What did they do in a practical way that showed that they believed the message?

NOAH: (Skim Genesis 6:11 – 22 for context to verses 13 – 15 and 22.)

ABRAHAM: Genesis 12:1 – 4

ANANIAS: Acts 9:10 – 19 (Skim vv. 1 – 9 for context.)

In each of the following verses, people trusted in something. What did they trust? Was this a good thing to trust?

Jeremiah 17:5, Proverbs 11:28, Isaiah 31:1, II Chronicles 14:11 – 13

PART 2: Questions & Reflection

1. According to the Hebrew word, *aman,* what does it mean to have faith? Why will true faith generally lead us to do an act of faith?

2. Thinking back, list three things you did within the past 24 hours without fanfare or emotion, that could be called acts of faith. What was the object of your faith in each case?

3. Describe a time when you chose to believe that a particular Bible promise was true. What did you do as a natural action that logically flowed out of your belief?

4. How would you summarize what it means to trust?

5. According to this chapter, why is it easier to have faith than to trust? Why is trust much more affected than faith by our emotions and our life experiences? Looking back at your own life, what would you say has most affected your ability to trust God or to trust other people?

6. Describe a time when you ran to God for refuge (doing the action included within the "hasa" term for trust). What happened? How easy is it for you to run to God when you run into trouble?

7. What did you find to be the most encouraging or intriguing idea in this chapter?

EXTRA CREDIT: *Pray about something troubling that is going on in your life right now. Ask yourself and ask the Lord: How can I exercise faith in this situation? What came to mind?*

Susan's Story

My three young sons and I were living on our own. My sons and I were hoping that my ex-husband would change his mind and that he and I could get back together again. After a few days he called to let me know that he got married and had to talk to the boys about it.

I was devastated. I was very anxious for my boys and their reaction to the news but also I didn't know how we would ever make it on our own as I had pinned my hopes on us getting back together again. I felt bitter toward God and I worried all the time. I didn't have a job. It seemed overwhelming. I was far away from my parents, who lived in another country, so I couldn't fall back on their help.

Even though I was a Christian, at this time I was not walking in obedience and I was unsure if I even wanted to follow the Lord. In the back of my mind I knew God was there and I had the head knowledge that God could provide for us. Even in the midst of this turmoil I cried out to God with some part of my heart but I was very upset by my situation.

One day I was cleaning up something in the closet of the home we were renting and I happened to find an old purse that I hadn't used for a long time. I looked through the compartments of the purse out of idle curiosity. I found a crisp one hundred dollar bill folded up in one of the pockets of the purse. It shocked me. I have no idea how it got there but it seemed like God was answering my prayers.

The first thing that occurred to me was the amazing truth that the Lord is faithful and He will provide. But most of all, I knew I needed to reconcile with the Lord mostly for the sake of my children. I was reassured that His faithfulness was something I could really count on. He was there for me even though I was confused and walking in disobedience. I couldn't believe that God would be so kind to me at such a time.

Finding that $100 bill played a major role in encouraging me to return to the Lord. Ever since then, God has been so faithful to provide everything that my boys and I have needed.

CHAPTER 3

Defining the Battle

❧

Be kind, for everyone you know is facing a great battle.
Philo of Alexandria

San Diego fire crews had braced themselves for possible brush fires because hot dry Santa Ana winds were whipping from the desert toward the cities on the coast. The winds broke a power line triggering a fire near the tiny mountain town of Ramona and it raced toward Rancho Bernardo and Escondido. Many miles further southeast, a few illegal immigrants crossing the border near Tecate made a small campfire that flared out of control, starting the Harris Fire that flew toward Chula Vista and Eastlake.

Seven fires raged in San Diego County during that terrible week and nothing could contain them. High winds and red tape grounded most of the fire fighting planes those first crucial days. Unchecked, the fires roared through dry creek beds and tinder-rich canyons. They gobbled up house after house, cutting vast blackened swaths through rural tourist attractions, up forested foothills toward Mt. Palomar, and deep into the heart of this beautiful city.

More than 600,000 San Diegans evacuated their homes. Most found shelter with friends or family but many fled to Qualcomm Stadium or other evacuation centers. Everyone spent that exhausting week glued to the news, hungry for any information about their neighborhoods.

By the end of the week most of the fires were contained, if not completely out. Finally, people could drive home to unpack the valuables they had frantically thrown into the car on their way to safety. They were the fortunate ones. Some people went back to sift through the ashes of homes and businesses. Some settled into an unhappy new routine visiting the burn ward. And a few made arrangements to bury their dead. Politicians and insurance adjusters posed for pictures at new help centers, and reporters began to interview the veterans of the 2003 Cedar Fire for tips on how to rebuild and recover from this disaster.

❧

That terrible week in October, 2007, illustrates on a number of levels the complex nature of trust battles. People assume that trusting God is a one-size-fits-all kind of thing. It used to frustrate me when people would tell me to trust God, and leave it at that, regardless of what situation I faced. "I know, I know, I'm supposed to trust God. But how do I trust God here – in this situation?"

In the same way that faith and trust are not identical, trust battles don't all look alike. One size does NOT fit all. A Christian fire fighter battling on the front lines would have needed to trust God in a far different way than an evacuee camped out at Qualcomm wondering if her house was still standing.

In this chapter we will explore a simple idea that has helped me enormously. After I give a basic definition of what I mean by *trust battle* we will talk about two main categories of trust battles: defensive battles and offensive battles. We will look at three common types of defensive battles and two types of offensive battles. I hope that, like me, you will find it much easier to trust God when you are able to identify what you're dealing with and what the trust issues are likely to be for that type of trust battle.

TRUST BATTLE: WHAT IT IS AND WHAT IT ISN'T

A *trust battle* can be any situation, problem or potential scenario that makes us feel afraid, worried, anxious, grief-stricken or perplexed. It can also be a decision-making time when we wonder what to do. A key element in any trust battle is that the outcome is up for grabs. We don't know what will happen and we also still have an opportunity to respond to the situation. Will we respond with confident faith and trust in God or will we respond by giving in to fear or unbelief? We also don't know for sure what God will do if we pray about it.

Trust battles can take the form of anything that disturbs our normal or our preferred life. It can be a health issue, a financial threat, an interpersonal conflict or a problem in our devotional life. Some (rare) people can go for a long time without any major trust battles. If something makes us feel afraid, worried, etc., then it's probably a trust battle to us, even if someone else wouldn't consider it a trust battle for themselves. Typically, we juggle several trust battles at any given time.

So a trust battle is mainly an internal struggle for the right attitude, the right actions and the right reactions when something inside us resists the idea of trusting God.

Before we go any further I need to get a **big disclaimer** out of the way. **By using the word "battle" I do not endorse any kind of combative, cantankerous or despicable behavior. That's NOT what I mean when I talk about battle.** It grieves me that some Christians jump at the chance to bicker or to put down other people. Jesus calls us to love everyone, even enemies or people who don't join our little group. Remember, *"If it is possible, as far as it depends on you, live at peace with everyone"* (Romans 12:18).

OK, having said all that, God uses trust battles to shape and refine our trust. In fact, in the history of Israel, He often used actual battles to teach His people to trust Him. He kept them away from battles until they had witnessed a few examples of His reliability.

When Pharaoh let the people go, God did not lead them on the road through the Philistine country, though that was shorter. For God said, "If they face war, they might change their minds and return to Egypt." So God led the people around by the desert road toward the Red Sea. Exodus 13:17, 18

In the wilderness, He led them through a series of battles that they won if they trusted and obeyed Him, and lost if they didn't. Even after the Israelites settled in the Promised Land, God deliberately left a few pockets of resistance to teach them to trust Him and to provide battle experience.

These are the nations the Lord left to test all those Israelites who had not experienced any of the wars in Canaan (He did this only to teach warfare to the descendants of the Israelites who had not had previous battle experience)... Judges 3:1, 2

The next time you read through the Old Testament, notice the close connection between whether people trusted God and whether they won or lost a particular battle.

Now, most of us don't face actual military battles very often, if ever. Still, the same principle applies to us. In this book I use the term *trust battle* quite loosely to refer to a wide variety of circumstances that we face. Let's explore two totally different kinds of trust battles: defensive and offensive battles.

DEFENSIVE TRUST BATTLES

In defensive trust battles, we're minding our own business when suddenly someone or something threatens us. We don't have any choice about whether to get involved. We might face a defensive battle when people do hurtful things to us, when a family member gets a serious illness or dies unexpectedly, when our boss fires us unfairly or when we find ourselves in some unexpected danger. No one in their right mind would ever willingly choose to trade their calm existence for a new defensive trust battle. Defensive trust battles happen to us against our will. The Bible gives many examples of defensive battles. For instance:

- Queen Esther heard Haman was plotting to massacre all the Jews, including her. (Esther 4)
- The disciples ran into a terrifying storm at sea while Jesus slept in the boat. (Mark 4:35 – 41)
- Jehoshaphat heard that three armies were heading straight for Jerusalem to wipe it out. (II Chronicles 20)
- Job lost his children, most of his wealth, and his health, all within a few very bad days. (Job 1)

As you can see, defensive trust battles come in different shapes and sizes. Let's look at **three typical kinds of defensive trust battles.**

Crisis. Most crises happen over a relatively short time span, marked by an unstable situation that quickly escalates to a life and death type of turning point or conclusion. The week that the fires raged and thousands fled their homes was a crisis week. Everybody in San Diego dropped everything to handle the emergency.

By definition, crises tend to be chaotic, emotional and scary times. Paradoxically, I've noticed that most people find it easier to trust God during a crisis. We cry out to God because, well, what else can we do? Even if we normally don't have a consistent prayer life, during a crisis our desperation drives us to God and we pray like crazy.

As we will discuss more fully in the next chapter, God uses these crises as part of His long-term strategy to teach us to trust Him. Most Christians get their biggest answers to prayer during a crisis. The memory of His faithfulness at such times can become a key ingredient to cultivate our trust. A crisis is the rarest kind of trust battle.

Challenges. These tend to last longer but at a lower level of terror. The dictionary defines a challenge as "the quality of requiring full use of one's abilities, energy or resources" and comments that a challenge is "difficult but stimulating." We face many more challenges than crises, such as –

- Financial worries,
- Relationships with difficult people,
- Dealing with someone else's persistent sinful habits or substance abuse,
- Waiting and waiting for something big that we really need or really want,
- Providing long-term care to a sickly child or dependent relative,
- Living far away from Christian fellowship or like-minded people.

After the fires, some people faced the long-term challenge of rebuilding their homes or finding new jobs. Some displaced people are still living with family members, all of whom deal with the challenge to adapt.

Often we try to handle these challenges from a survival mentality at first. We simply try to "get through it." Maybe we vaguely drift along without figuring out any particular strategy. But if we get frustrated enough or if the situation deteriorates, sometimes we look around for more constructive ways to handle it. Jesus waits patiently for us to turn to Him for help, for strategies, and most importantly, for patient endurance. These challenges provide plenty of opportunities to learn to trust God.

Significant Losses. The severity and significance of the loss will determine its role in our lives. Obviously, if someone we love dies it rocks our world and takes us a long time to grieve our loss. If our spouse or our mate betrays us, it throws us into a trust battle to process that loss. The fire victims digging through the debris to find mementos were just beginning to grieve the loss of their homes. Some of us try to ignore the wound we suffer from the loss of a treasured friend, or losses resulting from childhood trauma or devastating situations. People can grieve for years if they were part of a divisive church split.

When the time comes to stop ignoring the pain, God stands ready to help us through all the phases of our grief. He will guide us into wholeness again and teach us how to trust Him more in the process.

By the way, when we get into the next sections of this book we'll explore the phases before, during and after the battle to see how to handle each stage of our trust battles. Significant losses are unique, in that, for most people, it is from first to last an "after the battle" struggle.

The trust issue. In a defensive trust battle the trust issues focus mainly on our reaction to circumstances we didn't initiate. **The biggest trust issue in most defensive battles is whether to accept that God could love us and still allow it to happen.** After all, nothing happens to us without God's sovereign permission. He could have protected us from ever facing it. So, will we affirm the promise in Romans 8:28, that *"in all things God works for the good of those who love Him, who have been called according to His purpose?"* Will we run to God for help and guidance to face the threat? Or will we get mad at God or distance ourselves from Him?

Job gives us a great example of how to respond during defensive battles.

> *Naked I came from my mother's womb, and naked I will depart.*
> *The Lord gave and the Lord has taken away;*
> *may the name of the LORD be praised. Job 1:21*

That reaction doesn't come naturally for most people. And God allows us some latitude while we process our feelings and our reactions. But our goal in defensive battles is to come to the conclusion, as quickly as possible, that even though we may not know why something happened, we will trust that God allowed it to happen to us for reasons that reflect His character and His perfect love for us.

Before we move on, let me illustrate this idea of defensive trust battles with a personal story. Right before we moved to San Diego, Jim's elderly mother fell, landing her in the hospital. That was a crisis time because she was beginning to suffer from memory loss and didn't understand what was going on. Then we faced a much longer challenge after we found a nursing home for her – to help her to adapt to this better place even though she blamed us for all her troubles. It was also a challenge to make the right decisions to care for her while her memory deteriorated. After she died, I assumed that Jim would be the main one to grieve for her. I don't know why I thought that, but I did. It wasn't until this past year that I realized how much I missed her and grieved her passing.

So how was that a defensive trust battle for us? That whole season of our lives was marked by massive second-guessing and wondering what to do. It was also terrible to watch someone we loved deteriorate before our eyes. Would we trust that God was still a loving

God even though He had allowed that to happen to her and even though her troubles greatly complicated our lives? Would we trust God to give us wisdom for each new decision? Could we trust that her days were in God's hands, especially on days when she felt miserable and lashed out at us?

Later, when it finally occurred to me that I needed to mourn her death, was I willing to allow God to comfort me through all my complicated and half-perceived emotions? Was I willing to believe that He would stick by me even if my feelings didn't fit into a tidy little box?

OFFENSIVE TRUST BATTLES

Unlike defensive trust battles that hit us without our permission, we hold the power to choose what to do in an offensive trust battle. In Bible times, believers saw a problem or opportunity of some kind and had to decide what to do.

The actual trust battle was that window of time when they debated what to do. They had the choice to do nothing or to do something, and whether to rely on their own strength or on God's strength. If they figured out what God wanted them to do, and launched out to do it, then their whole project became an offensive trust battle.

But the key trust battle is always fought on the brink of the action, when people debate what to do. For example:

- At Kadesh-Barnea, the Israelites debated whether to invade the Promised Land. (Numbers 13 & 14)
- When David heard that the Philistines had ransacked a helpless town, he weighed whether to retaliate on their behalf. (I Sam. 23:1, 2)
- Nehemiah heard about the broken walls of Jerusalem and wondered what to do. (Neh. 1 & 2)
- Jesus prayed in the Garden of Gethsemane, agonizing about whether to endure the cross. (Mark 14:32 – 36)

We might face an offensive battle when we debate whether to clean up government corruption in our community, to bring a foster child into our home, to enter full-time Christian service, to confront a fellow Christian, to start a business or to go back to school. After the San Diego fires, if someone got an idea for a new way to help the fire victims, that period of time while they decided what to do would be their offensive trust battle. If they decided to go ahead with their idea, they would be launching out into an offensive trust battle to make their idea a reality.

If we decide not to act, we avoid risk, conflict, and hard work. But have you ever noticed how often people in the Bible got into trouble for NOT jumping into an offensive battle? Think about the Israelites. Wow, did they ever get into trouble! They chickened out at Kadesh Barnea and spent the rest of their days wandering around the desert. And if King David had gone to war with his soldiers – like he should have – he wouldn't have gotten into trouble with Bathsheba. Above all, praise God that Jesus chose to fight the offensive battle that took Him to the cross!

Let's look at **two main kinds of offensive trust battles:**

Challenges. You're right. I already used that word before. But challenges can be either defensive or offensive. For instance, let's say that "Mary" loses her job and has to move to another city to find a new job. That move would be a defensive trust battle. But if Mary has a decent job and a place to stay but she starts thinking about changing jobs or moving somewhere else, that would be her offensive trust battle. Mary makes the choice.

It's a defensive battle to deal with our mate's persistent sinful habit, but an offensive trust battle to think about tackling our own sinful habit or our own substance abuse problem. It's a defensive trust battle to help our child cope with his learning disability. We would never have chosen that for our child or for ourselves. But it's an offensive trust battle to ponder whether to home-school our child or whether to become an advocate for children with disabilities.

If we decide to home-school our child, home-schooling is our offensive trust battle. We choose to do it and if we decided tomorrow to quit, we could quit. Mary's new job would be an offensive trust battle. It's her choice to switch jobs and she could quit if the job didn't work out.

Intense ministry situations. Many of the trust training principles I share in this book came out of the pressure cooker of full-time Christian ministry. Make no mistake. Planting a church in a new community involves battle – spiritual warfare, strategy and struggle to win territory for Christ in a way that honors His name. And let's be honest, it includes winning the battle over bitterness with unlovable people, especially demanding and carnal Christians.

But let's focus on that first offensive trust battle – deciding what to do. I'll never forget the months that Jim and I debated about whether to leave our church plant in Temecula because someone challenged us to pray about moving up to the Antelope Valley to plant five churches in ten years. It killed us to think about leaving the Temecula church. We finally had a church building, with an actual office for Jim, instead of a makeshift office in our garage. That congregation was blessedly stable. I had a good job in town.

How would our boys adjust to a school change? Could we sell our house? Could we find a new house up there? Would I be able to find another job? Would Jim be able to raise enough support for that project to cover the shortfall for that project? Those worries and fears tumbled around in our heads along with the ever-present fear of failure that haunts any new venture.

This wasn't a choice between serving Christ and not serving Christ. We were already serving Him in Temecula. We prayed to find out what God wanted us to do. Did He want us to stay or to go?

All Christian service involves some kind of trust battle – Vacation Bible School, AWANA ministry, praying for others, worship ministry, missionary outreaches or local soup kitchens. It's all a voluntary choice on our part. I began to win the battles of Christian ministry when

I learned to recognize that they were trust battles. Throughout this book we will apply the various trust strategies to ministry situations.

The trust issue: While the trust issues in defensive battles focus on cultivating godly reactions, offensive battles focus on **godly action.** **The key trust issue in offensive battles is to figure out what it means to obey God. Are we willing to obey God, even if it means taking a risk? And if we launch out by taking a step of obedience, are we willing to stick it out even when it gets hard?**

What does obedience look like in this situation? If God promises to give us something and clearly leads us to take it, then we show trust by acting on what He says. For instance, God promised to give His people the land of Canaan and He led them to the brink at Kadesh Barnea. They would have demonstrated trust by marching in when He gave them the signal to go.

On the other hand, let's say that we face a big conflict with other Christians. Take it from me, Jesus does NOT care what color carpeting you choose for the church sanctuary. He clearly condemns bickering and wants us to maintain *"the unity of the Spirit through the bond of peace"* (Eph. 4:3). Jesus defended the truth but loved people. He counseled tolerance for true Christians who don't belong to our little group (Mark 9:39, 40).

God always expects us to love and forgive people even if they turn out to be our enemies. *"Do not be overcome by evil, but overcome evil with good"* (Rom. 12:21). If all else fails and God leads us to confront them, we need to cover it with prayer and use the procedure outlined in Matthew 18.

Most offensive trust battles don't involve confronting Christians (although sometimes they do involve holding people accountable for their behavior instead of continuing to be a doormat for bad behavior). Usually, though, offensive trust battles center on taking the next step of obedience in our walk with Christ, or acting with courage in our personal or professional lives. When we have clarified God's will for each situation, we need to step out in faith and follow wherever God leads us.

Whatever kind of battle we face can become a training opportunity just by asking God to make it so. Instead of drifting through the situation, we can ask God to help us to evaluate things based on what we've learned so far. We can ask Him how to exercise faith. Ask Him to use this situation to teach us how to trust Him better. We can talk over our doubts and fears, our insecurities, and our questions. That will automatically put us in the position of trusting God. Think about whether this situation is an offensive or a defensive struggle and look for where the struggle to trust is being played out in this battle.

If we commit the whole battle to the Lord, He will get us through it safely, teaching us lessons of trust along the way.

SUMMARY OF THE BIG IDEA
Defining the Battle

Clarifying what we mean by "Battle"	We *Don't* Mean – • Bickering with people; • Pursuing conflicts with people who aren't members of our little group; • Doing anything despicable or that does not bring honor to Jesus.	We *Do* Mean – • Any situation, problem or potential scenario that makes us feel afraid, worried, anxious, grief stricken or perplexed. • It can also be a decision-making time when we wonder what to do. • A key element in any trust battle is that the outcome is up for grabs.
Kinds of Battles	**DEFENSIVE BATTLES** The battle comes to us without our choice. These battles can take the form of: • **Crises:** Emergencies that quickly build to a highly charged conclusion; • **Challenges:** Difficult situations or hurdles that demand great energy to navigate; • **Significant Losses:** Whatever requires a grief process to mend.	**OFFENSIVE BATTLES** We make the choice whether to engage in the battle. These battles can take the form of: • **Challenges:** Choosing to make a change or take a risk in our personal or professional life. • **Intense Ministry Situations:** Big projects or service that tax our strength and resolve.
Examples	Job's troubles	The Israelites at Kadesh-Barnea
The Arena for Trust	Godly reaction	Godly action
Biggest Trust Issues	To accept that God could love us and still allow it to happen. To trust God even when we don't understand why something happened.	To figure out how to obey God. What would obedience look like? Are we willing to obey God, even if it means taking a risk? After we take that step of obedience, are we willing to stick it out even when it gets hard?

FACE TIME WITH MY TRAINER

PART 1: Answer these Bible study questions BEFORE reading the chapter

In each of the following stories, God's people faced a scary situation. For each story, jot down three things:

• *Who among God's people faced trouble or a dilemma in that story?*

• *From the main character's point of view, what was the nature of the threat or the dilemma?*

• *Did they have a choice about whether to become further involved, or were they already up to their eyeballs in a bad situation that they had not chosen and would never have chosen?*

Mark 4:35 - 41, Numbers 13 & 14, Job 1, I Samuel 23:1 - 2

1. What do we mean when we call something a trust battle?

2. What are the main differences between defensive trust battles and offensive trust battles? What are the most common trust issues for each?

3. **TRUST BATTLE LISTS:** Think back over your entire life and create two lists, one each for your most memorable defensive and offensive trust battles. Take your time and make these two lists as complete as possible because we will be referring back to these lists several times during this Bible study. (By the way, for purposes of this list, it doesn't matter whether you thought of these situations as trust battles at the time or whether you chose to trust God at the time.)

Here's how to set up the two lists, titles to use and some sample entries to give you the general idea.

> **MAIN DEFENSIVE BATTLES**
> *(Unwelcome experiences or major looming worries)*
> > My little brother got very sick
> > My parents got divorced
> > The time we thought we would lose our business
> > Etc.
>
> **MAIN OFFENSIVE BATTLES**
> *(Opportunities or circumstances in which I had some choice)*
> > Deciding which high school to attend
> > Choosing to move to Toledo
> > Debating about whether to teach Sunday school
> > Etc.

4. Now mark an "H" next to any episodes that HINDERED your trust in God, at least for awhile. Mark a "B" next to any episodes that, at the time or since then, have mostly BUILT your trust in God. If it didn't affect your trust, one way or the other, don't mark anything next to it. What did you notice as you evaluated your experiences? Lay these two lists before the Lord and pray however you feel led.

5. Think about your current situation. List the trust battles you're juggling right now. Are they more defensive or offensive struggles? What are your biggest current trust issues or your biggest obstacles to trusting God? What have you learned so far about trusting God that you could try out now?

6. What did you find to be the most encouraging or intriguing idea in this chapter?

Angela's Story

While living in Miami and working in the Miami City Attorney's Office, I fasted and prayed for three requests: a healthy pregnancy, a baby boy, and that my husband would get into a leadership training program that would move us from Miami to California. God answered all three of my prayers.

First, came the pregnancy. Second, my husband was accepted into the program and immediately went out of town for training. We did not want to find out the gender of the baby until the baby was born. In the meantime, I called our baby Brandon. I had a healthy pregnancy and refused all tests for women with advanced maternal age because, no matter what, we wanted to give birth to Brandon.

On February 7, 2002, we gave birth to Brandon. He was the spitting image of his father. During Brandon's development, I noticed that Brandon was not on target. At a well baby visit to his pediatrician, I mentioned that Brandon was not rolling over. At another well baby visit, I mentioned that he was not sitting up. And finally, I mentioned that he was not crawling. At each visit, the pediatrician assumed I was having first time mom's jitters or worries. At 9 months I insisted on help. Finally, the doctor mentioned that maybe he should refer me to the Tri-County Regional Center for an assessment. At that moment, I began to grieve that Brandon was developmentally delayed. I had suspected for months that Brandon was not on target but I did not know the diagnosis.

At first, I was terrified. I had so many bad thoughts. I looked at Brandon and thought, "He does not belong in the Special Olympics." I did not share any of these bad thoughts with my husband or God. I just worried myself bald. My hair began to fall out. But when Brandon turned 1 year old, he was tested for diseases and disorders. When I took Brandon to the lab to get tests for a chromosomal disorder, I cried in the waiting room. I stood Brandon up on my lap and hid my face in his stomach as people watched. I did not care what they thought of me. I was devastated and wondered where do we go from here? I felt so lost. What will our lives be like if my child has a disability? I did not pray for this. Why is God doing this to me? What did I do wrong? My husband was often out of town for training and at this time he was gone again. I felt so alone to deal with this bad news or this bad experience.

A month later, we got the test results confirming that Brandon had an extra 21st chromosomal disorder called Down's syndrome. I could not believe it. I asked myself, "He is Brandon. How can he also have Down's syndrome?" But later, I came to realize that he is in fact our Brandon and that Down's syndrome is a medical diagnosis and not a personality trait.

The moment I got the diagnosis, I trusted God and handed all of my fears and worries over to Him. I turned to God and He continues to lead me. He turned grief into unspeakable joy. Brandon is a miracle. We thank God for Brandon and his diagnosis because his diagnosis is a part of him. After trusting God, I found out that life is more than just okay when having a child with a disability. I cannot imagine a different kind of life other than the one that God has provided for my family and me. God is truly good.

CHAPTER 4

Clues About God's Master Plan For Trust Training

And we rejoice in the hope of the glory of God. Not only so, but we also rejoice in our sufferings, because we know that suffering produces perseverance; perseverance, character; and character, hope. And hope does not disappoint us, because God has poured out His love into our hearts by the Holy Spirit, whom He has given us.
Romans 5:2b - 5

By the time we moved to the Antelope Valley I had already learned to trust God a teeny tiny bit for our finances. I was not a bright pupil (and I'm still "in school" in this area). At first, God taught me mainly through my distrust. I would fixate on the gap between our bills and our income and get swamped with anxiety. Jim patiently helped me to turn that terror into some kind of constructive activity by encouraging me to pray for our needs. God provided every single time we needed something. It was truly amazing.

After several (OK, many) cycles of my getting freaked out during the crisis and then God providing, I gradually began to take notice. It occurred to me, "Oh, I don't need to waste all that energy on panic. God really is going to take care of this."

One year we got an unexpected tax bill, and it was a turning point for me. Instead of embarrassing myself by expressing a lot of fear and worry, and trusting God only in hindsight, I chose to trust God at the beginning, when we first found out that we owed $1000. It worked out fine. We had the money we needed by April 15. No problem. To this day, I have no idea how God did it. God used that experience to teach me that He would provide when we had some kind of unusual expense.

About then we moved to the Antelope Valley and Jim's salary structure included a component that called for him to raise support. God provided several dozen financial supporters. Every month we relied on these people to send what they had promised. This pushed me past my comfort level. I was used to that stable base of Jim's steady income. Plus, I didn't realize how much comfort my own job gave me. I liked getting a predictable paycheck to help us meet the growing needs of our little family.

Gradually I began to realize that I put my trust mainly in our jobs and in those particular people who wrote support checks. Some months we got a short check because some of them didn't send what they had committed to send. God used that period of insecurity to refine my trust.

It began to dawn on me that even though I felt safer trusting our jobs and our financial supporters, none of them was 100% reliable. My job or Jim's could be gone tomorrow. In fact, a few years after I left Temecula, I heard through the grapevine that they closed the manufacturing plant where I had worked and moved the whole operation back east. Come to think of it, we left the Antelope Valley after only four years because the district office went through a shakeup and the new director cancelled the church planting project!

God used our time in the Antelope Valley to show me that I divvied up my trust in chunks between Jim's job AND my job AND our financial supporters AND then God to provide anything over and above. Eventually I saw that it was much better to trust God, first and foremost, to provide for all our financial needs and to regard all those other things as vehicles for God's provision.

God might provide for us through Jim's job or He might provide for us through my job or through other people or through any of a hundred other means. Then again, some days He might just surprise us with manna from heaven or bread dropped by ravens. It's up to Him. No matter what, and no matter how, God has proven to me that He will meet every need I have.

Before we move on to examine how to trust God in a particular situation, let's stop for a moment to look at this subject from God's point of view. Now this can be tricky. As we've seen, God often teaches us to trust Him by using crises and other traumatic situations. However, I'll bet you find it as annoying as I do when I'm going through a hard time and some bystander wanders over claiming to know "the big reason for it all." We have to tread lightly here. God's ways lie veiled in mystery. God rarely answers "Why?" questions to our complete satisfaction.

However, because He chooses to reveal Himself (to some extent) we can draw some conclusions about His overall goals. He has revealed Himself in the Bible and in the person of Jesus who "put on skin" two thousand years ago. We can study how God behaved with people in the Bible. Why, sometimes He even gave them a running commentary as He taught them to trust Him that was as plain as the moral at the end of an Aesop's fable. We can apply the lessons they learned to our own situations.

Not only that, if we look back on our own life story sometimes we can pick up clues about why God did what He did in our lives. Hindsight can teach us much if we will pay attention. So, for a moment, can we step back from the painful details of a particular crisis and see what we can deduce about God's master plan?

Before jumping in, let's agree that God has an infinite number of reasons for doing what He does or for allowing what He does. So, we won't attempt to find any kind of unifying theory to explain everything. Let's just follow one strand, the strand of trust, because no matter how much the details may vary, in every circumstance God does seem to desire that we trust Him. Furthermore, He seems willing to help us to trust Him. Using that narrow scope, we can indeed evaluate every single situation as not only a problem to be solved, but also an opportunity to trust God.

Now, what can we deduce about God's master plan regarding this topic of trust? God passionately, joyfully, triumphantly, creatively does all things in order to bring glory to His name. God truly outshines everyone and everything else in all creation. He has no rival and no peer. When He claims to be the best, He says the simple truth. For Him to say anything less would make Him a liar.

One of the ways that God reveals Himself in Scripture is by giving us many names that hint at the infinite beauty of His glory. A cluster of these names apply especially to the issue of trust. Listen again to the names David uses to describe God.

> *The LORD is my **rock**, my **fortress** and my **deliverer**; my God is my **rock**, in whom I take refuge. He is my **shield** and the **horn of my salvation**, my **stronghold**.* Psalm 18:2

> *I will say of the LORD, "He is my **refuge** and my **fortress**, my God, in whom I trust."* Psalm 91:2

God is my rock – stable, solid, strong and changeless.

He is my Refuge – providing protection and shelter, a haven and a sanctuary. He gives reliable help, relief and escape.

He is my fortress and my stronghold – reminding us of a walled city with permanently stationed troops that courageously defend the people who live within its fortified walls. God defends His people by angelic warriors and by His own powerful right hand.

He is my shield – which in David's day meant that God takes on the good king's obligation to protect His own people from any outside threat. God welcomes anyone who runs to Him for refuge and allows us to live safely in His kingdom.

These names of refuge and protection express just a portion of God's glory. What an awesome God!

Now, if these names describe God, how can we best give Him the glory due His name? Simple. By trusting Him. By running to Him for refuge. By walking through every situation hand in hand with our heavenly Father, relying on Him to guide and protect us. By expressing confidence in the character of God. Non-Christians may quibble with us over doctrine, and they may laugh at us for going to church. But what can they say when we go through tragedy with unshakable peace, drawing on unseen reserves of strength and sustaining grace?

God places a high priority on teaching us to trust Him, not only for the sake of His glory, but also because He has designed us to function best when we trust Him. People who have learned to trust God go through life experiencing peace and fulfillment even in the middle of hard times. Instinctively, we know that's true. Part of our frustration comes from falling so far short of that ideal again and again, crisis after crisis.

But, thank God, He takes it upon Himself to teach us how to do what we cannot do apart from His help. So, how does God teach us to trust Him? Everyone has a slightly different life story. God tailors His specific plan to fit our individual needs. In general, though, I see a two pronged strategy as I study the stories in the Bible and the life stories around me. God sends us a steady supply of two things.

FIRST, GOD PROVIDES PLENTY OF EVIDENCE OF HIS TRUSTWORTHINESS.

This evidence comes in many forms. We see the encouraging *evidence of creation*. The cycles of the seasons and recovery give us hope when we are in the middle of our own "winter." Midwestern snows may seem to last forever. The snow banks pile higher and higher. But springtime always comes and the crocuses push their way through the last dirty snow. Birds find food to eat even though they don't punch a time clock. California poppies blanket the desert hillsides in a throwaway spectacle of God's provision. Rainbows twinkle a lovely farewell to thunderstorms. Charred meadows come to life after a forest fire. Redwood trees even incorporate forest fires into their life cycle and the fire quickens new shoots that spring up through the ashes.

We see the *evidence of God's character* as we learn more about the Bible. We listen to sermon after sermon that urges us to trust God. We study the attributes of God, sing songs about His goodness and celebrate the life and ministry of Christ who died to win our salvation.

Gradually, this "head knowledge" about God shifts into "heart assurance" as we see the *evidence of answered prayer.* When we face difficult times and cry out to God, He answers our prayers. After we have walked with God for awhile, we accumulate some favorite promises that God honored when we stood on them.

We begin to know God better. Our *evidence of relationship* grows stronger the more we seek out His presence. We move beyond merely knowing God's laws and begin to learn God's ways. When we run to Him through our tears, He hears our cry and comforts our heart.

God continually sends us evidence that He can be trusted. As Jeremiah put it, "*Because of the Lord's great love we are not consumed, for His compassions never fail. They are new every morning; great is Your faithfulness.*" Lam. 3:22

With all this evidence, why do we find it so hard to trust God? Blame it on Adam and Eve. When they ate the forbidden fruit, all of us turned away from a wholehearted trust in God. Now it doesn't come naturally to anyone. We would rather trust in our own abilities, our own goodness, our own resourcefulness, and most of all, our own control.

Like a crow that lines its nest with carefully chosen pretty rocks and brightly colored scraps of paper, we carefully cultivate a network of things and people to trust. We find friends who will watch our back. We pursue education and training and a good job so we can put food on our tables. We look for people and institutions to protect us from danger. We lock our doors and screen our phone calls.

When trouble knocks on our door, we run to our friends and family for help. We figure out our plan of action. If we tell the honest truth, before we became Christians, not many of us thought to turn to God for help. We figured we had it handled. And even after our conversion, we think to pray only as a last resort.

God described our situation using the analogy of water.

> *My people have committed two sins: They have forsaken Me, the spring of living water, and have dug their own cisterns, broken cisterns that cannot hold water. Jeremiah 2:13*

We have all dug our own cisterns instead of trusting God. And He grieves over our foolishness.

God could leave us there, trusting our leaky water tubs, our little sandcastle trust network. But, He loves us.

SO, SECONDLY, HE PROVIDES PLENTY OF OBSTACLES THAT THREATEN OUR TRUST NETWORKS

It might look something like this.

GOD BUILDS OUR TRUST BY SENDING: Evidence / Obstacles

These obstacles come in many forms. Maybe He lets our car break down; our job runs out or our best friend betrays us. He lets us go through scary situations and get huge bills that we have no idea how to pay. He allows someone we love to get sick. We put together big plans for the future and He lets our plans fall to pieces through unforeseen complications.

This does not amuse us. Most of us gripe and complain, worry and fret, and run around trying to handle things on our own. If we think about God at all, we grumble that He should have taken better care of us. After all, isn't He powerful enough to protect us from all of that?

Many new "believers" quit right away. Jesus talked about them in the parable of the soils. *"Those on the rock are the ones who receive the word with joy when they hear it, but they have no root. They believe for awhile, but in the time of testing they fall away"* (Luke 8:13).

Sooner or later, many Christians face what Chuck Swindoll calls the "Betrayal Barrier" when God seems to betray us. This happens when we pray for God to help us through something and He seems to let us down. He does something we can't understand.

Those who persevere may or may not learn to trust God. (Many Christians stay in church but close off their hearts to God.) Most Christians find it hard at first to see that God might have a loving purpose in allowing us to face challenges that shake our confidence in the things we have trusted so confidently.

Happily, some Christians figure out after awhile that when they went through trying times, they learned to trust God more. They figure out that God can use even Satan's attacks and the bad actions of evil people for His own good purposes. They figure out that God is faithful and He won't let us face any temptation beyond what we can bear – with His help (I Cor. 10:13).

God views our troubles differently than we do. When a crisis comes our way, we think the battle is "out there." We think God's main priority should be to bail us out: heal our sick friend; provide a job; give us a baby or a husband; defend us from the attacks by our enemies; and get rid of the annoyances that drip, drip, drip like Chinese water torture.

Of course, if we pray about them, our troubles do showcase God's grace. Time after time God delivers us. But, still, that's not His highest priority.

THE GREAT TRANSFER

We don't realize that God wages a careful and targeted campaign to win our hearts. God uses each new crisis to shake our grip on lesser refuges (like friends, our job, our 401K or our own control), so we'll transfer our trust to Him. He wants us to exchange the penny in our hand for the rubies in His. God works to win those areas of our heart that have never yielded to His control or known His glory. Sometimes He uses stressful situations to bring to light hidden regions of our heart just so He can heal our deep wounds.

In this campaign of tough love He often uses the pain of unanswered prayer, of slow progress, of perplexing dilemmas. He lets us fail. He puts us into situations that we cannot control. We try our best to abide in Christ the Vine and then He strips our branches of newly forming fruit (John 15:1 – 5).

A dozen times on our life journey, He brings us to a fork in the road and asks us to choose, "Will you trust this particular thing to Me?" Almost always, that question forces us to loosen our grip on something else that we've been trusting. Maybe this next diagram will help us to picture it more clearly.

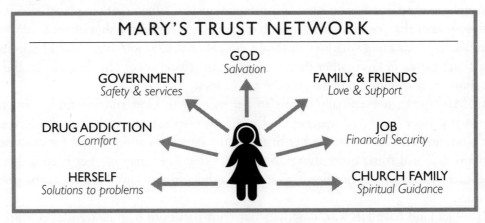

Let's assume that Mary has been a Christian for a few years. As you can see, even though Mary thinks she trusts God, she actually trusts a bunch of things more or less equally.

There is nothing wrong with this, as far as it goes. It's human to want to be able to trust our family and friends. It's fine to put some trust in our job or our church. It would be counterproductive to walk around filled with suspicion all the time. It is fine to assume that the government will do what it's supposed to do. And, in the middle of all those objects of trust, we trust God for our salvation.

There's only one problem. Every one of the things that Mary trusts, except for God, has some kind of limitation. It can be shaken. It can fall apart. To some degree or another, every other thing is a broken cistern that can't hold water. It is a "lesser refuge" than God our Great Refuge.

One way of looking at almost every trust battle is to see it as a time when God shakes up something in our trust network. Financial crises shake our trust in our job, conflicts shake our trust in the people involved, and church problems shake our trust in the church we attend. We assume that we'll always be able to count on our husband or our best friend. But even though they love us, they might get sick, or die, or just move away. Many of these situations can even shake our view of God.

When these things get shaken up, we have several typical reactions from which to choose. For instance, **we can unthinkingly redouble our efforts to trust that refuge.** If we lose one job, we can turn to another job. If one friend lets us down, we can look for another friend. We can go through the whole crisis without ever thinking about what it would mean to trust God for that area of our life.

Sometimes we react by rejecting that thing altogether. If we had a bad experience at one church we can quit going to church. If our friends betray us we can become a hermit. Now if we relied on some sinful refuge like lies or addictions, it's smart to quit. But it's generally a sign of deep woundedness to reject morally neutral refuges. And that's not the conclusion God favors.

We have a third option. **We can find refuge in God and learn to shift our primary trust to God.** Then God can provide healing for our woundedness and teach us the appropriate priority for that area. No one says we shouldn't have friends. But we should look to God, not people, to meet our deepest needs for companionship. When that's in place, friends are a blessing. It's not that we shouldn't get a job to pay our bills. But we should ask God to meet our financial needs using whatever method God chooses. Our job search would become an expression of trust in God rather than an exercise in self-reliance. The diagram on the next page shows how this third and best option might look.

In Mary's case, it eventually occurs to her to turn to God and she finds Him to be trustworthy. Now instead of trusting God merely for her salvation, she has also learned to trust God, first and foremost, for her finances, for safety, for support and for solutions to problems. She still trusts other things. She knows that God may use her friends, her job, her church, etc., to meet her needs. But those other things don't have the same grip on her heart.

If we let God have His way, God uses our trust battles to help us transfer our primary trust from things we see to God, whom we can't see. Over time, He teaches us to trust Him to meet our deepest needs whether directly or through human means.

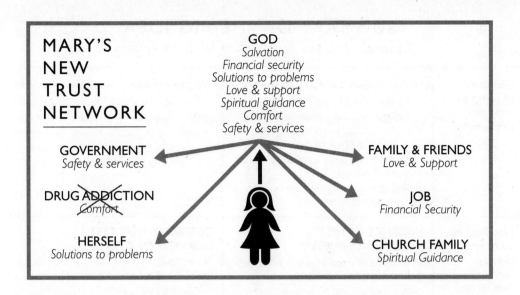

MARY'S NEW TRUST NETWORK

GOD
Salvation
Financial security
Solutions to problems
Love & support
Spiritual guidance
Comfort
Safety & services

GOVERNMENT
Safety & services

FAMILY & FRIENDS
Love & Support

DRUG ADDICTION
Comfort

JOB
Financial Security

HERSELF
Solutions to problems

CHURCH FAMILY
Spiritual Guidance

Those of us who steadfastly choose to trust God, one fork in the road at a time, find the hope that does not disappoint (Romans 5:5). We experience God's lavish love poured out into our hearts. We wake up one day and realize that God has never done us wrong. He has never been unkind. He stripped our branches of fruit only to channel our growth into strong roots that find and drink deeply at His hidden spring of water. Truly, He does all things well.

Every time we run to God to help us to deal with our trust battles we learn how to trust God a bit more. Gradually, the things we used to regard as *obstacles* switch sides, and we begin to see them as new *evidence* that He can be trusted.

When new troubles come along, we face them hand in hand with our faithful Friend. We set aside our control of situations and find security in His infinitely wise control. We begin to resemble Jesus who entrusted Himself to God (I Peter 2:23). And our calm trust blesses God by giving Him the glory due His name.

SUMMARY OF THE BIG IDEA
Clues about God's Master Plan for Trust Training

God does all things to bring glory to His name	**Names of God that Apply to Trust –** • **Rock:** stable, solid, changeless • **Refuge:** providing protection, shelter, haven, sanctuary, and rescue • **Fortress & Stronghold:** walled city guarded by troops assigned to protect and defend • **Shield:** King who protects His subjects from outside threats	**We give glory to these names of God by –** • Trusting God, especially during crisis • Running to God for refuge • Counting on God to defend and protect us • Expressing confidence in God's power and love during times of crisis
God Teaches Us to Trust Him By Sending Two Things	**EVIDENCE OF HIS TRUSTWORTHINESS** • Evidence of creation (especially cycles of seasons and recovery) • Evidence of God's character (Bible knowledge) • Evidence of answered prayer (personal experiences) • Evidence of relationship (personal and relational knowledge of God)	**OBSTACLES THAT TEST OUR VIEW OF GOD** • God deliberately shakes our trust network so we will transfer our trust to Him • God uses our troubles to win our hearts and teach us to yield everything to Him
Results	• These accumulated evidences build our confidence in God • Our trust brings glory to God	• These obstacles press us to choose to turn over unyielded areas to God's control • As we learn to entrust these obstacles to God, they become evidence of His trustworthiness

FACE TIME WITH MY TRAINER

PART 1: Answer these Bible study questions BEFORE reading the chapter

Read Matthew 6:25 – 34. *List at least five encouragements in this passage for trusting God.*
Read Isaiah 40:10 – 14. *List at least five reasons why God is worthy of my trust.*

PART 2: Questions & Reflection

1. Think about your own story. What evidence have you already found that assures you that God can be trusted? (For instance, when I look at birds it reminds me that God can be trusted to meet my financial needs.) For each of these four categories, jot down some things that encourage you to trust God.

> Evidence of creation;
> Evidence of God's character;
> Evidence of answered prayer;
> Evidence of relationship.

2. **TRUST NETWORK DIAGRAM:** Try drawing a diagram of your own trust network on a separate sheet of paper. You might start with the categories in Mary's chart, but include categories personal to you. If you used to rely on something, but don't any more, include it and mark an "X" over it. For instance, if you used to comfort yourself with alcohol and then quit, mark it down and put an "X" over it.

You might try making several of these diagrams, showing your trust network at different times in your life, say, one for when you were a child, one for when you finished school and one for now. That might make it easier to see what you used to rely on directly, and what items in your trust network you have been able to transfer more directly to God.

3. Now, refer back to those two lists you compiled at the end of Chapter 3. For each of those entries, note what parts of your trust network that situation affected. (Feel free to add categories to your trust network diagram as needed.) One situation might affect several categories. For instance, from the example "Choosing to move to Toledo," it would make sense to jot down "family, job, friends, and church."

4. Stop for a few minutes and just look at your lists and your diagram(s). What can you see regarding your life story that you haven't seen before? Spend some time praying about what this exercise brings to light. Meditate especially on what has happened in those parts of your trust network that have been most shaken. What have you learned already about how to trust God for those areas? Do any of these areas still cause some pain? Are you still holding on to some part of your trust network that you know, deep down, isn't worthy of your trust? What clues has this exercise given you about what God may be up to in your life?

5. What did you find to be the most encouraging or intriguing idea in this chapter?

Julie's Story

Both of my elderly parents were hospitalized for surgery within a day of each other, my dad for triple bypass heart surgery, and my mom for a ruptured appendix. I found myself leaving my six children daily, to stay at my parent's bedsides around the clock. It was pretty traumatic to see them both so ill and disoriented. During most of their three-week stay they were on different floors so my sisters and I were constantly going back and forth between them. It was hard because we always had to leave one of them to go sit with the other one.

Although I knew God was in control, I fought feelings of panic, not knowing how long the crisis would last and what God would decide to do. I desperately wanted life to go back to normal.

During those days, the song "Sometimes by Step" (written by Rich Mullins and Bebo Norman), gave me a lot of comfort. It was on a CD that I played constantly as I drove to and from the hospital. The words of that song reassured me that God would lead me step by step, even when I faltered.

Gradually, very gradually, I saw God's faithfulness as my parents both recovered and went home. They had insurance that provided for home health care help, so we didn't have to be there all the time while they adjusted to the changes in their routine. It is clear that this has evolved into a long-term challenge to deal with this new season in my parents' lives.

As I look back on that episode I can see several threads of evidence that have strengthened my trust in God. God has been so gentle with me as He builds my trust in Him. The situations with either of my parents could have turned out so differently. It has encouraged me that God answered my prayers and they both got better.

Also, I can see God's amazing timing. Two days before the hospitalization, my parents, my husband and I returned from a trip back East to revisit the sites from my mom's childhood. For years we had talked about taking such a trip but you know how those things can get postponed. But something urged me to make it happen when it did. The trip was full of divine appointments and incredible coincidences that allowed my mom to have a wonderful trip down memory lane. We were able to tour the inside of her childhood home, the house that her father had built. Against all odds we found the actual grave site of her grandfather. Only God knew what lay ahead for all of us. His timing made those memories even more precious.

Lastly, one of the biggest miracles occurred during those days at the hospital. God repaired the little animosities and misunderstandings that had built up over the years in my relationship with both of my sisters. As we cared for my parents we became a team and learned to appreciate the strengths that each of us brought to the situation. We are now very close and continue to talk often to make unified decisions regarding my parents and to enjoy our relationship as sisters.

CHAPTER 5

Preparing the Heart to Trust

But I have stilled and quieted my soul;
like a weaned child with its mother,
like a weaned child is my soul within me.
Psalm 131:2

Eight years ago I asked God to train me to trust Him. One day, early in this training, I asked Him to give me a clearer picture of my ultimate goal in this quest. My old idea of the Madonna sitting in the chair was clearly not sufficient for this new era of active trust.

"How will I recognize what it looks like to trust You?"

I waited in silence with my eyes closed. Then in my mind's eye I saw a little girl about five years old taking a walk with her daddy. Her chubby little fingers were tucked easily and confidently into her daddy's big hand as they walked along. She chattered happily, confiding her childish secrets and sharing the delights of her day. Daddy was focused on her and clearly enjoyed her company. They looked as if they liked each other, knew each other well, and felt comfortable together.

I watched them as they came to a fork in the road. Daddy told her which way to go and she didn't put up a fuss. She asked a few questions and then, tucking her hand more snugly in his, followed her daddy's lead.

That little picture reminded me of times I've noticed families in the grocery store or at the park. You can tell a lot about some relationships by their conversation and body language in such situations. If a child sulks or shrinks away from an outstretched hand, it might only mean he's having a bad day and could use a nap – or it might be a tip off to a troubled home life. That little glimpse in the store may reveal a parent handling a difficult child with grace and patience. Or you may watch in horror as a vicious woman shreds her helpless child with such cruelty that your stomach muscles clench with sympathy pain. A child's body language may betray secrets that the adults would rather keep hidden.

But every once in a while, that quick peek into their world, that you catch when you overhear their conversation while you scan the shelves for your favorite brand of cereal, can be a window into something wonderful.

I thought about what people see when they look at me. They can only get an impression of what's going on in my relationship with God. Unlike my mental picture show of that little girl with her father, when it comes to my relationship with God, people see only my side of the picture. They can't see my unseen heavenly Father.

But it occurred to me that when I talk about my life, I give people clues about my relationship with God. I paint a picture of what He's like by whether I tuck my hand easily into His big hand when troubles come my way, or whine and sulk and talk endlessly about my fears and worries. How often do I act as if God is not God, strong enough to handle anything that comes along in my life, and wise and kind enough to guide me through everything?

Back then I realized with sadness that I often gave people the wrong impression of God by my body language and by the things I said. I want my trust in God to be so bone deep that people catch glimpses of God's beauty even in my unguarded moments. When people overhear my conversations I want them to see the God that I'm coming to know and trust.

That mental picture of the little girl and her daddy has stuck with me. As I have studied about trust and learned to trust God in more kinds of circumstances, I've concluded that when it comes to trust, our goal is to see God as our wonderful daddy and to see ourselves as His dearly loved and well cared for little girls or boys. When you boil everything down to its essence, there is a core quality of **healthy childlikeness** in authentic trust in God.

Do you remember *hasa,* the Hebrew word for trust? *Hasa* means to run for refuge. It's an instinctual thing. When something takes us by surprise, when the adrenaline kicks in and we run for cover, if we have this quality of healthy childlikeness we will run to Jesus. But if not, we will run other places. We will try to handle things ourselves or crawl into a hole of isolation. We will trust our network of relationships, such as it is. Or worst of all, maybe we'll run for refuge right into the arms of abusers and users, of people who don't deserve our trust.

I'd like to explore this topic of healthy childlikeness and see how our life story either prepares us to trust God or throws roadblocks in our way. Even if we had a happy or uneventful life, by the time we become functioning adults we have picked up a few things that gum up the works when we try to trust God. I'd like to explore two areas that profoundly affect our aptitude for trusting God: our emotional development and our mind. We'll look at what is supposed to happen in each area, how life experiences can make it harder to trust God, and how to bring each area into healthy childlikeness.

PREPARATION IN OUR EMOTIONAL DEVELOPMENT

One day the disciples went to Jesus to settle an argument about who was the greatest in the kingdom of heaven. A little boy had been hanging around the group and Jesus called him over to stand in center stage. Then He replied, *"...unless you change and become like little children, you will never enter the kingdom of heaven. Therefore, whoever humbles himself like this child is the greatest in the kingdom of heaven"* (Matthew 18:3, 4).

The boy in Matthew 18 reminds me of my little girl with her daddy because that boy was attracted to Jesus. Why else was he hovering nearby? He came over willingly because he had a healthy childlike trust in Jesus.

With that little guy still standing there, Jesus expanded on this theme. In verse 6, He gave a solemn warning. *"But if anyone causes one of these little ones who believe in Me to sin, it would be better for him to have a large millstone hung around his neck and to be drowned in the depths of the sea."*

The adults who raise us bear a pivotal responsibility. They lay the foundation for trust before we can make any choices of our own. Our adult capacity to trust God and to trust people, particularly our ability to recognize and to gravitate toward emotionally healthy and safe people, is heavily influenced by what happens to us in our first formative years of life.

If they did a good job, by the time we were four or five, we learned the first crucial lessons about trust. And around that age, when we got fearful or nervous, they took extra care to show that they could be trusted. They consistently did what they said they would do.

If they did their job right, we learned some basic life truths, such as:

- My parents (or my caregivers) love me.
- They "see" the real me and accept me for who I am.
- They make wise decisions, even if I don't always see the wisdom at the time.
- I am safe when I am with them.
- They can and they do provide for my needs.
- I can depend on them to stay with me no matter what.

By this age we should have learned how to obey willingly because we made peace with their authority over us. They didn't set an impossible standard for our behavior. We could obey their rules with our chubby little fingers and they didn't change the rules without warning. Normally, they let us face the reasonable consequences of our behavior so that we could learn from our mistakes.

If we failed in some way, they spelled out a way to make things right again. They did a good job if we had confidence to go to them when we got into trouble, if we could confess our sins without terror, and if we could also share our worries or fears with the confidence that they would understand us, love us unconditionally, and make things right.

Children of such parents become like the weaned child mentioned in Psalm 131. Their parents have given them a childhood experience that equips them with the emotional ability to "still and quiet" their souls.

Unfortunately, many children have gaps of one kind or another and don't get such a good foundation. Many children deal with abandonment issues because of divorce or emotional neglect, or become warped by abuse of one kind or another. Many parents do not provide a good role model for authority. And even children with a good foundation can get hurt later on by teachers or classmates or early romantic relationships.

No matter how old we get, we still carry around that inner little girl inside our hearts, and she steers the ship, so to speak, when it comes to our adult relationships. If our "little girl" entered adulthood still and quiet, she will guide the adult woman toward good relationships. But if that little girl is wounded and troubled, she will unwittingly push the adult woman toward people who remind her of her abusive childhood home life, and she will choose abusive and untrustworthy people.

Incidentally, the same goes for men. If that vulnerable "little boy" was nurtured and loved, he will make the adult man strong and confident, someone whose strength translates into protectiveness toward the weak. But if that little boy was abused or demeaned, he will steer the adult man toward dysfunctional women who belittle or betray him. Or that little boy might make a child's vow never to get hurt that way again, and fulfill that vow by becoming an abuser himself.

The unfinished business of childhood haunts our adult relationships. If we had bad role models, we find it hard to recognize and gravitate toward trustworthy people. Many girls marry "daddy," for good or ill, and boys tend to become "daddy," whatever that means. Even if we vow never to become like those who hurt us, our efforts to swing the opposite way land us in the same dysfunctional place, if only through the back door. Even if we don't abuse others, we turn our rage inward to abuse and condemn ourselves. The fallout of our unhappiness affects others.

Our adult relationships become a stage on which we repeatedly reenact our little girl's unfinished business. Traumatic events or cutting words trigger our barely remembered memory of childhood pain and our reactions today reflect our pain from yesterday.

So why am I bringing this up in a study about trusting God? Simple. **We can't compartmentalize our lives and assume we can fix all of our spiritual problems by purely spiritual remedies like memorizing a Bible verse or praying harder. Our walk with God can't help but be affected by our emotional health, by our physical bodies, and by what's going on in our head.** In order to grow in our spiritual lives, sometimes we need to tackle problems in other areas. That especially applies to trust. What happened to us when we were children either made it easier, or made it harder, for us to trust God now in adulthood.

If we tend to choose romantic partners unwisely, those decisions probably had their roots in childhood pain. If that troubled little girl inside our adult body chooses an abusive partner instead of a more trustworthy one, that same woundedness often keeps us far away from God, who is the most trustworthy person of all. If our wounded little girl vowed never to let anyone see her vulnerability, the adult uses that same tough façade to guard against God's unpredictability. And we miss the chance to find our heart's true Father.

But there's good news. We don't have to remain slaves of our upbringing. We have more resources available than any generation before us. Good Christian counseling can help us to unravel the damage from the past and to set new patterns. Healing prayer also works well.

In the past few years I've been part of a number of healing prayer sessions. Again and again I've witnessed Jesus speak to the wounded child hidden within the adult and bring words of truth that heal and restore peace. He grieves over the woundedness of our little girl. Why else would He talk of such somber things as millstones? **More than we can ever imagine, He loves our hidden little girl and longs for the day when that part of us can freely run into His arms with a glad heart.**

Now let's get back on more comfortable ground. The good news is that by now we have entered adulthood and we have been able to deal with some of the problems we brought into our adult years. We can make choices. Isn't that great?

The Apostle Paul made an interesting observation in I Corinthians 13:11. *"When I was a child, I talked like a child, I thought like a child, I reasoned like a child. When I became a man, I put childish ways behind me."*

How can we do this? How can we put childish ways behind us? What childish ways are we talking about?

I think in context, Paul is contrasting our limited knowledge here on earth with the knowledge we'll have when we get to heaven. But taken with other verses, (like Ephesians 4:14, 15 and Romans 12:2) our goal is to become mature in our walk with God and to be transformed by the renewing of our minds. And one of the ways our mind becomes renewed is by learning to trust God wholeheartedly in every situation.

But let me share a little of my story as an illustration of how we can misinterpret Paul's words in a way that makes it harder to trust God. Maybe you have done some of these same things.

When I became an adult I "put away childish things" by moving a thousand miles from home. I also put away that little girl inside my heart and tried to ignore her completely. I went on about the business of being an adult woman with a husband and family. I sincerely forgave the people who hurt me, but because I didn't also address the underlying problems, my forgiveness was little more than a "spiritual band-aid." (It's always better to forgive than to harbor bitterness, but I didn't realize at the time that I forgave partly to avoid facing some serious issues.)

These strategies didn't work too well in the long run. Little things would happen that triggered memories of my childhood pain and I would explode in anger. I crawled my way through bouts of depression that lasted for months on end. As much as I loved my wonderful husband, the center of my emotional world continued to be my parents. I kept banging my head against a wall trying to get them to give me now what I had needed as a child.

I stuffed my pain for about ten years before my sweet husband encouraged me to get some counseling. That started a long season in which many people helped me through the process of renewing my mind. They helped me to take off that band-aid so I could look at the pain and deal with it.

Jesus is the Great Healer. I can tell you from experience, and from personally seeing how He has worked in the lives of many other people, that He loves that little girl inside of us. He came to save us completely (Hebrews 7:25), even that confused and wounded part.

When we grow up into maturity in Christ, that little child doesn't go away. Instead, we can more wisely take care of her. The Holy Spirit has come to live within us to guide us into that maturity. He works through many formats, such as Sunday sermons, insightful Christian books, good Bible studies, and our personal devotional lives that give us a good foundation in our walk with Christ. We need to be led by the Spirit in every aspect of our lives, developing the fruit of the Spirit if we are to become "adult" Christians.

By now, with eight years of trust training under my belt, I've noticed something interesting. If a situation rises to the level of becoming a trust battle or a trust challenge, it can be a training opportunity for both our renewed "adult" mind and for our little girl.

When we first become adults, we enjoy our independence. It's good to become functioning members of society who can stand on our own two feet. We like making our own decisions and controlling our own space. Unfortunately, we don't realize that some part of that independent spirit is actually plain old rebellious sin. It is mainly in scary situations that God teaches us to face the sinful aspects of our independence. He gives us the opportunity to let go of the superficial control we think we have and humble ourselves to submit to His control. Our renewed mind learns to make the truly adult decision to depend on God. Proverbs 3:5 puts it this way. *Trust in the Lord with all your heart and <u>lean not on your own understanding</u>.* [My highlight] We develop healthy childlikeness by learning to humble ourselves as adults and by relying on God's wisdom instead of our own.

God also uses scary situations to reveal Himself to our inner child. In the last chapter we talked about how God uses our life experience to transfer our trust from lesser refuges to Himself. Let me give a personal illustration of how this works with our little girl.

An odd thing used to happen whenever I was about to go out and look for a new job. Even though I don't get panic attacks, during these times I would get swamped with panicky feelings, worrying that I'd never find a job and dreading the day I'd have to go job hunting.

One morning in my devotional time I asked Jesus to show me the source of this anxiety. In answer to my prayer the Lord brought a childhood memory to the surface of my mind. I remembered a day when I was about eight years old. I remember sitting hunched on some stairs listening intently as my parents argued in the next room. One of my little brothers cried in one of the bedrooms while my other brother hid in his room. Jesus reminded me of one sentence in the argument.

My dad had yelled at my mother, "You'll never get a job."

Jesus stayed with me there in that memory, facing the pain and anxiety I felt that day when my parent's fears and insecurities engulfed me. Dad's angry words had pierced me that day and I thought they applied to me, then and forever. Jesus helped me to identify my faulty childish reasoning, and He spoke truth that renewed my mind.

The truth was that those words weren't directed at me at all, but at my mother. It wasn't even true for her. She went out and found a great job as an elementary teacher and did her job quite well. We never went hungry when I was little.

Jesus sat next to me on the steps. I didn't need to face that terror alone any more. Then He gently spoke the larger truth to that little girl part of me.

"Dionne, when you think about looking for a job, you go back to this time and place, sitting out of sight, surrounded by angry chaos and fear. Dionne, I control ALL jobs. I am generous. I am faithful. I have power."

As we sat there, He helped me to remember job after job that He has given me over the years. I've found work every time I needed a job.

Since that day I haven't had a panicked feeling when it comes to looking for a job. Jesus used that situation to shift my center of gravity away from my parents' house and toward His presence. As He has spoken healing truth to more and more of those leftover childhood traumas, the center of my focus has shifted to more healthy people. I don't keep looking to my parents to meet those deep needs. Jesus is becoming the center of my emotional world as He should.

Since Jesus has worked in my life to transfer my trust to Him, bit by bit, my husband has reaped some great benefits from my shift of focus. My emotions and my attention are now free to enjoy the here and now in the life we have together. That's what happens when the Lord restores our soul. We begin to gravitate toward trustworthy people.

Healthy childlikeness is a wonderful thing. John, the beloved disciple, understood and enjoyed this healthy childlikeness. Listen to his testimony. *"How great is the love the Father has lavished on us, that we should be called children of God! And that is what we are!"* (I John 3: 1) I hope that you can see yourself as a little girl boldly tucking your chubby little fingers in the big loving hand of your heavenly Father. That's the best preparation for facing every trust challenge that comes our way.

SUMMARY OF THE BIG IDEA
Healthy childlikeness prepares our hearts to trust God.

	EMOTIONAL DEVELOPMENT	OUR MIND
How healthy childlikeness is supposed to develop	**Good parenting helps a child to develop the foundations of trust. **Solid childhood experiences prepare us to make wise choices about who to trust when we grow up, making it easier to trust God.	**Good educational and life experiences train us to deal with situations in a mature, reasonable and skillful way. **After salvation, growth in Christ brings godly maturity and cultivates the mind of Christ within us.
If our parents left holes in our early childhood trust training, those gaps will...	...affect the choices we make in our adult relationships. These gaps will incline us to choose badly. ...return to haunt us as current situations remind us of childhood pain. ...keep us in a cycle of reacting to current stresses using flawed childish reasoning and responses.	...make us inclined to ignore or "stuff" our childhood pain. ...make it harder to move head knowledge about God into heart assurance. ...make us cling to our adult independence even when that independence represents rebellion against God.
The better way to deal with those gaps in our childhood (or early adult) trust training is to...	...bring them to the surface and bravely address the issues involved. This may involve counseling. ...bring them to Jesus for Him to speak truth and healing to our wounded little girl. ...shift the center of our emotional world toward Jesus and toward emotionally healthy people.	...cooperate with the Holy Spirit's ministry in our lives to renew our mind. ...humble ourselves by turning to God in stressful times instead of relying on our own understanding. ...learn how to become the parent to our own little girl as Jesus shows us how.

FACE TIME WITH MY TRAINER

PART 1: Answer these Bible study questions BEFORE reading the chapter

Each of the following verses either quotes God, or says something reassuring about God. Read each verse and then personalize it to complete the sentence: "I can trust God because..."

EXAMPLE: Numbers 23:19 *"God never lies to me and He always keeps His word."*

Philippians 4:19. Hebrews 13:5, Jeremiah 31:3, Psalm 32:7, I John 1:9, Psalm 103:13 – 14

Read Psalm 131*, and imagine that you are that weaned child. Now think about the other verses you just looked up. Why would it be easier for you to "still and quiet" your soul in God's presence if the truth found in those verses became real to you?*

PART 2: Questions & Reflection

1. Think back to your earliest childhood memories. Had someone taught you the basics of trust by then? (You can refer to the left side of the chart on the next page as you answer.) Which aspects did your parents or guardians do well and where did they have problems?

2. "The unfinished business of childhood haunts our adult relationships." Why will dealing with leftover childhood trauma ultimately have a positive effect on our ability to trust God?

3. Can you think of a situation in which Jesus helped you to unravel some childish reasoning and gave you a better way to look at things? What had you believed up until then, what happened that brought that to the surface, what truth did you hear, and how did Jesus bring you peace and newfound freedom?

4. On the right side of the chart on the next page, you'll find some things your heavenly Father says to you if you belong to Him. Spend some time praying and meditating on them. Has your "little girl" heard all of those assurances in a personal way? Remember back to when you heard Him say the ones you have heard. Rest in that sweetness of assurance and thank Him for loving you.

5. If you look over that column and some pain comes to the surface, ask the Lord to meet you now. Tell Him what that statement reminded you of, and ask Him to help you unravel your faulty childish reasoning. Give Jesus time to stand with you in that painful memory and listen to what He has for you now.

6. What did you find to be the most encouraging or intriguing idea in this chapter?

FURTHER HELP: *Check out the Trust Battle Prayer Guide at the end of this chapter. It is designed to help you to evaluate and clarify the issues you're dealing with when you find yourself in a new trust battle. It will become even more useful after you finish this entire Bible study. You might give it a test run by using it to evaluate something you're going through now.*

CONTRAST BETWEEN HUMAN PARENTS AND GOD

What we should have felt confident to say about our parents	*How God can provide what's missing*
They consistently do what they say they will do.	**I always keep My word.** *"God is not a man, that He should lie, nor a son of man, that He should change His mind. Does He speak and then not act? Does He promise and not fulfill?"* Numbers 23:19
My parents love me unconditionally.	**I will always love you.** *"I have loved you with an everlasting love."* Jer. 31:3
They "see" me and accept me for who I am.	**I know you and take delight in the "you" I created you to be.** *"O Lord, You have searched me and You know me....You are familiar with all my ways."* Ps. 139:1, 3 *"Accept one another, then, just as Christ accepted you, in order to bring praise to God."* Romans 15:7
They make wise decisions.	**My plans are always best.** *"Oh, the depths of the riches of the wisdom and knowledge of God! How unsearchable His judgments, and His paths beyond tracing out!"* Rom 11:33
I am safe when I am home with them.	**You are always safe with Me.** *"The eternal God is your refuge and underneath are the everlasting arms."* Deut. 33:27
They can and do provide for my needs.	**I take good care of My own.** *"And my God will meet all your needs according to His glorious riches in Christ Jesus."* Phil. 4:19
I can depend on them to stay with me no matter what.	**I will never abandon you.** *"Never will I leave you; never will I forsake you."* Heb. 13:5
They set an achievable standard for my behavior.	**I've taught you the path of life.** *"The ordinances of the LORD are sure and altogether righteous....By them is your servant warned; in keeping them there is great reward."* Psalm 19:9, 11 *"This is love for God: to obey His commands. And His commands are not burdensome,"* 1 John 5:3
When I mess up, I feel confident that I can get back into their good graces without demeaning myself.	**I've made a way for you and I forgive your sins.** *"For God was pleased to have all His fullness dwell in Him [Christ], and through Him to reconcile to Himself all things, whether things on earth or things in heaven, by making peace through His blood, shed on the cross."* Col. 1:19, 20 *"If we confess our sins, He is faithful and just and will forgive us our sins and purify us from all unrighteousness."* 1 John 1:9

Lynne's Story

It had been five years since we had painfully departed from our long-time church, and I was still hurting. I felt the familiar dull ache in my chest return. We had done everything we knew. For a year and a half we had followed the principles in Matthew 18, in letter and in spirit, including seeking mediation. Our private attempts toward a joint resolution had been repeatedly rebuffed. Then we had been blamed publicly and accused of non-cooperation.

Recently, I had been exposed to Healing Prayer. One day while taking a walk, I decided to use what I had been learning. I decided to take this ongoing pain to the Lord for help.

The ache in my chest felt like guilt, but I knew in my mind that I wasn't guilty. "What's this feeling, Lord?" I asked. As I continued to walk and focus on my feeling, I was amazed to hear, "It isn't guilt. It's shame." I asked, "What is this all about, Lord? Is there an earlier source of this shame feeling?"

Instantly, I remembered an incident that occurred when I was thirteen years old.

My algebra teacher had accused me falsely, in front of classmates, of having defaced my desk. Her accusation had made me feel confused, helpless, blindsided and humiliated. As I stood there in the pain of that vivid memory, I felt the Lord's presence. As I looked at the face of my teacher, I heard the words, "It wasn't about you. It was about her."

Immediately, compassion arose in me. I realized she had been an unattractive, aging spinster with problems of her own. She _had_ backed down somewhat, after class had been dismissed and everyone was gone, when I told her I had not done this. That felt better. But then a new pain surged up that found words. "But, she never _apologized_, Lord. She left me holding all the _blame_!"

Still absorbed in my memory, I continued to walk. I sensed that when I crossed the street, the Lord would meet me on the other side. As I walked across the street, the weight physically intensified to the point that I was bent over double. At the most crushing moment, I heard a stern, emphatic voice say, "_I_ am the scapegoat!" The weight immediately lifted. I began weeping, gratitude to Him overflowing. What had weighed me down had not disappeared. I could sense that it had been _transferred_ to the Presence still beside me. He had taken it off my back and was carrying it Himself. I could not believe it — that He had done that for me!

Later that night, at home, I was worshiping and reflecting on the words I had heard and what had happened that day on my walk. Once again, I heard His words, spoken casually (and with the suggestion of a gentle smile and a twinkling eye), "Yes. And do you know that church burden? I took that, too!" Astonished, I rapidly searched my memories of what had occurred five years before and found the familiar ache _gone_! There was nothing but peace.

I remembered something I had said to a board member back then, "If all of us could just meet together at the foot of the cross and humble ourselves, this could resolve. But, I guess, since they aren't willing to do that, for the good of the church, someone will have to be the scapegoat." I had taken on that role and that inappropriate weight.

I am so glad that the _Lord Jesus_ is the scapegoat and that He has set _me_ free! (In the last six years since the walk I took that day the pain has not returned.)

Trust Battle Prayer Guide

This is designed to help you prayerfully evaluate and clarify a new trust battle using information discussed mainly in the introduction to the *Trust Training Manual*. Since you have time to complete this prayer guide, assume God has given you an opportunity to practice active trust (instead of passive trust). For more information see the noted chapter or section.

SUGGESTED OPENING PRAYER

"Dear Father, thank You for promising, in James 1:5, to give wisdom if I need it. I need it now, so I ask for wisdom to evaluate and face this trust battle. Please open my eyes to see this situation from Your perspective. Thank You for offering to train my hands for battle. I lay this situation before You and ask that You use it to train me however You think best. Please increase my faith, and help me to trust You better for having faced it, in Jesus' name, Amen."

DESCRIBE THE PROBLEM. Include why it occurred to me to consider this a trust issue.

IS THIS A DEFENSIVE OR AN OFFENSIVE BATTLE? (Chapter 3) Am I wrestling with the typical trust issue for that kind of battle? If not, what is my trust issue regarding this battle?

- DEFENSIVE: I had no choice. I'm facing circumstances beyond my control.
  Biggest Typical Trust Issue: Whether to accept that God loves me and still allowed this to happen, and whether to trust God in the middle of these mystifying circumstances.

- OFFENSIVE: I can choose whether or not to fight this battle.
  Biggest Typical Trust Issue: To figure out what it would mean to obey God concerning this matter and whether I will obey His clear leading.

WHAT KIND OF TRUST BATTLE IS THIS? Is it a Crisis, a Challenge, a Significant Loss, an Intense Ministry Situation, or a combination of several options? (Chapter 3)

MY CURRENT TRUST NETWORK: (See Chapter 4)

"God views our troubles differently than we do. When a crisis comes our way, we think the battle is 'out there.' We think God's main priority should be to bail us out: heal our sick friend; provide a new job; give us a baby or a husband; defend us from attacks by our enemies; and get rid of the annoyances that drip, drip, drip like a Chinese water torture….

"We don't realize that God wages a careful and targeted campaign to win our hearts. God uses each new crisis to shake our grip on lesser refuges (like friends, our job, our 401K or our own control) so we will transfer our trust to Him….God works to win those areas of our heart that have never yielded to His control or known His glory. Sometimes He uses stressful situations to bring to light hidden regions of our heart just so He can heal our deep wounds".

- What piece of my current trust network has been shaken? Put another way, what was I relying on before this happened?

- What painful feelings, painful memories or insecurities has this stirred up?

- How willing am I to yield to God's nudging to transfer my deepest trust to Him instead of going back to relying mainly on something else in my current trust network?

- What evidence has God already given me that He can be trusted regarding this area of my trust network? What evidence have I already seen in other areas, which encourages me to trust Him for this area?

- Am I willing to give Him control of this area of my life to do whatever He thinks best?

WHERE AM I IN THIS BATTLE? (See applicable section of this *Trust Training* Manual.)

- <u>Before</u>: I've just become aware of the problem and I'm still evaluating how to handle it, or it won't happen for a long time (or may never happen) but I am worried and troubled about it now.

- <u>During</u>: It has been going on for awhile, or I'm already knee deep in dealing with it. I mainly need help to cope with it and to better trust God through it.

- <u>After</u>: The crisis or challenge has passed, but I'm still struggling to recover. I'm grieving a death or the loss of something, or I'm struggling to forgive people who hurt me in a recent situation. It may be that I'm still struggling to recover from things that happened long ago.

HOW CAN I EXERCISE FAITH IN THIS SITUATION? (Chapter 2)

Faith is a confident belief in the truth or trustworthiness of a person, idea or thing.
Faith means to regard something as true, to believe.
Faith centers mainly in the mind and the will, not in the emotions.
We exercise faith by doing an act of faith. An act of faith can be anything we do, or any attitude we hold, that logically flows out of believing that something is true.

- Has God given me any promises or do I know of any Bible verses that apply to this situation? (Use a concordance or Bible study help if needed.)
- What have I already learned about the character of God that applies to this situation?
- Even if I didn't feel particularly full of faith, what would I do differently if I acted as if those promises were true? How would I act if I believed God could and would help me to face this situation?
- Am I willing to continue to allow the Lord to show me how to exercise faith for each part of this trust battle? If so, ask for ongoing guidance about how to exercise faith.

HOW CAN I DEEPEN IN MY TRUST TOWARD GOD? (Chapter 2)

Trust is the firm reliance on the integrity, ability or character of a person or thing.
Trust can take the form of a conscious decision to seek refuge, flee for protection, or confide.
Trust usually takes the form of a less conscious feeling of safety, confidence, and reliance on someone or something.
Trust includes mind and will, but centers more in our emotions and our subconscious.
We trust God by pursuing a personal relationship with Him. We learn to trust God by getting to know Him and by finding Him to be reliable, especially in hard times. Trust grows when we take the risk to be honest and let God see the "real me."

- Be encouraged that I am already showing trust by running to God with this problem.
- Affirm that God loves me, He is eager to help me, and He doesn't condemn me.
- Talk to God about this problem as if I were talking to my best friend. Express my fears, my worries, my frustrations, and my emotions regarding this problem.
- How well did my childhood trust experiences prepare me to trust God? Does this situation stir up bad memories about someone else who failed me? How much of a stretch would it be for me to trust God for this, and that He will be more trustworthy? What promises has He made that I can cling to? (See chart at end of Chapter 5)

LISTENING PRAYER: (Helps on *Listening Prayer* are at the end of Chapter 7)

- Is there anything You want me to hear regarding this situation?
- Regarding a defensive battle, how would You like to encourage me?
- Regarding an offensive battle, what else should I do to seek Your will for this situation? Who else should I talk to? What additional research would help me come to a decision?

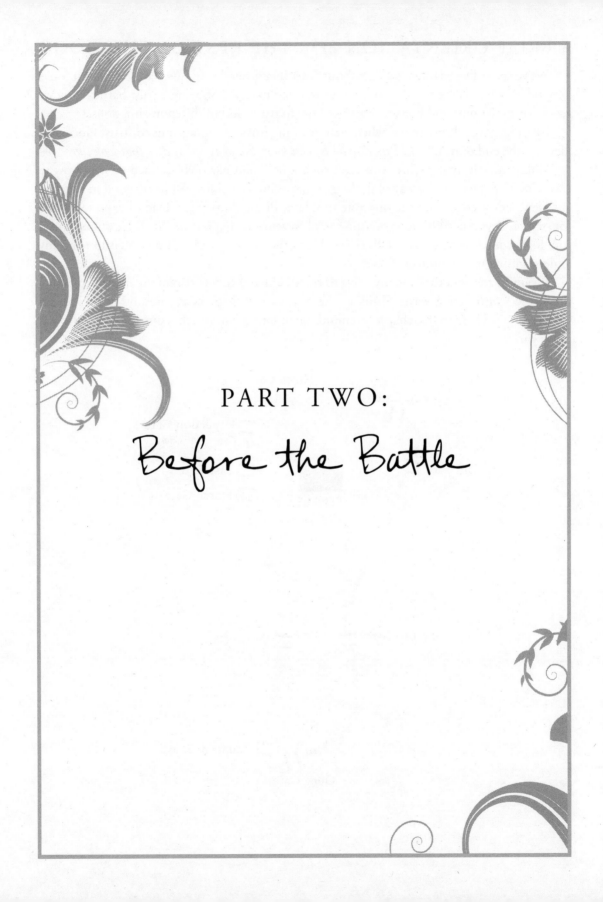

PART TWO:

Before the Battle

A BRIEF ORIENTATION FOR THE REST OF THIS BOOK

We've spent five chapters talking about trust in a general way. We clarified what it looks like and how to analyze a scary situation to frame it in terms of being a trust battle. Now we get down to the nuts and bolts of learning how to trust God in different situations.

All of us have felt frustrated when well meaning folks encouraged us to "trust God" as if that was the end of it. *Oh, all I need to do is trust God? So, okay, what does that look like?*

Unfortunately, many Christians have such a rigid and narrowly defined view of how to trust God that it gets in the way of dealing with specific situations. While it's good to broaden our view, let's not run into the opposite problem. Please don't pile a load of expectation on yourself, as if you need to do everything in all seventeen chapters of this Bible study, and if you don't, somehow your trust falls short. That's the exact opposite of my intention and my understanding of how to trust God.

I want to free you to see many ways to trust God and to feel confident about expressing trust in lots of different ways. Think of the next twelve chapters as gateways into God our Great Refuge. These twelve chapters remind me of Jerusalem, which, coincidentally, also has many gates.

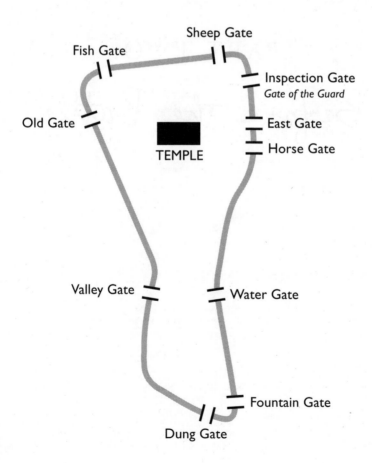

By now you know that we trust by running to God for refuge. **Any gate will work just fine.** We will look at four chapters about ways to trust God before the battle, four for during the battle and four for after the battle. In a big trust battle we will eventually use all four of these "gates," so to speak. Looking at the chapter overview below, you will see that no matter where we are in the cycle of a full-blown trust battle, God makes provision for four things:

- **The Safe Place** – providing protection;
- **The Feelings** – helping us process our emotions;
- **The Plan** – giving us guidance and direction; and
- **The God Factor** – getting involved in our battle.

By examining what suggestions work best in various situations, I hope you'll feel prepared to choose whichever trust strategy will best channel your trust day by day. It's as if people who find themselves in the "before the battle" phase look at the Refuge from that direction and so for them, the four gates "before the battle" are the quickest route into the Refuge. But *during the battle* we gravitate toward other gates, which will be closer during that period. And by the time we've reached the *after the battle* phase we've migrated to the opposite side of the city.

I hope you find each gate interesting and helpful and that you begin to beat your own footpaths into the Refuge, using gates you already know about and the new ones you discover in this study.

OVERVIEW FOR CHAPTER 6–17

	BEFORE	DURING	AFTER
#1 THE SAFE PLACE	CHAPTER 6 THE SAFE PLACE TO EVALUATE THE THREAT	CHAPTER 10 THE SAFE PLACE TO FIGHT THE BATTLE	CHAPTER 14 THE SAFE PLACE TO RECOVER
#2 THE FEELINGS	CHAPTER 7 HANDLING OUR FEELINGS	CHAPTER 11 FINDING THE HONEY	CHAPTER 16 (*) WRESTLING WITH GOD
#3 THE PLAN	CHAPTER 8 RECEIVING THE PLAN	CHAPTER 12 WORKING THE PLAN	CHAPTER 15 (*) DEBRIEFING THE PLAN
#4 THE GOD FACTOR	CHAPTER 9 PRAYER: ASKING GOD TO ACT	CHAPTER 13 POWER: WATCHING GOD ACT	CHAPTER 17 PRAISE: THANKING GOD FOR ACTING

(*) In the section *after the battle,* I've switched the order in which we study these four topics. That's because Chapter 15 is actually Part Two of material introduced in Chapter 14. Don't worry. It will make more sense when you get there. I've included a little note at the beginning of all the remaining chapters to help you keep track of where we are on this chapter overview.

CHAPTER 6

The Safe Place to Evaluate the Threat

For the eyes of the Lord range throughout the earth
to strengthen those whose hearts are fully committed to Him.
II Chronicles 16:9

A few years ago, I watched the fascinating *Extreme Survival Series* featuring Ray Mears, the British wood lore expert. In each episode he visited the terrain of an actual survival situation. He told the story of several World War II pilots shot down over the jungle and followed the route they took back to civilization. He retraced the trail of a young couple who ran out of gas in the middle of the Australian outback, the route of a family that got stuck in a blizzard, and people whose sailboat got damaged in a tropical storm.

In each situation, he reported what the people did to handle their predicament, commenting on what they did well and what they could have done better. He also discussed the wilderness resources they could have used if only they had known. So in the Outback, he pointed out the ordinary little plant the Aborigines dig up because its tubers provide food and water. He showed how you could make almost anything you need from bamboo for those "lucky" enough to find themselves stranded in the jungle. He showed how to make fresh water in the desert and on the open sea.

In almost every episode, regardless of the specific survival story, he emphasized one point. The pivotal choices generally get made at the beginning, when people first realize their danger. It's perfectly normal for a flood of panic and adrenaline to swamp most folks at first. Those who survive master that fear and then quickly move to assess the situation and choose wise survival strategies.

He commented that, even taking all that initial panic into account, people tend to have the clearest head and the most resources at the beginning. As their survival saga unfolds, people tend to become more disoriented and tired. Typically, they must fight hard to survive while coping with the draining effects of panic, dehydration, starvation, infection, and local hazards. Those who make sensible first choices and doggedly work their plan often find rescue. People who make foolish first choices sometimes aren't so lucky.

Now most of us will never find ourselves stranded on a desert island. Our crises tend to be less dramatic. But the same principle applies. When it comes to trusting God, we may talk a good show at church, but our first response to a crisis reveals our heart condition. And the choices we make right at the start set the stage for how the rest of the trust battle will unfold. In large part, that pivotal choice determines whether the crisis merely buffets us, or whether it strengthens our walk with God.

Do you remember those two Hebrew words for trust that we talked about in Chapter Two? In this chapter we will focus on the word *hasa*, which means "run for refuge." When we find ourselves in trouble, we have to choose *where* to run for refuge. When we quickly run to God we will discover the joy of partnering with Him to face and resolve each challenge.

ASA'S STORY

King Asa illustrates this pivotal choice. Three times during his reign as king of Judah he faced a challenge, twice from foreign invaders and once from a health condition. Each time, he had to choose whether to rely on God for help or run to someone else.

The first threat came from Egypt when Zerah the Cushite led a vast army against Judah. Although outnumbered, Asa bravely marched his army out to battle and then called out to God for help.

"Help us, O Lord our God, for we rely on You, and in Your name we have come against this vast army." (II Chronicles 14:11)

God answered Asa's prayer right away. Asa didn't fight the enemy alone. The Bible comments that the enemy was *"crushed before the Lord and His forces."* God jumped in and fought the battle that day using Asa's army.

The quantity of our resources is a matter of complete indifference to God. Jonathan put it this way in I Samuel 14:6. *"Nothing can hinder the Lord from saving, whether by many or by few."* God can always win the victory against any odds – He's the wild card that trumps everything else.

God waited to see whether Asa would rely on Him, and rewarded his choice with a huge and profitable victory. After Asa's army finished hauling in their plunder, a prophet praised Asa, passing along both a promise and a warning, recorded in II Chronicles 15:2.

"The Lord is with you when you are with Him. If you seek Him, He will be found by you, but if you forsake Him, He will forsake you."

What an encouragement! Asa and his people promised to seek God wholeheartedly. Good King Asa fought against idolatry. He made hard choices like the one to depose his wicked grandmother. He fortified cities and trained the army of Judah. For a long time the nation of Judah kept its word to worship and obey God.

Many years before Asa's time, part of the Israelite nation had broken off to become the Northern Kingdom of Israel. People up in Israel heard about the good things happening in Judah. Many of these northern relatives began to travel to Jerusalem three times a year to worship the true God, instead of worshipping the false gods provided by the King of Israel. In fact, some people even moved south and began to live in Judah just so they could worship the true God.

It angered the King of Israel to see his people traveling south to worship God in Jerusalem. It threatened his control over his people. The next thing you know, his people might want to reunite with Judah. He couldn't allow that! So he fortified the border town of Ramah to prevent his people from leaving his kingdom. Sort of like an olden day Berlin Wall.

By now, the kingdom of Judah was much stronger than the kingdom of Israel. When compared to the Egyptian enemy that Judah had defeated years before, Israel was a pitiful little kingdom that would have posed no big threat if Asa had relied on God. The Lord would have been happy to deliver them, especially for the sake of His dear people who traveled down to worship Him from the ten Northern tribes.

Asa had done many good things for God during his reign. But when he faced this new threat he forgot all about his promises to God and his good intentions went up in smoke. He decided to handle this problem himself. He ran to one of Israel's allies, a pagan king named Ben-Hadad, up in Damascus and proposed the idea that Ben-Hadad switch sides to partner with Judah instead. Asa took gold and silver out of the Lord's temple (some of which may well have come from that earlier battle against Egypt) and used it to sweeten the deal.

His plan seemed to work. Ben-Hadad attacked Israel forcing them to withdraw from Ramah. But, then Hanani the seer came and gave Asa God's assessment. Hanani reminded Asa that God had won the victory when he relied on Him to fight against the much larger Cushite threat.

"For the eyes of the Lord range throughout the earth to strengthen those whose hearts are fully committed to Him." (II Chronicles 16:9)

(If you study the history books in the Bible you will notice that "the eyes of the Lord" evaluated every king of Israel and Judah. God kept track of what each ruler did and how each one reacted to troubles.)

When Asa ran for refuge *(hasa)* to Ben-Hadad, instead of running to God, he made a foolish friendship alliance with a pagan king. He lost God's blessing because of that poor choice. By turning away from God he settled for something far less than God's best.

Now this feedback didn't sit well with Asa. He punished the prophet Hanani and mistreated his own people as well. How sad!

I think Asa resembles many of us who start out our Christian life with youthful enthusiasm. When we run into a few hard times we try out this business of running to God for help. Lo and behold, God helps us when we trust Him. We pile up some great stories about times that God rescued us from trouble.

But as time goes along, we may settle into a religious routine and drift away from the Lord. Then a new crisis comes along and, hopefully, it shakes us enough to return to God. Let's not make Asa's mistake. Not only did he forget to turn to God but he also got defensive when someone pointed out his error.

King Asa must have enjoyed the perks of being a king, like eating all that rich food and enjoying his wine, because most Bible experts agree that his foot disease was probably gout. (Uric acid builds up in the feet and joints forming crystals that make even the weight of a bed sheet unbearably painful.) He probably suffered a lot as his condition worsened.

Why didn't he cry out to God? Why did he turn instead to the Egyptian physicians he kept around at court for prestige sake, who made a show of treatment using pagan charms and mumbo jumbo?

By the way, Asa didn't get into trouble because he went to a doctor to treat his foot. He made the mistake of relying *only* on doctors. He didn't turn to God at all. (This story does not teach us that we shouldn't go to doctors if we get sick. The medical profession got God's big stamp of approval because of Luke the beloved physician, who wrote much of the New Testament and who served as Paul's personal doctor until the end of his life.)

OK, TIME FOR A STORY...

A few months ago I found myself at the start of a new trust battle. I had been operating on the assumption that I needed to look for a new job by September. Surely by then I would have healed enough from my surgeries. The clock was ticking. After all, we live in San Diego where housing costs are through the roof.

I love living on manna. That's how I had considered this season of my life, going on sixteen months now, when the surgery made it impossible for me to work. And yet God provided everything we needed.

But manna time doesn't last forever. I assumed that God would give me the high sign any day that I had to go back to work. I certainly didn't dread looking for work, like I did before Jesus healed that childhood memory. But I wasn't looking forward to it either. I have loved the flexibility of being able to write and to pray with people.

So it shocked me when I heard the Lord speak quite clearly to my heart one morning while I was dusting the loom in my living room. "Do you think I could take care of all of your financial needs if you stayed home and worked for Me?"

Say what?

I stood up and began to talk to Him out loud. "Of course, I believe. You've done it many times before. But is this Your answer? You know that I need to confirm this." I spent the afternoon crunching the numbers and adjusting our monthly budget. Could it work? By the way, it's a good idea to confirm anything that we hear from God that would mean a big change of direction. He doesn't mind. In fact, He honors it by sending confirmation when He sees that we sincerely want to obey Him.

Armed with papers and spreadsheets, Jim and I talked it over and Jim endorsed the idea enthusiastically. So, I stopped thinking about looking for a job. I put together a little journal in which to keep track of all the ways God took care of our financial needs. I included a section to list what we needed.

It looked good. After all, I'm an expert on trusting God, aren't I? Why, I even wrote a whole book about it! And Jim and I have gone through many financial tight spots. I'm an old pro at trusting God for financial needs. This'll be a piece of cake. No problem.

It took me about a month to finally acknowledge that, actually, there was a problem. A low hum of anxiety buzzed in my stomach all the time. All month long I felt as if I was holding my breath waiting for some catastrophic expense. What if we had a car accident?

What if the roof leaked? What if? What if?

It dawned on me that I had been acting like King Asa.

"Father, I'm sorry. I got good at the routine of being an expert at trust and forgot that I needed to trust You and not myself. Even though I've been through this type of trust battle a thousand times, I haven't gone through this one. I don't know what to do now. Please show me how to trust You now, in this situation."

Although I had started well by looking for confirmation and by setting up that trust journal, I had relied on myself and my previous experience instead of truly relying on God. In the next few weeks He showed me that He wasn't finished with me yet. He had more to teach me about trusting Him for financial needs. He knew what He wanted to accomplish in this season, and finally I was in step with Him. What a relief!

APPLICATION FOR OUR STORY

When we face a new challenge, God offers us a safe place to evaluate the threat. He always stands ready to protect and help us. *"The name of the Lord is a strong tower; the righteous run to it and are safe"* (Prov. 18:10). Furthermore, "the eyes of the Lord" see each one of us, too, not just kings and famous people. Nothing about our situation escapes His notice. Since He knows everything, He always knows the best strategy to handle our problem. God loves it when we run to Him for help. And James 1:5 tells us that God responds graciously, by generously giving us wisdom, without finding fault.

As you can see from my story, I spent some time evaluating. I had been trusting all along that God would help us regarding our financial situation. It wasn't a matter of wondering IF God would take care of us, it was a matter of wondering HOW He would do it. And when I began to hear His answer, it reflected trust on my part to test it out by crunching the numbers. God knew I needed to do that. He isn't arbitrary and He doesn't lead us into foolishness – into risk, yes; into faith, yes; but not into foolhardiness.

We show that we trust God by running to Him for help. Every new challenge gives us a new opportunity to trust God. We don't immediately know what to do most of the time. But by running to God, we have already shown that we trust Him. Right off the bat we did something right. In fact, we did the most important thing right. After that, it's much easier to trust God for the details as we navigate through the challenge.

Running to God triggers all of the blessings of the Refuge. He promises to help those who trust Him. You may not have found some of these blessings yet. Let me whet your appetite by sharing just a few of these wonderful promises. These promises are all tried and true ones that I've field-tested in actual situations, (assuming we fulfill the condition, if there is one).

When Asa ran to make an alliance with that pagan king, it's true that he got some help. When we run to God, it's as if we make an alliance with God and He fights on our behalf. Who do you think makes for a better ally?

THE PROMISE	THE VERSE
Safety	*"You are my hiding place; You will protect me from trouble and surround me with songs of deliverance." (Psalm 32:7)*
Wisdom	*"If any of you lacks wisdom, he should ask God, who gives generously to all without finding fault, and it will be given to him." (James 1:5)*
Deliverance	*"A righteous man may have many troubles, but the Lord delivers him out of them all." (Psalm 34:19)*
Endurance	*"When you pass through the waters, I will be with you; and when you pass through the rivers, they will not sweep over you. When you walk through the fire, you will not be burned; the flames will not set you ablaze." (Isaiah 43:2)*
Answered Prayer	*"This is the confidence we have in approaching God: that if we ask anything according to His will, He hears us. And if we know that He hears us – whatever we ask – we know that we have what we asked of Him." (I John 5:14, 15)*
Success	*"Do not let this Book of the Law depart from your mouth; meditate on it day and night, so that you may be careful to do everything written in it. Then you will be prosperous and successful." (Joshua 1:8)*

We trigger God's help when we learn to recognize the signs of the pivotal choice. Asa messed up because he didn't realize the choice he faced. When he looked at the Ramah problem and when his foot started hurting, he didn't frame the question as a matter of trust. He thought it was just another day at the office, dealing with the problems every king faces.

How can we recognize when we face that choice? A simple test: fear or worry. Did something happen that made us feel anxious or stressed or overwhelmed? Did we get news that made our heart sink? Every setback, every heartache, every danger, every obstacle, big or small, brings us to the pivotal test. Will we run to God to receive His help?

It's never too late to start trusting God. For many people, trusting God before, during and after a trust battle might be a new idea. Maybe that's because so many of us choose to rely on our own resources. We assume we can control everything by using our trust network. We run to our friends and cry on their shoulders. We look for another job to pay our bills. We call our lawyer to get justice.

Or we just worry, worry, worry. And complain to anyone who will listen. And toss and turn on our bed through sleepless nights. It doesn't occur to us to run to God until the middle of the crisis when our best efforts begin to unravel. By then we have made an even bigger mess of things.

Sound familiar? We've all done it. So let's try a new approach. Run to God at the first sign of trouble and see what happens. Let's venture into new territory and explore God's trustworthiness right from the start. Let's not just survive our troubles. Let's become trust experts and discover the joy of walking with God through every challenge. Like the greatest survival expert of all time, God will show us the secrets that turn our terrors into a trust adventure.

FACE TIME WITH MY TRAINER

This chapter will look at the example of King Asa. **Please read II Chronicles 14 - 16**, paying particular attention to these three sections. In each section, what challenge did Asa face? Who or what did he choose to rely on for a solution? What happened as a result?

14:9–15:7   16:1–9   16:12, 13

PART 2: Questions & Reflection

1. Describe a time you ran to God *first* when you faced a frightening situation. Describe a situation when you turned to other resources before, or instead of, turning to God. How did the story turn out in each case?

2. What is the pivotal choice?

3. Why does it show trust when we run to God first?

4. According to those six promises in the graph, what will God provide when we run to Him for help to deal with a situation? Describe a time when you have experienced each one.

5. What advice would you give to someone who has not turned to God for a situation that has been steadily deteriorating?

6. Try the simple test. Are you experiencing fear or worry about anything right now? If so, what? What do you choose to do about it?

7. What did you find to be the most encouraging or intriguing idea in this chapter?

Paula's Story

The first time my husband was deployed to Iraq I didn't handle it very well. I turned to food and alcohol to help me cope with the separation. That didn't work well at all. Obviously, I gained weight. I felt bitter and angry inside.

The second time Henry got deployed I decided to handle things differently. First of all, I committed the time to the Lord. It had been an unexpected deployment. The only thing I knew to do was to trust the Lord. That was my only option.

During that second deployment I got involved with the women's ministry at my church. I joined a small group Bible study, which got me connected with the church family. I also did several home improvement projects.

As a result, I had peace, confidence and a family that helped me to enjoy the deployment and be supportive of my husband. That time around I grew in my faith.

CHAPTER 7

Handling Our Feelings

I sought the Lord, and He answered me;
He delivered me from all my fears.
Psalm 34:4

"Beep! Beep! Beep!" I hated that sound. I was still in the critical care unit at the hospital hooked up to monitors of every kind. This particular one monitored my oxygen level. It went off whenever my breathing became too shallow or rapid. The nurses would come in and give me the same little pep talk.

"Slow down your breathing, honey. What are you worried about? Relax. Nice and slow. Breathe deeply. Everything's okay."

I couldn't understand why it kept going off. As far as I could tell I was relaxed. Sure, I felt uncomfortable, maybe I felt some pain, but I didn't feel anxious. Yet even if the nurses came because I called for them, my beeper would go off whenever they appeared. Over and over again that night I triggered that darned monitor.

What was going on? What was I worried about?

God had given me Psalm 34 to hold on to when I went into the hospital and I remembered verse four. *"I sought the Lord, and He heard me; He delivered me from all my fears."* After the nurses had plumped up my pillows and left me comfortable and warm for the umpteenth time, I took my questions to Jesus.

"I don't understand it. Why am I tripping that monitor so often? Why can't I control my breathing better? I know I'm strong enough to breathe just fine. What am I worried about? And what can I do about it?"

I never felt alone throughout that whole hospital stay because I always sensed the comforting presence of Jesus by my side. I heard Him clearly whenever I reached out to Him in prayer. About eight years before, I had learned how to practice a type of prayer called listening prayer in which I not only pray to God, but also quiet my spirit to tune in to hear His answer, which comes to me as a still, small voice. He speaks to my heart in words, phrases and impressions. His presence comforted me before He said a word. Here's the gist of what I heard Him say to me that night.

For the first few days in ICU I had been too foggy to know what the nurses were doing. But I'd been more or less aware of my surroundings for a few days by then. I was becoming familiar with the routine of my care. I sort of knew when I should get shots or food. I was learning a little bit about the strange gadgets hooked up to my arms and neck and belly.

I also had become aware that some nurses were better at their jobs than others. One night I watched my nurse set a shot on the counter by my bed, but I couldn't remember that she gave me the injection. Another nurse asked her supervisor to explain one of my monitors. They had chatted nonchalantly at my bedside about a sensitive tube that, unbeknownst to me – and more distressingly, apparently unbeknownst to my clueless nurse – went directly to my heart! Gulp! One great nurse did things I hadn't seen anyone else do. Did that mean those other nurses had forgotten to do essential things?

Jesus gently explained to me the source of my worry. My problem was that I more fully comprehended how helpless I was and I was afraid of what the nurses could do to me.

Then Jesus gave me a way to stop tripping my monitor. He told me that when I saw the nurses coming, I should think of them as being Jesus walking toward my bedside. I thought about the nurses putting on those latex gloves before they did anything. Jesus told me that, in the same way, He Himself would fill each nurse and personally work through whoever came to help me. He promised that He would make sure that every nurse, every doctor, and every stray technician would remember to do all they should and that no one would harm me by accident. He also reminded me that He is always with me and that I could always hold His hand.

I tried it out later that night when the nurse came in to give me my next shot. Under the sheets I made the small comforting motion of squeezing His hand when I saw her enter my room. I pictured Jesus behind her eyes, personally coming into my hospital room to take care of me. I smiled up at her and savored the silence of the monitor that didn't go off.

Most of us aren't hooked up to a monitor that beeps whenever we get worried or fearful. Thank goodness for small blessings! Sometimes we only notice that we're nervous when we catch ourselves nibbling on our fingernails or making extra trips to stand in front of the refrigerator. We can go for days with a knot in the pit of our stomach from free floating anxiety that has no particular cause we can identify. Other times, there's nothing subtle about our feelings. We get swamped with terror or overwhelmed by catastrophe. Whether on a large or small scale, all of us get worried or fearful from time to time.

Many Christians assume that trust can't coexist with any of those emotions like fear, anxiety, worry, anger, confusion or grief. They think that we need to get rid of them, or shove them out of sight, before we can truly trust the Lord.

My experience in trust training has taught me precisely the opposite. I've learned several big lessons that I'd like to explore in this chapter.

- Peace and confidence are the absolute birthright of everyone who trusts God.
- God cares about how we feel. He understands our human frailty.
- God wants to help us to process our feelings so that we can experience peace and confidence.

- Bringing our emotions to God in prayer is one of the best ways to deepen our trust in God.
- If we allow God access to our emotions, our emotions can become valuable tools to help us to learn how to trust God more completely.

As Christians we've probably been taught to downplay the significance of our emotions. Sometimes we have to ignore how we feel and choose to believe God. In general, that's a good habit to develop. Adults do lots of things they don't feel like doing, just because it's the right or mature thing to do. However, if we aren't careful, that good habit can contribute to a growing divide between our head knowledge and our heart experience.

Ignored emotions have enormous power. Unexamined emotions tend to degenerate into the lowest common denominators of fear, worry, resentment, confusion and discouragement. In this study we've emphasized that while faith is mainly a matter of the mind and the will, trust centers more in our emotional and subconscious reactions. If we want to bridge that gap between our head knowledge and our heart assurance we have to look at and deal with our emotions.

So emotions are pivotal if we want to trust God. Those emotions are the exact tools that God uses to develop our trust. Think about this example that particularly applies to us in this "before the battle" phase. This is the phase when we first realize we have a crisis or challenge on our hands. Let's say we get a huge bill in the mail. We can't possibly pay it. We react with a wave of fear and worry. What are we going to do? What will become of us?

We'd like to trust God by instantly feeling a deep sense of peace and calm regarding this bill. Of course, that's what our reaction should be. Part of trusting God is having that wonderful assurance that He will always provide for our needs. In our head, we know that God is powerful enough and resourceful enough to handle any financial challenge.

However, what if we don't have that immediate response of peace and calm? And, let's be honest, most people don't skip over the phase of feeling a little worried or fearful and zoom right to calm serenity. Have we lost out on our opportunity to trust God for that financial crisis? Certainly not. What hurdle prevents us from immediately trusting God in that way regarding this bill? The hurdle is our emotional reaction of fear and worry.

Since God has committed Himself to train us to trust Him, when we get that bill, where exactly will He want to train us? Right. Precisely at the point of our fear and worry. Our feelings. The cool thing is that the more we take our fears and worries to the Lord, the stronger our trust becomes. People who zoom right to peace and calm when they face a crisis usually didn't start out that way. They have gotten into the habit of going to God to process their emotions in His presence and gradually that has strengthened their ability to face new things with peace of mind.

So this is a win-win situation whether we instantly feel peace or whether we have some worries or fears at first. God is enormously kind and understanding, a wonderful friend who listens with compassion. God allows us to feel whatever we feel and doesn't condemn any emotion, just so long as we bring it to Him in prayer. But after we take our emotions to Him and talk them out in His presence, He gives us that sense of inner peace that helps us to deal with our troubles.

In this chapter we will look at David's example of trust. More than any other Bible character, David illustrates the mechanics about how to trust God. It's no coincidence that he is the most honest and persistent in expressing his feelings to God. Then we will explore how to use our own feelings as tools to build our trust in God.

DAVID'S STORY

David had troubles of all kinds. He was on the run from his own king who was insanely jealous of him. He had just said a wrenching goodbye to his best friend, Jonathan. He couldn't hide out with his family because that was the first place Saul would look. When he went to the priests for help, they had no bread except for the sacred bread from the tabernacle. You can't keep a band of merry men going for long on twelve loaves of flatbread.

As they camped out under the stars, I wonder who got the bright idea of asking the nearby Philistine king for protection. Whoever it was did David no favors. His reputation had preceded him, as the popular war hero who had killed Goliath, their Philistine champion. Suddenly David found himself in mortal danger as Philistines prepared to draw their swords.

Help! What should I do?

In a stroke of genius he pretended to be crazy. David felt limp with relief when the Philistines escorted him out of town. Later on when he thought back on that episode, he wrote a song of gratitude that we know as Psalm 34. In it he shows how he handled his emotions during this frightening time. By my count, this psalm touches on at least eight different negative emotions or dilemmas. The quickest way to show this might be in graph form.

The Emotion	The Verse	Notes about the word highlighted in bold letters
Fear or panic	I sought the LORD, and He answered me; He delivered me from all my **fears**. v. 4	Word used for "fear" means terror or extreme fear
Shame	Those who look to Him are radiant; their faces are never covered with **shame**. v. 5	"Shame" means embarrassment or shame
Worry about safety	The angel of the LORD **encamps** around those who fear Him, and He delivers them. v. 7	God "pitched His tent" to surround and protect them, especially comforting to David and his men camping non-stop
Financial worries	Fear the LORD, you His saints, for those who fear Him **lack** nothing. v. 9	The word for "lack" in v. 9 refers to financial poverty or need
Worries in general	The lions may grow weak and hungry, but those who seek the LORD **lack** no good thing. v. 10	The word for "lack" in v. 10 is a more general word for any kind of lack or need
Depression or discouragement	The LORD is close to the **brokenhearted** and saves those who are **crushed in spirit**. v. 18	"Brokenhearted" means broken in pieces, hurt or crushed. "Crushed" is stronger -- broken down to dust or very contrite
Fear about bad situations or hardships	A righteous man may have many **troubles**, but the LORD delivers him from them all; v. 19	"Troubles" refers more to bad or evil things that happen, afflictions
Guilt before God	The LORD redeems His servants; no one will be **condemned** who takes refuge in Him. v. 22	The word "condemned" refers to breaking the moral law or offending the law of God

David had no trouble bringing his emotions to God. In other psalms, he complained about friends who betrayed him and enemies who mistreated him. He expressed loneliness, anger and discouragement. Actually, he sounds a lot like you and me.

The next time you read through the Psalms why not look for the ones written by David. He wrote about half the psalms. Look at the emotions that he expressed in each one, especially the sad ones. Sometimes he starts right off expressing his praise to God. In other psalms he spends most of the time telling God his troubles. You'll notice, in either case, that by the end of each psalm he finds something that encourages him. He sees God by the time he finishes and that changes his whole perspective.

God used David's example to teach me some basic lessons about trust. If we learn how to bring our feelings to God, our trust will grow by leaps and bounds. Here's what I learned to do when I struggled with some emotion or when I felt confused and didn't know for sure what was going on in my heart. I hope it gives you some insight for your own situation.

FOUR WAYS TO TRUST GOD
REGARDING OUR EMOTIONS

1. Take them to Jesus and tell Him what you are feeling. Right off the bat this shows trust because we tend to share our feelings with people we trust.

I've noticed that just saying it out loud to Jesus tends to give us more clarity, especially when we remember who's listening and that we're not talking into the air. It's such a relief to talk to someone who hears. And cares. Sometimes that's all it takes for our usual good sense to kick in, or for us to remember what we already know, and feel much better.

Other times, verbalizing our feelings brings up the pain we were holding back. Talking about our pain might turn into crying or sobbing. Be encouraged, God understands the language of tears. He correctly interprets all of it. The tears <u>are</u> the prayer at times like this. He hears our salt water prayers and saves them in a bottle. The label of my bottle says "Dionne's tears." There's a bottle with your name on it, too.

2. When you've laid it all out there before the Lord, get quiet and wait for Him to respond. Psalm 46:10 says, *"Be still and know that I am God."* Stillness is an act of trust. People use noise to hide from God. God speaks in a still, small voice so stillness prepares us to hear Him.

Before I learned how to practice listening prayer I got only limited relief regarding my emotions. But after I said what was on my mind, while I waited in silence I began to hear more than just helpful promises, (which we'll talk more about in a minute).

God gave me insight about my emotions. He acknowledged them more deeply than I expected, and pushed me to go to the root of my worry or fear. One cool thing about God is that He knows everything about everything. He knows exactly what to say or how to respond. He knows when to give us a soft shoulder to cry on and when to give us a swift kick in the back side.

Maybe we don't understand why we feel what we feel. That night in the hospital when I was bothered by that beeper, I couldn't pinpoint the source of my anxiety. God can help us to sort out what we feel if we will lay it all out and ask Him for help. Once we get our feelings out in the open and see them for what they are it's much easier to move on to the next step.

3.   Look for God's point of view and receive His promise for today's problems. God likes us to bring our feelings into His presence, messy and sinful and tainted though they may be, because it opens our heart to begin to see Him as the great answer, wherever our heart is struggling. Even though we start by looking at our emotions, we need to end by looking at God.

God enters the equation when we finish talking. No fear seems as big if God is with us, encamped around us. No money problem seems as daunting when we remember that God has infinitely deep pockets to provide for our needs. No enemy seems as frightening, no disappointment so devastating in light of eternity. No sorrow seems as crushing if we share its weight with Jesus.

Often at this stage God reminds us of something that directly answers our fear or worry. That night in the hospital, God reminded me that Jesus is with me, that He is the best healer and that He would take care of me. It wasn't hard to let go of my anxiety in the face of those reminders. And did you notice how kindly God reminded me about those things? He didn't scold me. Instead, He helped me to see Him more clearly as it related to my fears.

Many times at this stage of prayer, the Lord has brought a promise to mind. Be on the alert for any phrase from a Bible verse or praise song that flits through your head. I've learned to track these down because they can be such a blessing.

It's at this point that a wonderful exchange can take place. In John 14:27, Jesus made this promise. *"Peace I leave with you; My peace I give you. I do not give to you as the world gives. Do not let your hearts be troubled and do not be afraid."* As I have gone to Jesus and laid out my emotions before Him, He has given me His peace in exchange for my fears and worries. He has calmed my heart. If I needed to confess some sin, He received my confession and freely gave me His forgiveness. Either way, He gave me peace.

God is not content just to hear about our fears. He promises to deliver us from them. When Jesus gives us peace, it chases away our fears. We don't need to stuff our fears. We plain aren't afraid anymore. If we get the same fear again tomorrow, it's easier to get over it more quickly because we can hold on to the promise we've received or remember the sufficiency of God to handle that particular thing. And we can always take that new fear to God as well.

4.   Start watching for God to deliver you out of all your troubles. A cool thing happens when we bring our emotions to God and lay them out before Him. It triggers some enormously broad promises. Psalm 34 is packed with them. Did you notice in that graph, earlier in this chapter, that every verse in column #2 was a promise?

God promises to deliver us from our fears when we take them to Him. More than that, He promises to deliver or save us out of all our troubles. Notice how often David used the word "all." God delivered him from *all* his fears and saved him out of *all* his troubles. No wonder David responded by extolling God *all* the time.

This chapter is in the "before the battle" phase and has explored the emotions we feel as we face a new, looming battle. In this phase we will likely experience many fears, worries and uncertainties. What a comfort to know that by laying our feelings before the Lord He will help us to make sense of them, give us peace and serenity as we navigate through the challenge and ultimately make everything work out for the best.

FACE TIME WITH MY TRAINER

PART 1: Answer these Bible Study questions BEFORE reading the chapter

Please read I Samuel 21:10 – 15, and briefly answer these questions before reading the rest of this chapter.

Who was David running from when he decided to go to King Achish? (v. 10)

How did David get into trouble when he went to Gath? (vv. 11, 12)

What strategy did he use to get out of this predicament? (v. 13)

Read Psalm 34.
List two or three things about which David cried out to God?

As you read this Psalm, what promise jumped out at you the most? Write it out, including the verse number.

PART 2: Questions & Reflection

1. How does it demonstrate trust in God to talk to Him about how we feel?

2. Many people guard their hearts, not really trusting God, even though they may pray for some requests. So why, if we discuss our feelings with God, does that tend to build more trust in Him than if we merely ask Him for things?

3. In what ways might it be safer to share our unedited feelings with God rather than with other friends or relatives?

4. At least once this week practice taking your emotions to Jesus using the four steps we discussed at the end of this chapter. What new insight or encouragement did you receive?

5. Read Psalm 34 at least twice this week, meditating on the promises you find. How does this deepen your trust in God?

6. What did you find to be the most encouraging or intriguing idea in this chapter?

FURTHER HELPS: *Several times in this book we have referred to listening prayer. Here are several resources about listening prayer that may make it easier to share your feelings with God. Sometime this week, try out the listening prayer exercise.*

LISTENING PRAYER

Listening prayer may be defined as a *responsive awareness of the presence of God.* Instead of merely talking *to* God when we pray, listening prayer is a conversation *with* God. Listening prayer does not replace any previous format of prayer we have used. It adds periods of silence to existing prayer times so we can hear God communicate to our heart in whatever way He chooses.

It takes time and practice to learn how to hear God's still, small voice. We should carefully evaluate what we think we have heard by the standard of Scripture. On the next few pages, you'll find several resources regarding listening prayer, including a simple listening prayer exercise and two resources that might be helpful for evaluating what we hear.

A LISTENING PRAYER EXERCISE

• *Find a quiet, solitary place.* Bring your Bible, notebook and pen but set them down beside you at first. Open with a short prayer asking God to speak to you. Pray for protection to hear only His voice. *

• *Present your unguarded self.* Focus on your breathing until you calm down and enter the present moment. Imagine that the *real you* waits behind the door of your heart. Imagine opening the door of your heart so that your unguarded heart comes out to pray.

• *Seek out the real God.* With your eyes shut, calmly cast about for God's presence. You might imagine Jesus coming toward you with a big welcoming smile on His face. You might pray using Psalm 46:10, "Be still and know that I am God."

• *Welcome God's presence and converse with Him.* If you have a question or concern, bring that before Him. If not, ask, "Is there anything You want me to hear?" Then listen quietly for His answer. Ask follow up questions. Continue talking and listening until the conversation winds to a natural conclusion.

• *When the time seems right, write down what you have heard.* If you begin to hear a lot, pause to make notes of what you have already heard. Then continue to converse with pen in hand. If you hear a little bit, write it down afterwards. When it seems like things wind to an end, ask God if He has anything more to say to you. Whether you hear a lot, a little, or nothing, end by thanking God for helping you to learn to listen.

• *Feel free to rest in God's presence without speaking.* Don't be afraid to just be quiet to enjoy God's presence. The goal of listening prayer is not primarily the words but the relationship.

---

*Like Lynne's example, in the story at the end of Chapter 5, some people find it easier to hear the Lord when they are on the move. If that's your case, you might try doing this listening prayer exercise on a walk. Maybe take along some 3 x 5 cards so you can jot down notes along the way.

SEVEN TESTS TO EVALUATE THE CONTENT OF LISTENING PRAYER

7 Tests	Likely to be God's Voice	Unlikely to be God's Voice
1. Test of conformity to the plain teaching of Scripture.	What I heard reinforces basic doctrines or Bible themes. Orthodox Christians would affirm the statement (allowing for different interpretations among true believers). When I look up a Bible verse to check the context, it will reinforce and amplify what I heard, or at least, not twist the meaning.	What I heard clashes with basic doctrines or Bible themes. The statement echoes positions taken in old heresies or modern cults. When I hear a Bible verse, if I look it up to check the context, I see that the meaning has been twisted somehow.
2. Test of heavenly wisdom. James 3:14 - 17	The statement meets the test of verse 17 *But the wisdom that comes from heaven is first of all pure; then peace-loving, considerate, submissive, full of mercy and good fruit, impartial and sincere.* Sounds like the "God's Voice" side of the next chart.	The statement has more in common with verses 14–16. *But if you harbor bitter envy and selfish ambition in your hearts, do not boast about it or deny the truth. Such "wisdom" does not come down from heaven but is earthly, unspiritual, of the devil. For where you have envy and selfish ambition, there you find disorder and every evil practice.* Sounds like the "Satan's Voice" side on the next chart.
3. The test of my own fallenness.	The statement shows grace even toward people with whom I disagree or who have caused me pain. If noting someone else's sin, it calls for prayer, sorrow and a godly, measured response. Tends to keep focus on my own sin – to overcome it, not to despair of it. The statement contradicts or combats some dysfunctional tendency within myself.	The statement tends to be critical, judgmental or condemning of church leaders, other people or myself. If noting someone else's sin, it incites me to attack, criticize or harbor anger. Tends to blame other people for my problems and gives up on fighting my own sin. The statement reinforces a dysfunctional tendency within me.
4. The test of vocabulary.	Shows respect, reverence, and adoration for the person of God. Uses pronouns consistent with something spoken from God's point of view, like I, Me or We, or by an angelic messenger.	Speaks about God with suspicion or distrust, betraying an us vs. Him mindset. Uses pronouns or nouns that betray a point of view other than God's, like he, him or God.
5. The test of the spirits. I John 4:1 – 3	*I John 4:1 – 3 Dear friends, do not believe every spirit, but test the spirits to see whether they are from God, because many false prophets have gone out into the world. This is how you can recognize the Spirit of God: Every spirit that acknowledges that Jesus Christ has come in the flesh is from God, but every spirit that does not acknowledge Jesus is not from God. This is the spirit of the antichrist, which you have heard is coming and even now is already in the world.*	
	The test: Do you affirm that Jesus is truly God and truly man? Do you affirm that Jesus is Lord? When I ask the test question, I hear the answer yes and sometimes an elaboration with verifiable statements that affirm the person and work of Christ. Anything said about Jesus Christ elevates, honors and blesses His person and work.	When I ask the test question, I hear the answer no, silence, a wimpy answer or an evasive answer. Anything said about Jesus Christ downplays or dishonors the person or work of Christ.
6. The test to confirm.	I run across Bible verses on the same theme, confirming circumstances, unsolicited comments from people or further listening prayer that confirms the original point. What I heard in prayer happens.	I don't hear anything else and no other evidence comes up to confirm the original point. Or, I hear a direct contradiction in listening prayer, further Bible study or from closed doors of circumstance. What I thought I heard doesn't come to pass.
7. The test of submission to godly advisers. (These advisers are mature believers who know how to listen to God. Preferably, they also know me well.)	When I share what I think I heard, my advisers affirm the big idea even if they offer counsel to fine-tune the details. The conversation remains an open one, exploring together to see what God has to say. My advisers affirm that what I heard points me in a healthy, obedient, and God-honoring direction.	My advisers express concern, skepticism or caution about the big idea, not just advice about side issues. The discussion becomes tense and I act defensively about what I think I heard. My advisers point out areas of dysfunction or vulnerability that might have blinded me from evaluating things in a healthy way.

DISTINGUISHING GOD'S VOICE FROM SATAN'S VOICE

Evaluating By:	GOD'S VOICE	SATAN'S VOICE
The Approach *"Tone of voice"*	Gentle, quiet, deeply internal; The voice of the shepherd Loving, accepting; Full of calm authority	Intrusive, buzzing, demanding; The voice of the thief Accusatory, sometimes falsely loving but with a seductive quality
The Content *"What we hear"*	Conforms to the major principles of scripture AND applies verses properly within their context Expresses mercy and grace toward us and others; non-condemning of personal worth; When convicting us of sin, names the precise behavior and reminds us only of past grace, not confessed sin. Most often focuses on the here and now; Counsel is usually practical and simple; Emphasizes who He has called us to be; Appeals to our identity in Christ, our unique calling and to our more mature side. Gives the glory to Jesus; throws the spotlight on God's sufficiency.	Although sometimes a genuine word from God may pull a word or phrase out of context, hearing a verse that's used out of context should be viewed with extra skepticism and caution; Fosters feelings of condemnation toward ourselves and others; Condemns the total person & taunts us about past sins, failures and embarrassments Exploits our natural tendency to live in the past or the future; Counsel is confusing, generates anxiety or gets us into trouble; Emphasizes the more difficult aspects of what we should do; Appeals to our desire for approval, applause, and to our less mature side. Gives the glory to anything else; throws the spotlight on our resources or lack of resources.
The Effects *"Likely response"* Greatly expanded from seed thoughts found in *Hearing God*, by Peter Lord	We feel love and gratitude toward God; We develop more empathy toward others and we see their pain; We see at least our one next step; We find greater peace and courage, even in fearful or difficult circumstances; We hunger more for God Himself.	We feel fear or shame toward God; We tend to despise, resent or envy others. We get a bad attitude; We feel confused or paralyzed; We feel more anxious, fearful, ungrateful or dissatisfied; We back away from seeking God.

THREE COOL LISTENING PRAYER STORIES

Jerleen's Story

I had been reading in the book of Hebrews that God provides a place of rest for His people. I was going through an overwhelming time dealing with some family problems, and I felt no rest. God showed my friend Dionne that I was carrying heavy burdens, like a soldier with a heavy pack on. With Dionne's help I was mentally able to take off my pack. Then I rested for a long time in God's presence.

I was given His perspective of me. Rather than seeing myself within my roles of mother, wife, homeowner, even woman, I was able to see myself as just a child of God. It was just me and Jesus. I always knew I would one day leave all this behind. He gave me the perspective that these roles were not my identity, but rather were temporary assignments. I was able to separate from my problems and roles long enough to lay them at God's feet and receive His rest.

Karen's Story

I sat down with all my concerns and some notebook paper and wrote down my conversation with God. I began telling God all the things that bugged me. I filled up six pages. In reviewing my notes I saw that I was calming down. I was seeking some insight on how to deal with loved ones who are living sinful lifestyles, and how disconnected and unloved I feel by them. I wanted to show them love and still show loyalty to Jesus.

I realized that I have contentment in my relationship with Jesus, but I don't have peace when I consider the possible fate of others. I asked God to help me hear His voice. As I reviewed my notes again, I noticed that my writing had changed, as the intensity of the pencil is lighter in tone. I wrote down what I heard God saying through my thoughts.

"Don't condemn. Don't voice your judgments right now. Not your jurisdiction. I (God) am perfectly capable of dealing with the issues in that camp. The errors there will be exposed for all to see. Remember Solomon. His divided heart did not please Me. Keep on the path I have chosen for you, and be My beacon, a source of light to this fallen world."

I finished by praying, "Lord Jesus, let my life be worthy of that calling. I know You will sustain me in all things."

Danielle's Story

I was experiencing something like listening prayer even before I became a Christian. It has been a relief to find out I'm not crazy! One day after I accepted Jesus, the word "Corinthians" flashed into my mind, and I thought, "What's that?" It kept coming to mind during a time I was having difficulty in my behavior and my character. So, I thought, let me open the Bible, and sure enough, there was Corinthians! It was about character, and learning to become what I am now becoming.

God doesn't speak to me only in quiet times. It could be when I'm driving in rush hour or in the middle of chaos. When I feel lost, He tells me to let Him be the light that guides my feet and that He's going to light my way.

CHAPTER 8

Receiving the Plan

We do not know what to do, but our eyes are upon You.
II Chronicles 20:12b

"'For I know the plans that I have for you,' declares the Lord, 'plans to prosper you and not to harm you, plans to give you hope and a future.'" Jim and I were dating when we found this promise in Jeremiah 29:11 and we claimed it as *our* verse. As teenage college classmates we wrestled with the big questions of young adulthood. What major should I pick? Who am I anyway? Who should I marry? What should I do with the rest of my life?

Sobered by the consequences if we made the wrong choices, we hung on to that verse. Like travelers slowly picking our way through ground fog at night, we looked up and saw God's promise, bright and steady as a fixed star above all our questions and uncertainties. That promise comforted us. *Don't be afraid. God has a plan for us, for Jim and Dionne.*

The promise has been our personal touchstone ever since, through countless trust battles. We clung to it when we wondered what jobs to take, when we encountered turbulent days in church ministry, when God seemed to slam doors in our face, when we couldn't figure out how to solve parenting dilemmas or when problems remained unfixable after years of our best effort.

That promise assured us that even our most miserable experiences would someday break through into blessing. Looking back, in every situation that has come full circle, we have seen God's good plan unfold. Let me share one funny example.

All through seminary Jim knew he wanted to be a church planter. We prayed like crazy for God to lead us to the place He had planned for us.

Our friends, Bob and Nancy, were also interested in church planting and when the director of a California denominational district (whom I'll call Dr. Frank) came to interview candidates, Jim and Bob both signed up for an interview. Now, Bob had grown up in Southern California and he and Nancy had good friends in the area. They let Dr. Frank know they would love, love, love to plant churches, especially in California.

I wasn't so sure. I had picked up the strong Colorado prejudice against all things Californian. In a fit of temporary insanity, or at least stupidity, I expressed all my misgivings to Dr. Frank. What about the earthquakes? What about those crazy people in California? What about all the hippies and gangs? On and on. You're right, I was a complete idiot.

Imagine our shock, six months later, when Dr. Frank called Jim and offered to fly him out to California for a second interview – Jim, not Bob. My hesitancy about California evaporated with that phone call. If God led us to California, it was fine by me. We prayed about the offer and asked God to confirm His plan. We could have accepted that job either under the supervision and funding of the national headquarters or under the California regional office. We laid out a fleece to make sure. We went through the interview process for both the local and the national group and decided only to go to California if both groups accepted us.

They both did. So we moved to California. I was eight months pregnant with our first child. We felt confident that we had done a great job of seeking God's good plan and that we had landed in California based on our fabulous qualifications.

A month later we had Andy. Dr. Frank came out to see us in the hospital maternity ward. While he and Jim chatted in the waiting room Jim asked him a question that had puzzled us.

"Dr. Frank, why did you pick us to come out to California instead of Bob and Nancy?"

"Well, Jim, you both had great qualifications. But Bob's wife had the weirdest ideas. I got the impression that she hated California."

Jim's jaw dropped. Dr. Frank had confused the interviews! In an odd way, that bit of information became our clearest confirmation that God put us right where He wanted us. He didn't even allow my stupidity in the interview to mess things up.

As it turned out, God led Bob and Nancy to a job with Wycliffe Bible Translators which has been a far better fit for their gifts and abilities. Jim and I went on to a productive ministry in church planting. And I have come to love California.

Thus far in these chapters "before the battle," we've discussed what to do when we first recognize a looming battle. We've also explored how to take our initial emotional reactions to God to receive His comfort and encouragement. Now that we've dried off our tears, we're ready to tackle the next logical question.

"OK, Lord, what do I do now? How should I handle this situation?"

Based on my long experience of living with Jeremiah 29:11, I've noticed a few things that will help us to answer that question.

#1 God always, always, always has a plan. Whenever Jim and I asked God to show us His plans He always gave us some kind of plan. You see this all through the Bible as well. When people asked God what to do, God never once replied, "I don't know." He always had a plan.

I've seen God display His glory as both mastermind and micromanager. He is the chess master on the game boards of our lives. But He also plays multidimensional chess. The pawn that He moves on one board affects the game on many other game boards. He effortlessly coordinates the game boards represented by each person, by every nation in the sweep of history, by every church, every marriage, and every business. He has a personalized game plan for the sanctification of every person who comes to faith in Christ.

His plans can zero in to the tiny details about how big to make the bronze altar for the tabernacle or how to fulfill all 332 Old Testament predictions about the life of Jesus. Or they can span the massive choreography of numberless stars and galaxies spinning in perfect harmony within the great celestial dance.

Every time we face a new trust battle we can count on the fact that He has a specific plan. He either directly planned for us to have that trust battle at that particular time or signed off on allowing it to happen to us. And He has a specific plan for how to deal with it.

#2 God throws the full force of His power and wisdom into accomplishing His plans. Job 42:2 says, *"I know that You can do all things; no plan of Yours can be thwarted."* *"The LORD does whatever pleases Him, in the heavens and on the earth, in the seas and all their depths"* (Psalm 135:6). Isaiah 46:9-11 echoes this theme. Listen to what God says and be amazed.

> *…I am God, and there is none like Me. I make known the end from the beginning, from ancient times, what is still to come. I say: My purpose will stand, and I will do all that I please…What I have said, that will I bring about; what I have planned, that will I do.*

#3 God will let us follow our plans instead of His, but works against us if we do. I found this out when wrestling with the truth in Psalm 33:10 – 11.

> *The Lord foils the plans of the nations; He thwarts the purposes of the peoples. But the plans of the Lord stand firm forever, the purposes of His heart through all generations.*

I sort of hoped this applied only on a national scale, but I've learned the hard way that it applies to little old me as well. If I come up with some plan of action that doesn't take God into account or, worse yet, if I see what God wants me to do and do something else instead, God is under no obligation to bless my plans. In fact, He frustrates them and me. He messes them up somehow. That explains why so many Christians get half way through some trust battle and have to rethink everything because things have fallen apart and they're so frustrated they could scream. Well, duh. God wants us to follow His plan.

On the flip side, this principle can provide enormous comfort when our trust battle involves people who plot evil against us. One time I agreed to pray for a group of people. A malicious opponent was harassing them, bragged loudly about all the experts on their side who had thought up a sure-fire strategy to grind my friends into certain defeat. They seemed unstoppable. God gave me a fabulous promise to use. *"There is no wisdom, no insight, no plan that can succeed against the Lord"* (Prov. 21:30). We prayed for God to frustrate their plans and bring confusion to their experts. God did exactly that. Their plans collapsed like a house of cards.

I've concluded that it's stupid to waste time trying to figure out my own plan. Why bother when God isn't going to bless it anyway? Why waste time on a plan that will put me at odds with God when, with just a little effort, I can find out His plan? His plans are rock solid. They will last through generations. God will throw all His power into accomplishing His plans.

#4 God has a plan especially when He doesn't share that plan with us. This happens so often that after awhile we get so used to fumbling around that we assume God *never* wants to share the plan with us and we stop asking. But let's clarify something that might help us out here.

There are different kinds of plans. When we face a crisis, God has a plan of action to help us deal with it. (Let's call this a "plan" with a small "p.") God promises to reveal His guidance to us if we ask and to walk with us through every circumstance. But we want another kind of plan. We want to see the big picture about why God has allowed this particular thing to happen to us and how it fits into His master plan for our lives. (Let's call that the "Plan" with a big "P.") God rarely tips His hand on this part of the plan until the whole thing has unfolded. Truth to tell, we probably wouldn't understand it if He did tell us.

And this is precisely where trust comes in. Every time we face a dilemma and don't know what to do or how it will work out, trust boils down to believing that God has a plan for this particular problem even if He hasn't shared it all with us yet. We trust God by being willing to walk with God blindly.

A few years ago, during one of these confusing "blind" trust battles, I found a great verse that became one of my most reliable promises. *"I will lead the blind by ways they have not known, along unfamiliar paths I will guide them; I will turn the darkness into light before them and make the rough places smooth. These are the things I will do; I will not forsake them"* (Isaiah 42:16).

Do you feel blind? Is the trust battle you're facing an "unfamiliar path?" Maybe your firstborn just became a teenager. That's unfamiliar territory to you. Maybe you just got fired for the first time. That's new territory. Surgery and convalescence has been an unfamiliar path for me in this past year.

That verse doesn't promise that God will take away our blindness. But He promises to turn the darkness into light (eventually) and to make the rough places smooth (eventually). Best of all, He promises to stay with us each step of the way. Even though it's so dark we can't see our hand in front of our face, take heart, God sees in the dark. He will guide us safely through every twist and turn into the safety of daylight.

THE BIBLE STORIES

Let's take a minute to review those stories we scanned at the top of this chapter. They illustrate some basic points that we can easily apply to our own trust battles.

You'll notice that whether God's people faced an offensive or a defensive battle, God answered their big question about what to do. (A few times God refused to answer because of sin in the camp. When the people handled the sin issue, God answered their question.

Check out I Samuel 14:37-38 and Micah 3:4, for instance.)

You'll also notice that, while God always gave a general piece of guidance about what to do, on occasion He also gave His people a promise of victory and sometimes He gave them a specific battle strategy. Twice David went into battle armed only with God's instruction to go, no promise and no strategy. On rare occasions, God gave all three things.

IDEAS FOR RECEIVING GOD'S PLAN

Now, let's work our way through these four elements making some observations about how to receive God's plan in our own situations. Keep in mind two things:

- We "receive God's plan" by looking for God's specific <u>guidance</u> for how to handle this trust battle ("plan" with a little "p"). God seldom shows us the Big Plan ("Plan" with a big "P"). So think guidance, not foreknowledge.

- Think short and sweet. Most of the time, I've been able to put everything I got by way of guidance on a 3 x 5 card. That became my game plan for the trust battle. In Chapter 12 we'll discuss receiving daily guidance going through the trust battle.

Offensive/Defensive Battles. I've become convinced that God will always give clear guidance about whether to launch out into an offensive battle if we will wait for it. This covers things like starting new ministries, making a job change or tackling some big problem. To put it mildly, God has an opinion about what we do with our time and energy. Our job in this "before the battle" phase of an offensive battle is to find out what God wants us to do – or not do. God will pour into us more than enough strength and grace to accomplish the *"good works, which God has prepared in advance for us to do"* (Eph. 2:10). He makes no such promise if we decide to go off and do our own thing.

In defensive battles, the plan God provides usually helps us to figure out how to react to the situation or how to weather the storm. This keeps us thinking proactively even in situations like people problems, illness or financial stresses, when it can feel as if other people or other factors hold the upper hand.

Receiving an answer – a plan. Many Christians don't get a plan when they go through trust battles simply because they don't ask. James 4:2 says, *"You do not have because you do not ask God."* In Matthew 7:7, Jesus gave us an incredible promise. *"Ask and it will be given to you; seek and you will find; knock and the door will be opened to you."*

We don't have to just muddle through. Here's where the idea of trust training can be a huge advantage to us. By expecting to receive a plan for each battle, we can ask God for something we might not have thought to mention in our prayers. Having said that, most trust battles are pretty confusing and God teaches us to trust Him by letting us fly blind at times.

In both kinds of trust battles, God will give us some kind of guidance if we ask for it. In offensive battles this usually amounts to at least a thumbs up or thumbs down. It might take one prayer session in simple decisions. In larger decisions like whether to move or switch jobs, the answer might delay for several months or more than a year. We can make good use of that time delay by putting into practice all we've learned about how to seek God's will. Study the Bible, pray, get input from wise advisers, and watch for confirming circumstances and that sense of inner peace.

In defensive battles, the plan will often be more basic and bare-bones. It might take the form of a simple reminder to hold on to God's hand or a general statement, like "Trust Me."

Don't get shook if you don't sense God's presence or His answer. Often that's precisely where God is training your trust. If you hang in there, you'll begin to hear from God. Sometimes we get too overwhelmed with pain or grief to hear anything clearly. God tends to wait until we quiet down enough to listen. That might just mean waiting until we finish sobbing and breathe that deep sigh, or it might mean waiting until we quit thrashing around in the situation. When I've connected with God after a long silent spell, He has tenderly given me comfort and a simple plan. He was there all along, like He promised.

Focus on how to respond in a Christlike way even if you haven't received clear guidance yet. I've noticed that God often waits for us to begin obeying what we know before He answers our questions about what to do in this particular situation. We know He wants to glorify Himself, to teach us to trust Him and to make us like Christ. Start there.

Particularly if the trust battle is an interpersonal conflict, I've learned to focus on humbling myself. If someone criticized me, have they pointed out something I need to address now? That might well be God's way of revealing His plan, much as it grieves me to admit it.

Do I even need to mention that God will never contradict His word? It's never God's plan for us to steal, to be cruel to people or to have an affair. God doesn't need to send us a sign in the sky to obey the Ten Commandments. The plan often comes straight out of a Bible command. He expects us to find it and obey. That's where Bible study and advisers come in handy.

Promises. Frankly, I don't know how people can learn to trust God, and really know Him, without adopting a few promises. People who survive rugged trust battles and emerge with a vigorous trust in God's goodness usually build up a collection of favorite promises. That's no accident. Promises are often the only thing we have to hang on to when we're slogging through the underbrush. Promises that we've used and found to work become trusty weapons in our future trust battles. We can go back to the same promise again and again.

I look for two kinds of promises. God has given me one or the other, and sometimes both, in most of my recent trust battles. This may sound vague, but I watch for God to highlight a promise. You know how a verse sometimes leaps off the page? Something in my spirit vibrates or resonates as if to say, "Pay attention. This is for you." Faith wells up within me when I hear it.

1. Bible Promises. Some promises can cover many years. I used Joel 2:25a for over twenty

years while I worked through recovery from childhood abuse. *"I will restore to you the years the locusts have eaten...."* I asked God not to waste my pain. He has begun to restore those lost years. The very fact that you're reading this Bible study is one of many fulfillments of that promise God made to me.

Some promises cover a particular situation. I felt pretty scared when we drove across the desert toward California in our VW bug, watching for hospital signs in case I went into labor. I found John 10:4. *"When He has brought out all His own, He goes on ahead of them, and His sheep follow Him because they know His voice."* Jesus had gone ahead of us out to California.

2. <u>Words of encouragement.</u> Sometimes during sessions of listening prayer I will hear a promise for a particular situation. Jim and I have had several big financial crises since we learned about listening prayer and each time God gave one or both of us assurance that He would meet our need. This was in addition to promises we rely on like Matthew 6:33 and Philippians 4:19.

One time God sent the word of encouragement through a mutual friend named Laura. We were seeking God's will about a job change. When Laura prayed for us she got the idea of God as chess master. We were pieces on this chess board, and God knew where to move us, but He had to move other pieces on the board to open the way for us. That analogy gave us peace to wait patiently for over eighteen months. We even saw the last few pieces that God moved when the time was right. We still bless God as *The Chess Master*, our personal code for exalting His sovereignty.

Strategy. God's people won the victory in all seven battle stories we studied, even though God gave them a strategy for victory only twice. Isn't that curious? How does that apply to us? For our purposes, I see strategy as a more detailed bit of guidance. God gives us a plan that tells us "What to do." But on rare occasions He also tells us "How to do it." That's strategy.

I've concluded that God is like a film director who gets everything together to make a movie, including writing a wonderful script and hiring the crew and the actors. When shooting starts, he tells them what he wants to accomplish in a particular scene, but instead of insisting that his actors memorize all the lines, he allows them freedom to improvise within the scene.

In the same way, although God holds us responsible for whatever instructions He gives us, God apparently gives us plenty of latitude as to how to obey Him otherwise.

We need to ask God to give us direction. Give us a plan of action. If we need it, also give us a promise and a strategy for this trust battle. When we receive whatever God has for us, we need to obey everything we've been given. Twenty people can each receive the plan to "Trust God" in a similar trust battle, and each find a totally different and perfectly acceptable way to do it. I find that enormously reassuring, don't you?

Having said that, let me give some modern day examples of strategies. Last year God gave me a simple plan when I went into the hospital. "Trust Me." I can't recall how He did it, but He also gave me a strategy, "Hold on to Psalm 34." That's it. That gave me enough to go on, and as a bonus it gave me access to all the promises found in Psalm 34. Do you see how bare-bones that was? And it got me through just fine.

I recall one time when Jim and I were going through a "blind" trust battle. We felt helpless and forsaken. Looking back, I'd say that the plan was simply to "Trust God." By way of strategy, we crafted a catch phrase that went something like this. "God is in control and He is acting." We would encourage each other with that phrase and remind God of it when we prayed together. That phrase helped us to shift our focus away from the scary circumstances we could see and fix our faith on the unseen activity we believed, but couldn't see, was happening in the supernatural. The day finally arrived when we finally saw what God had been doing all along to answer to our prayers.

I mentioned handling criticism and interpersonal struggles, regarding which I've experienced three different types of strategy depending on the circumstances. The plan is usually some variation on Romans 12:18. *"If it is possible, as far as it depends on you, live at peace with everyone."* Usually, the strategy to obey that command involves reaching out to restore the relationship. Sometimes God's strategy puts the focus on breaking a tendency toward people pleasing. In one such situation, God told us, "Be quiet. Don't defend yourselves. Let Me defend you." In a third ongoing situation, God has made it clear that I am to trust Him by setting strict boundaries regarding the relationship.

I hope this chapter has encouraged you to ask God to give you a plan to deal with trust battles and to keep your eyes open for promises and for strategies, as well. Anything we get is a blessing. If we don't hear anything, we can always default to a basic plan: "Trust God."

No matter how much we receive in the way of guidance, we can trust that God has an overall plan for our lives and for those we love, and that His plans are good. Even if we walk blindly through this trust battle, He holds our hand and He will get us through to safe haven.

FACE TIME WITH MY TRAINER

PART 1: Answer these Bible study questions BEFORE reading the chapter

Quickly scan the following passages looking for the guidance God gave in each case.
Write "O" if God's people faced an offensive battle; "D" if it was a defensive battle.
If God answered the request for guidance, write ANSWER, if not, write NO ANSWER.
If God gave a promise, write PROMISE, if not, write NO PROMISE.
If God gave a specific battle strategy, write STRATEGY, if not, write NO STRATEGY.

EXAMPLE: Deut. 3:1 – 2: D, ANSWER, PROMISE, NO STRATEGY

Joshua 5:13 – 6:5

I Samuel 23:1, 2

I Samuel 23:3 – 5

II Samuel 5:17 – 21

II Samuel 5:22 – 25

II Chronicles 20:1 – 17;
(Especially note vv. 1 – 3; 12 – 17)

PART 2: Questions & Reflection

1. This chapter began by discussing four observations about God's plan. Which ones had you already discovered for yourself and which ones were a new thought to you? What gives you most encouragement and where do you still struggle a bit?

2. What is the difference between the "plan" with a small "p" and the "Plan" with a capital "P?" Which is God more willing to give us?

3. How does it show trust to ask God to show us His plan for our trust battle?

4. Have you ever been through a "blind" trust battle such as the one connected with Isaiah 42:16? What was the situation? How well were you able to handle the uncomfortable sensation of walking blind or having to wait? Have you come through into daylight yet or are you still walking blind? How might this verse apply in your situation?

5. Think about one promise that has become meaningful in your life. What happened in your life that made that promise come alive for you?

6. Are you going through a trust battle now? Have you received a plan, a promise or a strategy yet? If so, describe what you've gotten so far. If not, spend some time praying about this situation asking for direction about a simple plan, and anything else God will give you.

7. What did you find to be the most encouraging or intriguing idea in this chapter?

Karen's Story

When my youngest child graduated from elementary school, I began chomping at the bit regarding a possible career opportunity waiting for me at the local police department where my younger sister was already employed. I longed to reestablish a closer tie with my sister reminiscent of our younger days, before we were so entrenched in the demands of rearing young kids and keeping busy family schedules.

I had always taken advantage of opportunities to volunteer at the schools my children attended to stay better connected to their worlds, so now I would seek an opportunity to volunteer at the police department where my sister worked. When I finally got my foot in the door, I jumped in with my entire being by also enrolling at the community college to complete an A.S. degree, Criminal Investigator. This made my volunteer experience that much richer and more meaningful and also put me in a better position to secure employment.

The lure of government employment was very strong. It met all my desires to be more financially secure, have health benefits, a retirement plan and an opportunity to be near my sister. It was close to home so I could walk to work. My parents would be so proud. This was how I felt I could help my husband. In case anything ever happened to him, my job would pick up the slack, pay for any medical emergencies, and my eventual retirement income would help us both, right? I'm a very practical person and I knew that this was my answer. My plan. But was it God's plan?

With my degree in hand, and an opportunity to interview for an internship in the Crime Lab, I was also dealing with some unforeseen occurrences. Two things happened, over which I had no control, which jolted my world. My sister and her family decided to move to Missouri. I knew all along that they were considering this move, but I kept hoping it wouldn't really happen. The other devastating blow was that my husband's long time friend and co-worker passed away after a life long battle with diabetes. He had counted on Mike for being that extra set of hands that are so often needed in construction jobs. Surely, one of our teenage sons could take his place, I thought. But this would not be the case.

How to be a helpmate to my husband, and a mom to my now teenage daughter were coming back into focus. What did God want me to do? My husband was very clear in reminding me that the business that he was running was "our" business. All along he had hoped that I would become more involved in "our business." Now that Mike was gone, he felt overwhelmed both by getting the construction jobs done as well as the paperwork part of it. I knew that God had been faithfully providing for our family through our business. What would it take for me to fully commit to this?

Just then things started getting weird at the Crime Lab, so I made a decision not to compete for the internship. Crazy as it sounds I would come alongside my husband to enter the world of construction, with all its unknowns, risks and apparent insecurity. I made a decision to work with my husband and to 100% trust God to provide and protect.

God blessed that plan in many ways. Working side by side deepened my relationship with my husband and my respect for him. It allowed me to spend more time with my daughter, my family and my friends. It also gave me flexibility to take on projects I wouldn't have been able to do if I worked for the police department.

CHAPTER 9

Prayer: Asking God to Act

*And who knows but that you have come to royal position
for such a time as this?*
Esther 4:14b

Frank Peretti's novel, *This Present Darkness*, forever changed my perspective on prayer. He tells two stories side by side. One story follows the adventures of several ordinary people who face challenges and enemies far larger than they realize. Hank Busche pastors a tiny church torn by conflict. His sound Bible preaching has angered some powerful church members who schedule a vote of confidence, hoping to kick him out. Marshal Hogan edits the local newspaper. His only reporter happened to snap a picture of something suspicious. He's not sure what they've uncovered and their investigation hits one roadblock after another. Both men seem terribly alone, little nobodies fighting daunting power blocs and political factions.

To make matters worse, in Peretti's second plot line, he lifts the curtain between the physical universe and the supernatural and shows the angels and demons drawn to this sleepy little town to fight a cosmic battle with far reaching consequences. The demons already scuttle about, executing their plot. They use unwitting humans like pawns in their game. The angels hang back, gathering reinforcements but waiting, except for strategic moves such as putting the reporter in the right place at the right time.

Why do the angels wait? The situation gets grimmer by the page for our heroes as evil characters score victory after victory. When will the tide turn?

Well, apparently the angels are waiting for prayer cover. God, who knows all plots hatched in secret, has sent the angels to encourage and protect Hank Busche as he prays alone in the church. But Hank and the angels wait for others to take up the challenge to pray, and to stand up and be counted. First one, then another finally rise up – a little old lady, a married couple, a repentant man – each one oblivious to their importance and strategic value in affecting both the story in the town and the larger story unfolding in the unseen realms above the town.

That book opened my eyes to the power of prayer. It took Bible truth about prayer, angels and demons and brought it to life in a story that rang true. When we go through our little or big trust battles, we can get discouraged looking at the forces gathered against us. Illness or family disputes, job challenges or financial troubles can make us feel so small and helpless.

That's where great stories can come to our rescue. Reading *This Present Darkness* added a whole new layer of understanding regarding a crisis Jim and I experienced. We could identify with Hank Busche because some people plotted to kick us out of the first church Jim planted.

We even glimpsed the supernatural enemy assigned to our case. One night, Jim and I jolted awake out of a sound sleep, suddenly aware of an oppressive evil presence in our bedroom. Without a word, Jim and I rolled out of bed and joined hands across the sheets. "Jesus, cover us. We plead the blood of Jesus." We prayed until the entity left.

That night marked a turning point in that crisis. Until then we had concentrated on humbling ourselves, sifting through their criticism to see if maybe they were right. After that night, we saw the battle more clearly, and threw ourselves on God's mercy. *God, please help us.*

Jim happened to be preaching through the life of Abraham. At the height of the crisis he came to the story in Genesis 22 about Abraham offering Isaac. All week he wrestled with God. This church had been Jim's "child of promise," his dream for years. By the end of the week he laid the church down and yielded it to the Lord. If God chose to allow people to kick him out of the church he had started, he would submit. It wasn't his church anymore; it was Jesus' church. We asked for help but entrusted ourselves to His will, no matter what.

The elder board found the courage to call for church discipline against the main agitating family. Church members began to pray and research the background of the contentious family. Turns out they had caused church splits in all four of the previous churches they had attended!

About 135 sad and battle weary people attended church that Sunday morning before the evening church discipline meeting. Rancor hung like smog over the service. Until I read Peretti's book, I didn't recognize the hints of angelic activity that brought people from that divisive family's last church to offer moral support, and that gave our people courage to speak out when most Christians head for the hills during such confrontations. I didn't put it together why I had such a profound sense of peace. I experienced a palpable bubble around me that muffled and deflected every malicious word from piercing my heart.

When the church voted to remove that family from church membership, five families left with them. We dreaded seeing all those empty seats. We were all too numb to do anything constructive that week. So it must have been the angels. The next Sunday we were awash with visitors and our attendance topped 165, increasing steadily into the summer. Even without the insight from Peretti's book we knew God had answered prayer. To this day we thank God for saving us and for saving that church.

It may seem odd to have a whole chapter on prayer. Hey, we've been talking about prayer all along. Trust in God often expresses itself as prayer. However, these first three chapters have laid some crucial groundwork to address some preliminary trust issues surrounding this trust battle, namely:

- Who or what will I run to for refuge?
- How do I process my feelings?
- What plan of action should I pick to handle this problem?

Finally, in this chapter we will tackle the $64,000 question: **How can I draw God's power and participation into my trust battle so that He answers the prayers I desperately need answered? How do I trigger** *the God factor?*

Near the end of *The Princess Bride*, the swordsman Inigo Montoya and Fezzik, the gentle giant, take their friend, Westley, to a stone embankment overlooking the castle gate. Before sundown they have to rescue Princess Buttercup from the villain. They hoist up Westley for a peek at the sixty soldiers guarding the closed door. The odds are stacked against them. It doesn't help that Westley isn't moving too well since he's been "mostly dead" all day. Westley asks his friends an excellent question.

"What are our assets?"

Inigo replies, "Your brains, Fezzik's fists, and my steel."

As we wonder how to pray effectively for our trust battle, this chapter will borrow Westley's question. We also have three assets that can help us to trigger God's help, each of which requires us to exercise some trust. **Those assets, in the order we will take them are: Myself, God and Other Christians.** Of course, we know about the first two. But, hang with me and we'll see how our partnership with a few vital but ordinary prayer partners can vastly increase our odds of success, not only to get our prayers answered, but also for staying on track to trust God throughout our whole trust battle.

MYSELF

I became a much more effective pray-er when I began to regard myself more like a character in one of the great myths and legends I love like *The Wizard of Oz, The Lord of the Rings* and *The Narnia Chronicles*. Not so coincidentally, that occurred after I asked God to teach me to trust Him. It took awhile to move from the helplessness of the first half of Psalm 18, into the active trust illustrated by the second half of that Psalm. But gradually an amazing thing happened. Like David, the more I trusted God, the more confidently I wielded the weapons in God's training program. I found that I, too, <u>can</u> bend a bow of bronze. I <u>can</u> run up a hill. I <u>can</u> scale a wall, and I <u>can</u> chase down and conquer my enemies.

In John Eldredge's wonderful book, *Waking the Dead*, he notes that the old myths and great stories spotlight **Three Eternal Truths** which especially apply to Christians.

1. **Things are not what they seem.**
2. **This is a world at war.**
3. **We have a crucial part to play.**

Of all the Eternal Truths we don't believe, this [third one] is the one we doubt most of all. Our days are not extraordinary. They are filled with the mundane, with hassles mostly. And we? We are … a dime a dozen. Nothing special really. Probably a disappointment to God. But as Lewis wrote, "The value of … myth is that it takes all the things we know and restores to them the rich significance which has been hidden by the veil of familiarity." You are not what you think you are. There is a glory to your life that your Enemy fears, and he is hell-bent on destroying that glory before you act on it.

John Eldredge, *Waking the Dead*

Something happens when we spend time in God's presence, doggedly bringing our little fears and worries to Him, and timidly cultivating a friendship with God. We begin to see ourselves through His loving eyes. He helps us see our dignity and identity as people made in His image. He shows us that we really are royal priests (I Peter 2:9) – royal because we are children of the King, and priests with powerful authority to pray for others. We lost so much when Adam sinned, but He shows us what Christ won back for us at the cross.

Most amazing of all, He gives us a glimpse of the glory He intends as our birthright. God still looks for people who will be His agents to channel His power and presence into this fallen world.

When you look around at the chaos in your world, your frustrations at work, the sadness of your family infighting, the financial mess, has it occurred to you that God has already started to address that problem?

He put YOU there.

It doesn't matter if you feel inadequate or if you don't feel like a prayer warrior. It's no accident that in *The Narnia Chronicles* the main heroes are children. Lucy, the youngest child, often saw Aslan first and the grownups frequently dismissed what she said. Dorothy was just a teenager when she plopped down into the Land of Oz. Frodo and Sam Gamgee, hobbit heroes of *The Lord of the Rings*, were half-lings compared to the great warriors, wizards and goblin Orcs they dodged in completing their quest. Esther was petrified of the king when Mordecai challenged her to stop Haman's plot. What could one pretty girl do?

But like Esther, God has put us into our circumstances *"for such a time as this."* God could bend the laws of physics to give us a miracle. He could zap an answer to the problems we face. But for reasons He keeps to Himself, He usually chooses to work through the prayers and actions of ordinary people like you and me.

C.S. Lewis put it this way in *The World's Last Night:* "For He seems to do nothing of Himself which He can possibly delegate to His creatures. He commands us to do slowly and blunderingly what He could do perfectly in the twinkling of an eye."

God values our prayers. He promises to take them into account. Active trust has affected my own prayers in several ways. I have come to value my importance in the story because

God values me. Active trust has helped me to see myself as a conduit of God's presence to others. My friendship with God has taught me something of what He likes to do – and what He can do – both of which encourage me to pray bigger.

To the best of our ability and insight, active trust prays big, specific requests that dangle out there, big as life. We risk more unanswered prayer, but we trust God to do what's best, regardless of the outcome.

We can't know what would have happened in our circumstances if we hadn't prayed. Active trust believes that it made a difference. As Archbishop William Temple once said, "When I pray, coincidences happen, when I don't, they don't."[1]

GOD

Early on in my own trust training, God prompted me to study most of the Israelite battles in the Old Testament. God clearly used real live battles to teach them to trust Him. Here's what puzzled me: What did the Israelites need to do to show that they trusted God? The battles didn't look much different from one another. Soldiers usually lined up in formation in roughly the same way and used the same basic battle strategies.

I spent a long time bogged down in the details of each battle. What did God want them to figure out? One day it dawned on me. Aha! The difference wasn't so much in what they did down in the trenches of the battlefield. The difference was in the role they chose to give to God for that particular battle.

They trusted God by looking around to find out where God "stood" regarding that particular threat, and then by choosing whether or not to align themselves with God's perspective and let God run the show for that battle. It wasn't complicated. Every time trouble hit, they (and I) had one simple task:

OUR ONE SIMPLE TASK is to align ourselves with God's purposes, to the best of our ability, so that we set the stage for God to fight along side us, or better yet, for God to fight the battle for us.

According to the dictionary, we *align* several parts of a machine by moving them to bring them into correct relationship to one another. We meticulously *align* two strips of fabric before we sew them together to make the next quilt block.

We align with God by looking around to see where He is, and then adjusting ourselves so that we move over to stand with Him. "The way of trust is a movement into obscurity, into the undefined, into ambiguity, not into some predetermined, clearly delineated plan for the future. The next step discloses itself only out of a discernment of God acting in the

---

[1] But wait a minute. What if we find ourselves in a horrible situation? We'd like to say thanks, but no thanks, if God put us there. That's not the point I'm making. Some situations inflict a lot of damage and the quicker we can escape the better. However, I'm suggesting that we stop feeling so helpless about our circumstances and begin to see ourselves in a more proactive light. If we're in a tight spot right now, we can push back to overcome evil with good. And if we carry pain from other traumatic days, we can find healing so we don't stay emotionally trapped back there. OK?

desert of the present moment. The reality of naked trust is the life of a pilgrim who leaves what is nailed down, obvious, and secure, and walks into the unknown without any rational explanation to justify the decision or guarantee the future. Why? Because God has signaled the movement and offered it His presence and His promise" (Brennan Manning, *Ruthless Trust*).

Aligning ourselves with God sets us up for the release of all His blessings beginning with His presence and His promise. When the Israelites trusted God, it also released His power to perform His most amazing miracles.

Let's look at how this shows up in the story we read in Exodus 17. That battle between the Israelites and the Amalekites introduced a new name of God: **Jehovah Nissi,** *The Lord is my banner.* A banner was used in battle as a rallying point or a standard. It drew people together for some common action. The banner helped to communicate important information. In battle, the commander would position the banners on some high place that everyone could see, so that the battalions would all work together to defeat the enemy. Battleships still fly pennants that serve the same purpose. **So when we say that God is my banner, it means that God calls the shots and all of us rally to Him and take our orders from Him.**

It also means that when we begin to pray about our problems, we climb over to God's point of view and ask Him, not just to answer our prayers, but more basically, to show us what to pray. Maybe you find this easy to do. I don't. Ephesians 2:6 says, *"And God raised us up with Christ and seated us with Him in the heavenly realms in Christ Jesus."* Unfortunately, when I start to pray for something, I often don't feel as if I'm seated with Christ. I feel like I'm little old me, caught like a deer in the headlights staring up at this looming catastrophe. I feel far away from God's throne.

When I have something deadly serious to pray about, I've found that I need to take some time to get myself into the right mindset before I even start to pray for the problem. For me, that involves a step-by-step "climbing up" into God's presence. I generally begin by confessing my sins and then remind myself of who I am in Christ, reviewing all the rights and privileges that are mine because I am "in Christ." With that in mind, I focus on worship, praising God by singing, by remembering His names, and by remembering what He has already done. God becomes bigger in the eyes of my spirit with every song and recollection. Step by step I climb above my earthbound viewpoint, step over that daunting problem I came to pray about, until I stand face to face before the awesome Creator, my Savior and King, who spoke the universe into existence by the breath of His mouth.

I stand there as a royal priest, confident of my welcome, and then I sit down next to Him and begin to talk to Him about my troubles like one friend to another. The best way to pray for problems is from high up above them, seated next to God. That problem that seemed insurmountable shrinks in my sight until it looks as small as an anthill.

I've learned to wait until I'm seated with Christ to frame my requests. I tell God what the problem is and then ask Him, "What's Your perspective? How should I look at this problem? What should I pray for?" Graham Cooke commented that "prayer is finding out what God wants to do and then asking Him to do it."

By the way, doing this one thing has vastly improved my percentage of answered prayer. The prayers I would have prayed "on the ground" looking up at the problem often voiced my fears and selfish motives and lack of faith. I'm more content to let God guard His mystery by delaying the answers to prayers I ask when He has helped me to craft the prayer requests. But when I ask God to do what He wants to do, I have aligned myself with God. Over and over again I have seen Him do battle along side me and a few times He has fought the battle for me.

One last thing, I've learned to write those prayer requests down and to keep track of the answers to prayer. **The single biggest hindrance to trust in new trust battles is amnesia regarding God's faithfulness in previous battles.** Now is the best time to start the prayer log.

OTHER CHRISTIANS

Back in Chapter 6, we talked about the comment made by Ray Mears, the survivalist. The decisions made at the beginning of the crisis tend to shape the chances for ultimate success. We wrap up the four chapters in this section by discussing one of the most crucial elements to set in place as we prepare to deal with a trust battle – trustworthy prayer partners.

God never intended for believers to face most trust battles alone. The Israelites illustrate this. It pleased God when they worked together as a team to face their enemies. In Exodus 17, Joshua led the army but it couldn't defeat the enemy without help. High on a hill, Moses held up his staff praying for God's intervention. Joshua's fortunes in battle rose or fell with Moses' arms. Moses couldn't win the victory alone either. When Moses couldn't hold up his arms any longer, his brother Aaron took time off from his regular job as high priest, and spent the day holding up one arm, while Hur held up the other one.

That victory gave the Israelites a new, deeper knowledge of God: *The Lord is my banner.* Isn't it fascinating that this name of God, so perfect for us as we face either figurative or literal trust battles, includes within it not only a vertical dimension of letting God run the show, but also a horizontal dimension of united prayer, of people working together? When the Amalekites raised their fists against God and His people, the Israelites defeated them by lifting their hands in united prayer and by working together. God set the agenda for that day, and because they prayed, He joined the battle. That day God made their enemies His own, *"The Lord will be at war against the Amalekites from generation to generation."* [My highlight]

Throughout their history, the Israelites often got into trouble when they formed unholy alliances with pagan neighbor kingdoms instead of trusting God. But **God wants us to share our prayer requests with fellow believers. These are good alliances if they make it easier for us to trust God.** We see this in Esther's story. Many Jews fasted and prayed for three days asking God to give her a successful audience with the king. Knowing they had prayed for her made it easier for Esther to trust God as she faced the king.

The older I get, the more I value support networks, and the best time to set these in place is usually before the trust battle hits us. I hate it when I'm knee deep in a trust battle and I have to bring someone up to speed before they can even pray intelligently. It feels like I'm grabbing at straws because they haven't proven their reliability or whether my crisis information is safe with them. It happened more often than I care to admit before I wised up. Now I cultivate these friendships during the boring stretches between crises.

Assuming we find some prayer partners who know how to maintain confidentiality, we should share our requests. Fight the impulse to keep your burdens a secret from prayer partners who have proven their trustworthiness. The Bible specifically commands us to confess our sins to one another (James 5:16), and that's usually the hardest trust battle to share. Don't worry that you feel like a horrible parent. Let your friend know what you're going through with your rebellious child. Or whatever.

I've run across only two exceptions. On rare occasions my trust battle involves carrying someone else's secret. And several times, during financial crisis, God told me to keep the need hidden. God always provided lavishly, displaying His glory to me in a most personal way.

In general, though, God seems to encourage our reliance on trusted friends. Sometimes, a whole church can mobilize to pray, or to fast and pray. When we invite others to come along side us to pray, they can focus on praying for us while we focus on fighting our battle.

RESISTING OUR OVERWHELMING IMPULSE TO ISOLATE

I know what some of you are thinking as you read this. Yes, you say, I agree that we should pray to God, and I'm perfectly happy to try to align myself with God's purposes. But, to be honest, I just don't trust the folks I know any further than I can throw them. They've stabbed me in the back and laughed at me and looked down their noses at me. It would embarrass me to death to let anyone know what was really going on in my life, especially during one of my meltdowns.

To you I say, welcome to the club. A curious thing happened a few months ago in one of my Bible studies. I was feeling extra self-disclosing that day and confessed that when a new trust battle comes along, my first impulse is never to rush out and trust God or to share it with people. My first impulse is ALWAYS to run away and isolate myself from everyone. I asked if anyone else felt the same way. To my astonishment, every single woman raised her hand and started nodding her head. I was so taken aback that I asked the same question of the women in my other Bible study. The same thing happened. Every woman raised her hand.

Yet I look around at those two circles of women, many of whom have gone through deep waters since we began to meet together. We made the deliberate decision to be honest with each other about where we struggled – it's no coincidence that we were willing to come clean about our urge to isolate. Bit by bit we have grown to trust one another with the details of our stories. We've made this leg of the journey together and grown mightily in our ability and confidence to trust God. **The best prayer partnerships rest on the foundation of self-disclosing friendships with believers who would rather grow in their faith than keep up a front.**

On the other hand, it has broken my heart during that same timeframe to see a few women who have chosen to isolate themselves when disaster befell them. As I observe their body language and recall what has always happened when I've opted for isolation, I can well imagine their grim struggle to stay connected with God and to keep up their spirits. It's tough to go it alone.

You may be right that nobody in your circle can be trusted. But, if you're holding out for perfect people who won't ever betray you, you won't find anybody. Dorothy didn't find perfect people in Oz. She found an ordinary scarecrow and a cowardly lion and a tin man, all of them stuck until she came along. More than one of Frodo's companions tried to kill him. The people who rose to the occasion for Hank Busche in the Peretti story had plenty of personal problems. The Apostle Paul traveled with teammates, several of whom deserted him. Even our Lord Jesus gathered disciples knowing which ones would desert or betray Him.

So, I'm really aware that this can be very scary. Don't get me wrong, I have a few knife scars in my back, too. That's why I made the suggestion to cultivate prayer partners before we run into trouble so we build a little history and have some time to kick the tires with each other before letting down our guard. It's also why it's a good idea to entrust our story to a few well-chosen people instead of broadcasting our secrets at random. Jesus said not to cast our pearls before swine.

But I know two things. First: When I have allowed a few well-chosen people to see what was really going on in my life and where I struggled, even though some of them reacted badly or thought less of me, my self-disclosure helped me connect with others who gladly and gratefully set aside their façade and joined me on the journey. Finding them was worth the risk. I'm positive that if you thought about it you could come up with at least one ordinary person who might have potential.

Because, Secondly: All I know is that many times it was my fellow companions who kept me connected with God. I would never have learned how to trust God at all if it hadn't been for Jim. And even though I wrote this Bible study on trusting God, it's so ironic that since I began to teach it, more than once it's been my friends in the Bible study who pointed me back to the God I trust. They helped keep me between the ditches when I got discouraged. That's what happens in these holy alliances. The roles switch around as to who helps whom. If you think about it from the point of view of the cowardly lion or the tin man or the scarecrow, Dorothy was one of the ordinary people traveling with each of them in their entourage.

That's why we show trust *in God* when we resist the temptation to isolate ourselves, and instead, open up to our prayer partners. Like Dorothy and her friends, we all have a much better chance of getting to our goal when we travel together. Although, by ourselves we may be pretty ordinary little people who inhabit one of the great legends, together we will dare to do heroic deeds we would never have attempted on our own, and we will have a much happier experience traveling together until we see Jesus face to face at last.

FACE TIME WITH MY TRAINER

PART 1: Answer these Bible study questions BEFORE reading the chapter

Read Exodus 17:8 – 15 and answer the following questions.

How did Moses help Joshua to win the battle against the Amalekites? (vv. 9 – 11)

How did Aaron and Hur help Moses complete his mission? (v. 12)

How did prayer help Joshua to defeat the Amalekites? (Look at the significance of the name of God revealed in that battle.) (v. 15)

Read Esther 4:5 – 17.

What plot had Mordecai discovered that threatened the Jews? (vv. 7, 8)

What did Mordecai ask Esther to do? (v. 8)

How did the Jews living in Susa help Esther to prepare to go into the king's presence (risking death)? (vv. 15, 16)

PART 2: Questions & Reflection

1. Have you ever gotten a hint of supernatural help or opposition in one of your trust battles? What happened? Looking back, do you spot activity you missed at the time?

2. The chapter raised the question: "How can I draw God's power and participation into my trust battle so that He answers the prayers I desperately need answered? How do I trigger the God factor?" What three assets will help us? (Hint: Each of them has its own section.) What are they and how does each of them require that we exercise some trust?

3. When trouble comes, what is our one simple goal? Describe several ways to do that.

4. What was your reaction to those Three Eternal Truths? Have you ever suddenly realized that "things are not what they seem?" Describe what happened and what you figured out.

5. How do you see yourself? Do you see yourself as someone who has a crucial part to play? What is your favorite mythical or epic story?

6. Describe a time when people prayed for you during a trust battle. Did they turn out to be dependable prayer partners? What do you look for in a prayer partner?

7. What did you find to be the most encouraging or intriguing idea in this chapter?

EXTRA CREDIT: *When you have some time, go back and review all four of the chapters in this section, looking for the tips that you found most helpful to deal with this before the battle phase. Write a "Note to Self" checklist of things to remember or suggestions to follow the next time you launch into a new trust battle. Include the four Trust Gate statements, found at the beginning of these four chapters.*

Debbie's Story

I had been married for a few years but I wasn't walking with the Lord. I was a Christian in my head and I knew that there was a God. But I mainly went to church so that I could play the piano.

I was struggling to come to terms with the divorce of my parents years before. It had become an abandonment issue because my mother left the family when I was still a child. Years later I was still hurting and, without realizing it, I slipped into alcoholism.

Although I thought I hid it well, two of my friends recognized the signs and they began to pray for me. They prayed for two years.

One of them was a recovering alcoholic herself. One day she invited me to go with her to a meeting but she didn't say what kind of meeting it was. I agreed to go and at first I was taken aback when I realized it was an Alcoholics Anonymous meeting. My friend assured me that I didn't need to do anything. All she asked me to do was listen.

But God had prepared my heart. I got emotional that night which I just don't do. By the end of that first meeting I was able to admit that I was an alcoholic. My friend became my sponsor and I became accountable to her. I embraced the program and it helped me to open my heart to God. My faith deepened into a personal relationship with God. I still loved to play the piano but now I played for Him.

After awhile, my sister-in-law, Barb, let me in on the secret of the many people who had prayed for me, even in addition to those first two friends. With their love and support, I've been able to rely on God to keep me sober. I've been sober for the last 17 years. Praise God many times over!

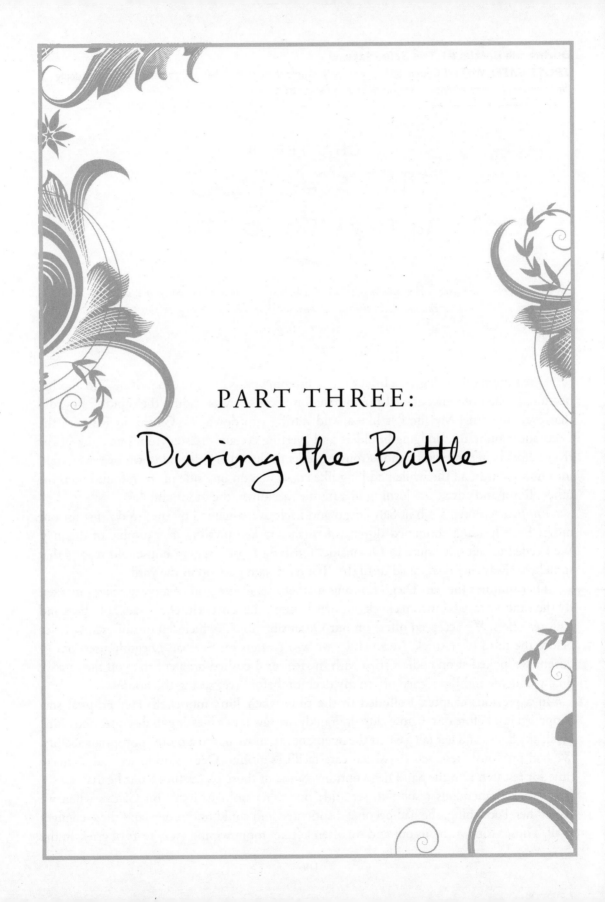

PART THREE:

During the Battle

CHAPTER 10

The Safe Place to Fight the Battle

How great is Your goodness, which You have stored up for those who fear You, which You bestow in the sight of men on those who take refuge in You.
Psalm 31:19

One summer morning, in a brief time of listening prayer before catapulting into another hectic day, the Lord encouraged me to hang on because I was "riding the rapids." Boy, did that ever ring true! My life felt like a wild rafting trip down the Gunnison River in the Colorado mountains, dodging boulders and averting certain disaster from one bank of the river before being thrown by monstrous currents to the other side and down over waterfalls into new hazards, all the while paddling like crazy, first on one side of the raft and then the other. Terror and adventure jostling in a frantic race down the mountain pass.

Jim had accepted a job in San Diego and I felt overwhelmed by the "to do" list for our move. Each heading contained dozens of smaller tasks tumbling in a jumble of urgency. We needed to sell our house in Oceanside, finishing those nagging household repairs that somehow always get postponed until the "For Sale" sign goes up in the yard.

That summer the San Diego housing market was in the grip of a crazy seller's market. By the time we raced down to check out new listings, the sellers clutched stacks of offers and counter-offers. We accepted offers on our Oceanside house, which fell out of escrow twice before the third offer stuck. Meanwhile, we wrote offers on five San Diego houses, out of dozens we looked at on endless trips with the realtor. I dashed off a contract on the one we finally bought, and Jim signed off on my decision before ever seeing the house.

In a previous chapter, I alluded to the time when Jim's mom fell. Her hospital stay happened just before our escrow closed. Frankly, we saw it as a blessing in disguise. She didn't break any bones and her fall gave us the open door to move her to a more appropriate facility. We had previously researched assisted care facilities around Oceanside so we had to make time for research into the San Diego options. Some of those places broke our hearts.

It took tremendous resolve to set aside our other tasks to focus on Gladys when we visited her. Poor thing, she had become disoriented and could not understand these changes at all. Those visits wrung us out and we often left her room wiping away tears of grief. In the middle of our own move, we packed up and disposed of her belongings in the apartment she couldn't handle any more.

Even the easier transitions took time and energy, like Jim's commute to San Diego during the interim, his new duties as pastor of the church we had come to know and love, and our son's transition to a different community college. And I knew that the clock was ticking until I found a job to help pay the house payment.

You'd think that after so many moves I'd have the packing down to a science. I started well, de-cluttering the drawers and closets and doing the yard sale. But somewhere along the line it broke down and the last few belongings didn't wind up in neatly marked boxes. I threw the last stuff into trash bags, tossed them into the moving van, and hoped for the best.

BATTLES ARE MESSY

The single biggest thing I've learned about trust battles is that, when we're in the middle of one, it will feel messy, chaotic and confusing. This is particularly true of defensive battles. Normally, people debating about whether to launch into the offensive battle of a new ministry or a new job may have the luxury of more time to do the things we suggested in the "before the battle" section. But often the defensive battles clobber us without warning. We find ourselves scrambling to catch up, trust-wise, as we race to the hospital because our husband just had a heart attack.

Maybe we land in conflict. We had no idea we had offended our best friend so deeply. Her angry accusations hit us like body blows. Or worse yet, we get blindsided by our husband's confession. We dread its impact on ourselves or the children. So many jumbled feelings fight it out under the black cloud of our panic – embarrassment, second guessing, the hurt, the anger, the unfair treatment, and the confusion about how to resolve the problem. We feel helpless that we can't force people to see things our way and grief if we think they're making mistakes. We see them about to jump off a cliff and we can't stop them.

Their words sting even if they speak the truth to us in a loving way. We struggle against the urge to justify our own wrong behavior and we often resist changes we need to make.

At times like this, nobody calmly sits down with a manual and works through a three-point outline about how to trust God. The spade work we did in calmer days and previous trust battles will have to do. As you read this chapter and the rest of this section about what to do "during the battle," imagine the loud background noise of this messy confusion. If you tend to demand perfection of yourself, you might as well forget it. Trust me, you will not do everything perfectly. Some days you will sail serenely through the chaos. Other days you'll snap at your children or your mate, kick the dog and yell at God.

Usually this is not the time to set lofty goals. Postpone that in-depth study of Leviticus. Bible study goes into survival mode searching for answers and comfort. Our prayers shift to prayers of desperation, arrow prayers that fly upwards on the way into the doctor's office or on the commute to the company that's downsizing our department.

Normal routines often get turned on their ear. Exercise and good eating habits get dumped in the chaos of frantic schedules. We have no time for leisurely chats with our best friends. Organizing our photos into albums will just have to wait. Offensive trust battles eventually settle down into calmer routines and, after the initial scramble, long term challenges, like dealing with a disabled child, often do, too. It's wise to return to healthy habits as soon as possible. However, defensive battles often consume our energy to the very end.

THE REUBENITES, GADITES AND THE HALF TRIBE OF MANASSEH

During the battle, trust shows up in short, strategic bursts. The two and a half tribes illustrate this well. They came to the battlefield well trained, veterans of campaigns to win the Promised Land for the rest of Israel before tackling their own enemies. They didn't stop for a church service when the battle raged around them and the swords clanked and arrows whizzed by and the enemy seemed unstoppable. These battle hardened soldiers cried out in the middle of the battle. Their prayers were probably short.

"God, help us!"

The Israelites in the wilderness illustrate that sometimes we don't even have to speak to show trust. For instance, Numbers 21 tells the story of snakes that attacked the Israelites after they grumbled about God's provision. Many died before Moses made a bronze snake that he held high over the camp. They only had to look at the bronze snake to receive healing.

THE REFUGE

A short cry for help. A look up. That's all it takes to run into the refuge of God's presence. God responds with all the resources at His disposal when He hears one heartfelt cry. In this chapter, we'll look at how to fight the battle from within the protection of the Refuge, and we'll focus on what to do in the most extreme crises. You can draw your own application for less frantic trust battles. If I had only one word of advice for how to show trust during the battle it would be this:

Ask God to show you one easy, simple thing to do and keep doing that one thing whenever you wonder how to show trust.

To that end we'll look at a great trust training tool that you may not know about yet, called **breath prayers**. A *breath prayer* is a short prayer, no more than four to six words that you pray in rhythm with your breathing. For example: Breathe out whispering or thinking the word, "Jesus," and breathe in whispering or thinking the words, "Hold me." Stop right now and try it. Other great breath prayer ideas might be:

- Father / I trust You;
- Jesus / I look to You;
- I know that / You're in control.

Breath prayers have been around for centuries. The most famous breath prayer draws from Jesus' parable about the Pharisee and the tax gatherer (Luke 18:13). God accepted the tax gatherer's prayer for mercy, *"God, have mercy on me, a sinner."* The people who thought up breath prayers modified that into this breath prayer: "Lord Jesus Christ / have mercy on me, a sinner." It's a little long for a breath prayer but it still works well. (You can pray for others by inserting someone's name in place of "me." "Lord Jesus Christ / have mercy on Bob, a sinner.")

Sometimes I use a phrase from a promise in this way. For instance, Breathe out: "My God shall," breathe in: "supply all my needs."

We can pray *breath prayers* anywhere. They express trust and connection. They have a great physiological benefit because they remind us to slow down our breathing. One slow, deep breath does wonders to push away panic. Three deep breaths in a row, in which we mentally re-center ourselves behind the walls of God our Refuge can fortify us to face crises with more serenity.

The best part of breath prayers is that they trigger fabulous resources to help us in our time of trouble. We will give breath prayer suggestions as we explore three of these blessings found in the Refuge: A place to hide, Strength, and Resources.

A PLACE TO HIDE

I learned a lot about the hiding place during an excruciating interpersonal conflict when I worked at a Christian organization. Two people high in the hierarchy had been good friends of mine. When they ran into their own problems, they took it out on me. In the process, they rejected me as a person. Then they paraded their rejection of me and their favoritism toward another employee instead of me. I dreaded going to work.

During that crisis, the Lord deepened my understanding of the Refuge. I began to see it as a place of many rooms with different purposes. The hiding place became a favorite room. Psalm 91:1 refers to God as the shelter. *"He who dwells in the shelter of the Most High will rest in the shadow of the Almighty."* We can set up camp in this shelter. We don't have to take quick trips into the hiding place and then return to the battle. We can fight the battle from inside the shelter.

Years before, when I sat in that church discipline meeting I was holding on to Psalm 31: 20. I used the NASV Bible in those days which reads: *"Thou dost hide them in the secret place of Thy presence from the conspiracies of men. Thou dost keep them secretly in a shelter from the strife of tongues."*

Notice that we run for shelter but then God goes into action. He hides us and He keeps us secretly.

Breath prayer: *Father / hide me.*

I've also learned to cry out to God by praising God in the middle of the battle. This helped me survive the hospital stay, one of the messiest, most chaotic times of my life. To top it off, during the worst days, I was drugged to my eyeballs to manage the pain (unsuccessfully). It is so scary when doctors don't know what's wrong. Fear would rise up inside like a physical thing, like I was about to throw up. The only thing that helped was to use Psalm 34. I couldn't remember the names of God to praise God in some coherent, impromptu prayer. But I could say Psalm 34:1 out loud. *"I will extol the Lord at ALL times; His praise will ALWAYS be on my lips."* Somehow, that helped. The fear would subside.

Breath prayer: *Father / I praise You now.*

STRENGTH

One of the things I love most about God is that He is all-powerful and yet He shares His strength. He reminds me of a giant who lets little children play at his feet and hide in his coat pockets. Psalm 18:1 says *"I love you, O Lord, my strength."* I learned about this name of God when I did a forty-day juice fast. The upside of full-blown water fasts is that people lose their appetite within about four days, but juice keeps the stomach working just enough to feel periodic hunger and to feel faintness. I discovered that I could ask Jesus to be bread to me when I had no bread (He is the Bread of Life), and I asked Him to be strength to me because I had no strength. Each time I prayed, He gave me renewed energy. I didn't run any marathons during that fast. But He sustained me and gave me grace when I needed it.

I found another access into His strength during the trial at work I mentioned a page ago. To add insult to injury, my so-called friends criticized me for not being strong enough to handle their relentless criticism. They despised my weakness.

Truth to tell, I, too, despised my weakness until God gently let me see that He had an entirely different perspective. He led me to Prov. 30:24, 26.

Four things on earth are small, yet they are extremely wise… Coneys [rock badgers, similar to jack rabbits] are creatures of little power, yet they make their home in the crags.

It doesn't matter how small or how powerless we are. If we make our home in the Rock, God promises to channel His strength through us. He promises to be our defender. We learn to rely on His strength, not our own.

Breath Prayer: *O Lord / be my strength.*

This strength shows up in different ways depending on our situation. Let's look at two.

Offensive battles: When Jim and I planted churches, the process was like we've described – messy, chaotic, confusing, and uncertain. So many things needed to be done. We faced many unknowns. The crush of ministry always included messy interpersonal problems and missteps as people got to know each other and learned how to work together. In those times we trusted God by remembering that He had called us to that task. There's a saying that rolls around in Christian circles, "God will never lead you where His grace cannot keep you." It's true. We would remind ourselves that there was no safer place on earth than in the center of God's will. We would ask for strength to obey and He always gave it.

Breath Prayer: *Keep me / in the center of Your will.*

Defensive battles: The main source of strength has been the reminder of God's past faithfulness to us, His unchangeableness (that just like He took care of us in the past He will take care of us in the future) and His promises for our future. We hung on to promises applied to us personally. "I know that God has good plans for us." No matter what catastrophe happens to us, God is bigger than that and He will make it all work out for good in the end. In those situations, God gave us strength to endure and to keep the faith.

Breath Prayer: *I trust You / to turn this into good.*

RESOURCES

Psalm 31:19 – 21 is one of my favorite passages. We've already looked at verse 20, so let's go back to the other two verses.

> *How great is your goodness, which You have stored up for those who fear You, which You bestow in the sight of men on those who take refuge in You.... Praise be to the LORD, for He showed His wonderful love to me when I was in a besieged city.*

The Hebrew words in these verses are fascinating. The phrase "stored up" means "to conceal something (often a treasure of some kind) with a definite purpose in mind." Think of the emergency supplies of water, blankets and first aid kits stored up by the Red Cross ready and waiting for the next disaster. **God has stored up specific necessities that He knows we'll need in the middle of the battle.** He has stored up His "goodness" which includes good things like practical help, and, more importantly, Himself. God is good. He has stored up sides of His personality and His glory. He waits for just the right moment to "bestow" them. Have you noticed yet how often I mention that a name of God became a living reality to me during one trust battle or another? God bestows both Himself and whatever specific thing we need.

In verse 21 David praised God who showed His "wonderful love" to him in a besieged city. The word "wonderful" means "to cause a wonderful thing to happen, things beyond human capability." The word "love" refers to God's loving-kindness, His commitment to us, and His loyalty to stick with us even if we blow it from time to time. Because God loves us, He freely helps us when we need it. He's the Friend who walks in when the rest of the world walks out.

Did you catch that this was all happening while David was in a besieged city? The whole point of a siege is to starve people out by cutting them off from supplies like food and ammunition. Yet God stands with us, inside those walls, and provides everything we need. Outside, the enemy congratulates himself for cutting us off from any supplies. Inside our city walls, a hidden spring suddenly gushes up water in the middle of Main Street. We find the treasure that Elijah gave the poor widow – the jar of flour that never gets used up and the jug of oil that never runs dry (I Kings 17:16). And we happen upon warehouses stacked to the rafters with every weapon we'll ever need to win this trust battle.

Breath Prayer: *Thank You / for stored up goodness.*

THINGS ARE NOT AS THEY APPEAR

Battles are messy, chaotic, and uncertain. We don't know how things are going to turn out. Disaster crouches at the door. Frank Peretti pulled back the curtain between the natural world and the supernatural. Let's do the same thing.

During the battle we feel like we are riding the rapids, tossed and turned by people and forces beyond our control. When we cry out, we feel as if our prayers get swallowed up by the rushing chaos. We see nothing but risk and uncertainty. Did anyone hear? Will we make it through to calm water? Will anyone pull us to safety? What if we die? What if we fail?

But here is the reality. We may feel all wobbly during a trust battle. But the Bible says that people who trust God are like trees. What does that mean? Listen to Jeremiah 17:5–8.

> *This is what the LORD says:*
>
> *"Cursed is the one who trusts in man, who depends on flesh for his strength and whose heart turns away from the LORD. He will be like a bush in the wastelands; he will not see prosperity when it comes. He will dwell in the parched places of the desert, in a salt land where no one lives.*
>
> *But blessed is the man who trusts in the LORD, whose confidence is in Him. He will be like a tree planted by the water that sends out its roots by the stream. It does not fear when heat comes; its leaves are always green. It has no worries in a year of drought and never fails to bear fruit."*

Trees are stable, strong and tall. Every time the Bible refers to us as trees, it also says that we flourish. These tree roots find water even during drought, and enough nutrients to bear fruit every year. It gets even better. Some trees have to tough it out in windy places. But Psalm 92:13 promises that we are *"planted in the House of the Lord."* Think of graceful poplars lovingly tended in the quiet gardens of a monastery or cloister.

That's who we are. That's where we are.

All it takes to be the tree is to cry out in the middle of the battle. Isn't it kind of God to make it so easy? In this chapter we've given many examples of breath prayers to jumpstart your own ideas about turning verses and thoughts into a breath prayer. In an actual trust battle ask God to give you one thing to say, one breath prayer, or one promise to latch onto, and stick with it. Let God reveal His glory to you through that one thing. Repeat it whenever you need it.

Breath prayer: *I'm a tree / planted in the house of the Lord.*

> Fluency is a questionable endowment, especially when it is not accompanied with the weight of thought and depth of feeling. Some brethren pray by the yard, but <u>true prayer is measured by weight – not by length.</u> A single groan before God may have more fullness of prayer in it than a fine oration of great length.
>
> Charles Spurgeon *The Power of Prayer in a Believer's Life*

FACE TIME WITH MY TRAINER

PART 1: Answer these Bible study questions BEFORE reading the chapter

Read I Chronicles 5:18 - 22 and answer the following questions. (The Reubenites, Gadites and the half tribe of Manasseh were the Israelite tribes that settled on the east side of the Jordan River.)

Describe the training of their warriors.

How did they exhibit trust in God?

How did God get involved in their battle and why?

Look for several ways that their trust in God reaped rich rewards for them, both short term and long term.

Read Psalm 31:19 – 22 in preparation for this chapter.

PART 2: Questions & Reflection

1. Have you ever used a breath prayer before (even if you didn't call it that)? What were the circumstances and what was the prayer? How did it turn out?

2. Describe a time in your life when you ran to God to hide you during a crisis. Did that crisis deepen your trust in God or did it shake your trust? What unexpected resources did you find to handle that situation?

3. Slowly read over Psalm 31:19 – 22, meditating on the ways God provides the hiding place, strength and resources. What do you notice about David's attitude, what he focused on and what he reported regarding his own experience?

4. How can you follow David's example as you deal with one of your current trust battles? Practice whatever you figured out to do and be prepared to share how it went.

5. How would the thought that you are a tree, with all the security and stability that includes, change the way you might react to a new crisis? How do you react to that aspect of your identity in Christ?

6. What did you find to be the most encouraging or intriguing idea in this chapter?

THREE BREATH PRAYER STORIES

Pat's Story

I work for my brother and I seem to take on my brother's stress. I prayed before going to the office one day because it can be chaotic there. My breath prayer was, **"Lord, You are my peace!"** (Isa. 26:3). This time I was unaffected and very thankful for it. Sometimes I'm afraid God won't answer that prayer, but that is a lie – His peace is always accessible to me and I praise Him for that.

Jerleen's Story

This spring we have been caught up in the mortgage crisis in California. Our house payment suddenly doubled. We were not able to refinance our home because the value of our house had dropped quite drastically. It feels like we are at the mercy of our mortgage company to refinance us. They have been taking forever to evaluate our income and budget.

There are many days when it seems certain that we will lose our home. What grieves me the most is the thought that, if we lose our house, our two children will have no yard to play in.

In my devotions one morning I ran across Proverbs 14:26. **"Those who fear the Lord are secure. He will be a Refuge for their children."** I have turned this verse into a breath prayer. That verse has given me peace of mind knowing that whatever happens, God is in control, not the mortgage company.

Lois' Story

Whenever the pager sounds in the middle of the night; whenever I'm asked to rush to intensive care or the emergency room; whenever I encounter someone in deep distress – it's clear that supernatural direction and protection will be required. There's no time to dwell in intercession or pour out my feelings. As a hospital chaplain, the people with whom I'm going to minister don't need me, they need the Lord. I need courage summoned and to know that He's entering the situation with me, partnering with me to extend mercy, compassion, comfort, strength, wisdom, and hope, sometimes in desperately painful circumstances – a terminal diagnosis just given, the decision whether to remove life support, the death of a child.

That's when the only two words that there's time to pray before opening the curtain or knocking on the door come to mind. **"Okay Lord"** is my breath prayer that acknowledges that He has prepared the way. It invites Him to go with me. It helps prepare my heart and mind for what's coming. It's me aligning myself with what He desires to do in that situation and seeking His powerful grace.

CHAPTER 11

Finding the Honey

But you would be fed with the finest of wheat;
with honey from the rock I would satisfy you.
Psalm 81:16

Recently Jim and I saw the movie *The Pursuit of Happyness* (spelled with a *y*.) In it the little boy tells his father a joke that I'm sure you've heard before. It goes something like this.

A man was stranded on the roof of his house during a flood. Some neighbors come by in a boat and offer him a ride. He waves them off saying, "No, I'm trusting God to save me." Reluctantly, they shove off and leave him behind.

A little while later a rescue helicopter flies over and the rescuers lower a basket to take him to safety. Again, he waves them off with the assurance, "No, I'm trusting God to save me." Shaking their heads in disbelief, they raise the basket and fly away.

Some time later the flood rises above the man's roof and he drowns. When he gets to heaven he's pretty mad at God and he asks, "Why didn't You rescue me? I trusted in You."

"What are you talking about?" replies the Lord. "I sent you a boat and a helicopter!"

The overarching premise of this Bible study is that trusting God looks different at different phases of a trust battle. It looks different in offensive battles than in defensive battles. Granted, some differences may be more pronounced than others. And our study of these distinctions has also highlighted some common denominators. Trust will always involve turning to God to rely on Him in some fashion. It will tap into a relationship with God in some way. It will usually express itself in some kind of prayer, and with handling fears about the unknown.

This chapter focuses on handling our feelings during a trust battle. In some situations, we can keep doing whatever we found helpful from Chapter 7 (the feeling chapter that corresponds with this chapter in this section). But during the battle, we often don't have time to stop and process our feelings. We're up to our eyeballs in alligators. This chapter will focus on how to maintain our emotional equilibrium in the middle of chaos. Before the battle we asked God to help us. Now, we show trust by keeping our eyes open for help that God sends our way and by receiving help, even if it arrives in a form we didn't expect. Say, for instance, a boat or a helicopter.

We laugh at the man in that joke. He had such a skewed view of what it means to trust God. But I've seen many people with his exact misconception. They set the bar too strictly. They expect God to reward them for trusting Him by answering their prayers in one certain way, preferably a miraculous way. In the process they miss or dismiss the help God offers.

Let me pull in another thread of thought while we're at it. Back in Chapter 4 we talked about how God sends obstacles so that we'll shift our primary trust from lesser refuges to God, the best Refuge. In this chapter we'll put the spotlight on one of our favorite lesser refuges – ourselves. We want to keep control in our own hands and to meet our needs in ways we control. We want to keep bragging rights afterwards that we did it our way, and that we made it through a crisis because of our brilliance or our strength or even our towering faith in God.

Unfortunately, if we survived solely by our own efforts, the trust battle strengthened our trust in our own abilities instead of in God's reliability. That's why God sometimes plops us into situations beyond what we can handle alone, and throws us curve balls to try to shake loose whatever part of our self-reliance reflects a lack of reliance on God.

Saul and the story of the honey on the ground opened my eyes to a whole new way to trust God. So let's look at what his mostly bad example can teach us and then explore how to spot honey in our own circumstances.

SAUL'S STORY

King Saul led his Israelite troops in battle against the Philistines. God fought on the side of the Israelites and sent the enemy into a panic. Saul could have trusted God by just rejoicing in God's involvement and by keeping his big mouth shut. Instead, he put his army under an oath, saying, *"Cursed be any man who eats food before evening comes, before I have avenged myself on my enemies!"* This oath was a terrible idea for several reasons.

His oath was motivated by his ego… *"until I have avenged myself on my enemies."* It's all about me, me, me. Contrast that to David's motivation when he faced Goliath: *"Who is this uncircumcised Philistine that he should defy the armies of the living God"* (I Sam. 17:26). David cared about God's reputation and the reputation of the whole Israelite army. That unselfish motivation prompted David to trust God when he defeated Goliath.

Saul, on the other hand, was pretty oblivious to God's help and didn't trust God to win the battle that day. He didn't get the point that his actions should enhance God's reputation. Instead, he wanted to win the victory to pad his own reputation.

His oath caused distress for his men. His ego blinded him to the impact his oath had on his men. It was common practice for soldiers to carry a few edibles but also to graze along the way if they ran into some food or to confiscate food from captured enemy soldiers. He blocked all of that for his men. Verse 24 says that *"the men of Israel were in distress that day"* because of Saul's oath.

When they trudged into the woods they found some honey on the ground. You can just picture them licking their lips and rubbing their hungry stomachs when they saw it. Jonathan hadn't heard his father put the people under the oath so he ate some of it. It perked him right up. Only then did a soldier tell him why the others didn't eat, concluding, *"That is why the men are faint"* (verse 28). Verse 31 says that *"they were exhausted"* by the end of that grueling day. What a dismal downward spiral from distress to faintness to exhaustion!

His oath hindered the degree of victory. Jonathan pinpointed one of the consequences of Saul's oath. In verse 30, he observed, *"How much better it would have been if the men had eaten today some of the plunder they took from their enemies. Would not the slaughter of the Philistines have been even greater?"* He was right. The Philistines were on the run that day, but because of Saul's stupid oath, his men were too weak to press their advantage.

His oath left his men vulnerable to temptation. By sunset, his soldiers had been reduced to quivering exhaustion and when they found some livestock they pounced on the animals and ate the meat raw. What they did was considered a shocking sin, and normally they would never have done it. They wildly overreacted because they had been wrongly deprived of what would have kept them rational. They sinned, but Saul's oath weakened their ability to eat correctly.

HONEY ON THE GROUND

So, what do we mean when we talk about honey? **It's anything that "brightens the eye" during the trust battle. It's any little unexpected blessing that we happen upon that helps us to renew or reinvigorate.** It can come in many forms.

It might be *a physical thing*, maybe a lovely painting or a praise tape that someone loans us that blesses our spirit. It might be an alcove in the hospital with a beautiful view. It might be a twenty dollar bill that we find on the ground just when we need it.

One way you can spot honey is by observing the timing of its arrival and its effect on people going through a trust battle. For instance, Jim loves bread pudding and he just "happened" to whip up his first batch a day or so before my first operation. He wrapped and froze individual portions. When the spaghetti hit the fan, and my routine surgery turned into a life and death crisis, he spent many wrenching days at my side. He would stumble home late at night to a bleak and empty house.

Some nights he would think of the bread pudding. It pulled his thoughts away from the hospital worries into the present moment and he could savor. And breathe. And refresh. Curiously, he ate the last piece of the bread pudding near the end of my hospital stay.

It might come in the form of *a person who offers help* of some kind. I'll never forget Esther Smelser. She was an elderly lady who loved babies. I was so bent around the axle trying (unsuccessfully) to be the perfect mother to our firstborn. So many transitions to deal with left my head spinning; the move to California, and the transition from a career in teaching to a new identity as pastor's wife and stay-at-home mom. I felt like a failure most of the time.

Esther offered to watch Andy every Monday. Jim and I took her up on her offer. I seem to recall that she did this for more than a year. By all appearances she enjoyed her time with Andy and never felt stressed about it. She gave us a badly needed break from the pressures of ministry. Frankly, she saved my sanity. Esther was honey on the ground, an unsolicited help.

It might come in the form of *support networks or special needs groups*. I have a friend, Leslie, who used to run a ministry to caregivers of Alzheimer's patients. Her group offered break opportunities to caregivers to take a day or a week off while trained people cared for their loved ones. Leslie used to marvel at the number of caregivers who refused to get involved with her wonderful organization and refused to accept the free help they offered. How short-sighted!

Lots of honey comes our way if we belong to a healthy *church family*. A friend, whom I'll call Joan, used to struggle with the question, "Does God give us more than we can handle?" I'm sure she expected me to agree with the usual cliché response of "no." But I've seen too many people crushed under the weight of unbearable sorrow or catastrophe. Maybe they could handle it in theory, but they sure didn't handle it in practice.

It's true, looking at I Corinthians 10:13, that God doesn't allow us to face temptations beyond what we are able to bear. We have no excuse for sin. But Galatians 6:2, 5 speaks more to the point of Joan's question. *"Carry each other's burdens, and in this way you will fulfill the law of Christ...for each one should carry his own load."* When Paul told the Galatian believers to "carry [their] own load," he selected the word for backpack. We need to handle our normal adult responsibilities like taking care of our own house and paying our monthly bills. But in verse two, Paul urged them to "carry each other's *burdens* [meaning *heavy load*]." Some burdens are too heavy for one person to handle. God has designed the body of Christ to pitch in and help carry what one person can't carry alone.

Many trust battles qualify as heavy loads, rather than backpacks. If we don't go through deep trust battles very often, we might not realize all the honey that's available. But, I'll tell you what, land in the hospital like I did, and honey starts flowing freely. Some people kept Jim company in the waiting room during my six operations. Some people brought him food and shopped for us after I came home. Others cleaned our house. Two ladies ironed Jim's shirts. One lady came over every morning for the first two weeks after I got out of the hospital to care for me so Jim could go to the office. Several people sent me books to read. Others sent praise tapes. One family babysat our dog. Many people kept us in prayer and the church took up an offering to help with the hospital bills. The list goes on and on.

It was all honey on the ground, lovely kindnesses that brightened our eyes and helped us to make it through. Each kindness reminded us that God was in control and that He was taking care of our needs. Each person contributed in a unique way, encouraging us during the battle.

HOW DOES EATING THE HONEY
DEMONSTRATE TRUST IN GOD?

We show that we expect God to help us. We tend to find what we set out to find. It reminds me of banana slugs. When our sons were small, we enjoyed camping in the coastal redwood forests in northern California. The four of us would set out on nature hikes through some of the most gorgeous old growth forests on earth. Andy and Zach were fascinated by banana slugs, bright yellow blobby creatures that sometimes grew to four inches or more. They would keep track of the number of slugs they spotted.

I've often wondered what delights we missed when we focused only on those slimy things. Birdwatchers hiking those same trails noticed the birds, because that's what they were looking for, and botanists found many kinds of ferns and took delight in those incredible trees.

It was easy to spot banana slugs because their bright color clashed with the soft earth tones of the forest floor. Worries and fears are like that. It's like they have built-in neon lights. Look at me! Look at me! Honey on the ground tends to blend in with the background and we can miss it if we aren't on the lookout for it.

God isn't like Saul. God treats His people well. He lets us make use of every good resource to get through trials. He lets us eat the MRE's in our backpack and graze along the way. People who trust God expect this. And furthermore, they expect that God will send them honey on the ground, little bonuses, little serendipities, little love notes tucked into their lunch buckets.

We show that we don't need to control everything. You'd think that people would eat the honey without a second thought, but you'd be surprised how often people (like those Alzheimer's caregivers) refuse honey because of control issues. It often requires humility to accept honey. Notice, it's on the ground. One reason why it's more blessed to give than to receive is that it takes humility to admit we need help. We'd rather keep up the facade that we're coping just fine.

For example, someone may offer to clean our house when we're going through a hard time. But then we think about our messy bathrooms or our cluttered bedrooms. So we refuse the help, or run around frantically "cleaning the house for the maid." Perhaps God put it into their heart to help us with our housework, but our own insecurity turned it into a stressful situation.

Sometimes we can refuse help because we set too high a standard. I confess I've been guilty of this. I didn't want anyone else to load my dishwasher because they didn't do it "the right way." How foolish is that? Here is God, sending a volunteer to give us the honey of companionship and shared tasks, and we turn it into a fight over where to put the cereal bowls!

Sometimes we refuse help because we insist we don't need help. However, God favors interdependence over independence. We Christians are supposed to *"fulfill the law of Christ"* by helping each other when we feel prompted to do so. But when we refuse help, even though we need it, we hinder that process. They wanted to be Jesus' hands and feet to us and we didn't let them.

On a related subject, I've seen some parents shoot themselves in the foot by trying to over-control their children's lives. I'm sensitive to this issue because part of the dysfunction in my childhood home was because my parents discouraged normal contact with friends and others whom they tellingly called "outsiders." We can harm our family members by cutting them off from honey or other appropriate sources of renewal.

Saul hurt his troops by forbidding them to eat food. Some rugged trust battles affect everyone in the family. If someone invites our children to a sleepover, be inclined to say yes. Be wise, of course. That's a given. But let them have a break. Let them be children during childhood, instead of pint-sized soldiers in our adult trust battles.

We show that we are willing to let God decide how help comes to us. Sometimes we can get into a snit if we want a particular person to help us and they don't. That can blind us to other people who are trying to reach out to us. During my hospital stay I noticed that people offered particular help. No one person did everything. Their offers of help reflected their personality, their spiritual gifts and their availability. It sucks all the joy out of it if people feel obligated to help.

We can also get into a snit if we want God to send us help in a certain way. We'd rather find the twenty dollar bill on the ground than enjoy the praise tape that redirects our worry into praising God. We demonstrate our trust by letting God surprise us.

WHAT IF YOU'RE THINKING, "WHY AREN'T I GETTING ANY HONEY?"

Maybe God knows that you don't need any honey now. Maybe you're not in a trust battle at the moment so you don't need an unusual method of help. Thank God for your calm, boring day.

Maybe you've already eaten your fill and you need to go back to carrying your own backpack. Proverbs 25:16 gives this good advice. *"If you find honey, eat just enough — too much of it, and you will vomit."* It's a sad fact of life in most churches that 20% of the people demand 80% of the attention. Oddly, the 20% rarely recognize that they demand too much and the 80% feel inhibited about expressing legitimate requests for help. (We're here to encourage the 80%. If you hesitate to ask for help, that's a good sign you aren't among the 20%.)

However, if you feel resentment or a sense of entitlement, stop demanding that people help you and start looking for ways to offer honey to others. When you carry honey to somebody else, you can't avoid dripping some honey on yourself. We reap what we sow.

Maybe people have offered help and small blessings have been there but you didn't notice. A heart full of gratitude will always spot additional things for which to thank God. Ask for grace to see what's already under your nose. Quit counting the banana slugs of worries and fears and grievances and start counting your blessings.

Sometimes we can become so consumed by our pain that we withdraw from people. That's a perfectly normal response to trauma. I hope this chapter has encouraged you to open up a little and let people help you to carry your heavy load.

Maybe as you navigate through this trust battle, you just haven't trudged into the woods yet. Keep your eyes open. Sooner or later, people who hang out in the Refuge find the honey in the Rock because the honey's there. God eagerly waits to give us what we need when the time is right. He has stockpiled jars and jars of honey for just the right occasion.

The main point of many of our early lessons in trust training is to teach us how to recognize what God is doing in both good times and bad. It's so much easier to trust God when we have an idea about what He's up to. So when bad things happen to us, trust training helps us to understand that we can trust God because He is sovereignly and totally in control of every single event in our lives. He either sent that seemingly bad experience or allowed it to happen. He didn't do it to be mean, but because He loves us and understands perfectly what will help us the most in the long run.

Even if evil people set out to harm us, God set a strict limit to what He would permit them to do. Part of trusting God is learning to look past the actors on the ground to receive even bad circumstances from His hand. To trust Him to work things out for good no matter what other people intended.

But now, in the middle of the battle, when we are often so fixated on all of our woes, our trust training teaches us how to spot the daily kindnesses and helpful nudges from God we might have otherwise missed. It's learning to see Jesus in the lady who offers to watch our kids for the afternoon or the bureaucrat who takes it upon himself to audit our account and sends us an unexpected refund. It's learning to receive the sunset as a gift from God. It's learning to recognize God's whisper when we overhear the guy on the bus tell his friend all about a support group that addresses the exact thing we're going through now.

Once we figure out that God is always good, it's much easier to trust Him. And, my friend, He *never* stops doing good to us. The trust battles we go through are a precious gift because they train us to spot God's goodness shining through any disguise.

FACE TIME WITH MY TRAINER

PART 1: Answer these Bible study questions BEFORE reading the chapter

Quickly scan I Samuel 14:1 – 23 to orient yourself so the main part of this story makes sense.

How did Jonathan show courage? What did he say that demonstrated his trust in God? (vv. 1, 6 – 10, 12 – 14)

How did God reward Jonathan's faith? (vv. 13, 14)

What evidence can you find that God used more than just natural methods to help the Israelites fight the battle against the Philistines? (v. 15)

Read verses 24 – 35.
Why couldn't the soldiers eat the honey? (v. 24)

How did eating the honey affect Jonathan's ability to fight well? (v. 27)

PART 2: Questions & Reflection

1. What do we mean by the term *honey on the ground?*

2. As you read this chapter did it remind you of some examples in your own life of finding honey on the ground? Describe a few instances. What were you going through? What form did the honey take?

3. Why might we refuse to accept, or fail to notice, honey on the ground that God has sent to us? Why does accepting honey on the ground shake us loose from our dependence on ourselves and our own ability to control things?

4. Thinking back to one of your more stressful trust battles, what did God provide for you in the way of ongoing support? Did you take full advantage of what was offered? Why or why not?

5. Have you ever felt prompted, out of the blue, to do something nice for someone in need? Did you do it? How did they respond to your offer of help? How does the fact that God called on you to help that person in their time of need reinforce your trust in God to meet your own needs?

6. What did you find to be the most encouraging or intriguing idea in this chapter?

Paula' Story

My month had started off with a quick business trip to the East Coast. On the way home, between missed connections and delays, it took 26 exhausting hours to get back to San Diego. I returned just as my in-laws arrived to spend the weekend. Instead of resting like I longed to do, I had to entertain them without my husband's help because he was back in Iraq again.

Then I spent two weeks in non-stop briefings with long hours every day getting ready for a six-day trip to Mississippi for yet another week packed with briefs and meetings.

On Sunday afternoon I went directly from church to catch my plane to Mississippi. That flight was delayed and the airline personnel gave me two options. I could either reroute to a different connecting city or chance making the original connection. (There was still 45 minutes to spare.)

My two co-workers chose to leave immediately to the alternative connector and they had a grueling trip with lots of layovers and delays. They arrived with barely time enough to catch only three hours of sleep before the meetings started.

I, on the other hand, accepted the delayed flight to Denver, the original connecting city, based on their assurance that I'd be able to make the connecting flight. When I returned to the gate in San Diego, I learned that my outbound flight was delayed two hours, and I would most definitely be stuck in Denver overnight.

It was déjà vu – another 24-hour trip. My heart sank.

Then it occurred to me to call my friend, Kathy, who had just moved to Denver. I asked if she could put me up for the night. She quickly agreed. We had a joyful visit and a relaxing morning before my trip continued. It did me a world of good to spend time catching up with my dear friend.

I arrived in Mississippi just in time for a leisurely dinner, with an opportunity for a full night's sleep. I took full advantage of it.

The next morning I caught up with my fellow naval officers and we compared travel stories. I realized how the Lord had provided me with an oasis of rest and recovery in the middle of my crazy month. It was honey on the ground. Remembering that made the rest of the week much easier to endure.

CHAPTER 12

Working the Plan

Have I not commanded you? Be strong and courageous.
Do not be terrified; do not be discouraged,
for the LORD your God is with you wherever you go.
Joshua 1:9

On a prayer retreat about a year ago, I asked God why I had reached an impasse in my devotional life. Seven years before, listening prayer had transformed my life. I had enthusiastically explored the implications of that discovery. But it made me uneasy that my testimony kept harking back to that event, "Four years ago when I discovered listening prayer…" "Five years ago …" "Six years ago…" I knew in my bones that God doesn't like us to camp too long on one experience. I felt restless but map-less until I heard the cryptic reply, "Study the Philistines."

The Philistines? What could I learn from them?

Puzzled, I pulled out my *Strong's Concordance* and got to work. By the time I reached the book of Judges, I began to understand what the Philistines represent, at least for me. Then I studied four men who mainly fought the Philistines: Samson, Samuel, Saul and David.

As I prepared for this chapter, it occurred to me that several of the insights from my Philistine studies might help all of us who find ourselves in the middle of trust battles. Philistines have a crucial lesson for us about how to work the plan we received when our trust battle started. In fact, we will explore the secret to defeating Philistines. After all, we want to do more than get through our trust battles. We want to win them.

The Philistines were culturally advanced pagan people who settled in the coastal area known today as the Gaza Strip. They lived on the westernmost edge of the territory God promised to give to Abraham's descendants – the Israelites. Although the Philistines helped Abraham and Isaac, they had become a powerful opponent by the time God delivered the Israelites out of Egypt four hundred years later.

God protected the new Israelite nation from fighting the Philistines prematurely. So, on their way out of Egypt, He led them down into the Sinai Peninsula, away from the powerful Philistine territory, even though going through Philistia would have been the shortest route into the Promised Land (Exodus 13:17, 18). In the wilderness God reaffirmed His pledge to help the Israelites conquer the nations occupying the Promised Land. He also promised that if they obeyed His directions, He would fight on their side and send a supernatural terror against their enemies to defeat them (Ex. 23:27 – 30).

Moses sent twelve spies to go check out the Promised Land. When the spies gave their report, ten spies focused on all the difficulties, including giants that lived in the land. Joshua and Caleb were the only two spies who gave a great report. They described the land's bounty and expressed confidence in God's promises. Unfortunately, the nation opted for unbelief and rejected Joshua and Caleb's good report. God punished the Israelite's national unbelief by making them wander in the wilderness for forty more years.

The second time around, the Israelites chose to believe God. Led by Joshua, the Israelite army launched the war in the east, at Jericho, far away from the powerful Philistines in the west. Israelites conquered the hill country that went down the center of the land, establishing what should have been a solid foothold to conquer the rest. But they fell short of their goal. When Joshua divided the Promised Land among the twelve tribes, God directed him to include chunks of unconquered land within the borders of many tribes. Each tribe was assigned the task of winning the unconquered territory within its borders.

As we've mentioned earlier, God reserved these unconquered neighbors, including the Philistines, as training tools to teach the next generation of Israelites how to fight (Judges 3: 1 – 4). He wanted the Israelites to learn how to trust Him. Unfortunately, the tribes gave up and, because they didn't conquer their neighbors, these neighbors led them into idol worship and enslaved the Israelites from time to time. **That which remains unconquered becomes a snare.**

The Book of Judges and the Two Books of Samuel trace four hundred years in the history of the Israelite efforts to conquer the Philistines, among other enemy neighbors. Samson, Samuel and Saul whittled away at the task of conquering the Philistines, but David had the most success. His victory over the Philistines lasted for 150 years.

HOW IT APPLIES TODAY

What I learned from studying the Philistines gave me more new insights and principles than I have space to share in this chapter. And what I came to regard as Philistines in my life may not resonate with you. So, let's make it easy on ourselves and just call whatever we're dealing with in our current trust battle a Philistine. So a *Philistine* **is just another name for a trust battle.** OK?

Just as the Philistines controlled five cities, most of us juggle several Philistine challenges at any given time. God wants us to rise to the occasion and conquer them. He recognizes it will be hard and take time. If we step out in faith to tackle them under His direction, He promises to help us. *"Little by little I will drive them out before you, until you have increased enough to take possession of the land"* (Ex. 23:30).

Now, let's switch gears a little and orient ourselves about where this chapter fits with the rest of this book. Depending on the circumstances, sometimes people can zip through the entire *before the battle* phase in a day or two. Sometimes we have to scramble to catch up when we find ourselves plopped into the middle of a trust battle. For most people, though, this chapter lasts the longest by far in many trust battles. This chapter talks about slogging it out day after day or month after month, working the plan God gave us in Chapter Eight. This is the nuts and bolts of enduring the battle until it ends in some way.

Studying the Philistines gave me tons of encouragement regarding these trust battles. I saw that God kept total control over the Philistines and really did use them as a training tool. Even though Philistines posed a huge challenge, and even though they terrified and frustrated God's people, the minute they outlived their usefulness God shut them down easily and completely – as effortlessly as if He flipped off a light switch.

I looked for strategies. What could Samson and Samuel – Israel's last two judges, and Saul and David – Israel's first two kings, teach us about how to conquer our own personal Philistines? Studying what worked for each of these four men, and what didn't work, revealed a common thread – an amazing secret to defeating Philistines! We'll also look at how to set the stage for this secret strategy to work and what results to expect.

SETTING THE STAGE

Obedience and yieldedness set the stage for victory. The Israelites prepared to defeat the Philistines by being in the right place at the right time. Usually they did this by inquiring of the Lord. You can't read David's story without seeing that repeated theme of inquiring of the Lord.

That's why we made such a big deal in Chapter 8 about receiving the plan. As soon as we recognize a problem, we need to ask God what to do. We talked about getting guidance, a promise, and/or a strategy. It is crucial to stay yielded to God, to know what God wants us to do and to do it.

That's also why we emphasized the importance of asking for guidance as soon as possible, before the situation gets too far out of hand. In the story of Goliath, Saul illustrates the danger of not inquiring of the Lord. By the time David showed up, Goliath had been taunting the Israelites for about six weeks. The Israelite army had been camped out on one hill and the Philistine army on another. We can read between the lines that Saul had not asked God what to do. Let me guess what God might have replied (based on I Sam. 9:2; 13:22).

"Well, Saul, why do you think I created you a head and shoulder taller than any other Israelite? And, let's see, only two people in all Israel own a sword and spear, and you're one of them. Quit stalling, Saul. Put on your fancy armor and go fight Goliath."

Saul had a bad habit of dragging his feet. Back in Chapter 11, we studied about another occasion when two armies lined up on separate hills. And then they sat around. Saul didn't have a plan because he didn't ask God for one. Eventually, Jonathan got bored and went off to find some action. When Jonathan defeated his batch of Philistines, the rest retreated in a panic. But Saul didn't realize that. Saul only noticed the general chaos of a bunch of soldiers running around. At the last minute, He hastily tried to inquire of God and then stopped the priest in mid-inquiry. Saul had no clue what God was doing and made no attempt to align himself with God's plans. He stumbled around without direction and hurt his side more than he helped.

By contrast, David consistently and immediately asked God what to do. And obeyed promptly. In the story of Goliath, he was just a kid, so he wasn't in a position to inquire of the Lord in a formal way using the high priest's ephod. But it couldn't have been more obvious that Israel needed a champion and Saul's cowardice left the door wide open for David to volunteer.

Hopefully, we already have a plan. We should obey what we know. We can always ask for more guidance when we run into new dilemmas within the trust battle. Isaiah 30:21 gives us this lovely reassurance. *"Whether you turn to the right or to the left, your ears will hear a voice behind you, saying, 'This is the way, walk in it.'"*

If my trust battle lasts for a long time, I've learned to build in regular review days to take stock. I pull out that 3 x 5 card of guidance. I tend to do this on the first of the month for longer projects. It is so easy to drift away from the plan. This review day helps me to remember God's promises, to check my progress, to rejoice in intermediate answers to prayer and to get new direction. It's much easier to make small adjustments if I've gotten a little off track.

THE SECRET TO DEFEATING PHILISTINES

When it became clear that the Israelite tribes weren't going to conquer the territory within their borders, God chose to work through individual men and women. They would rally the people and lead the charge to defeat the enemy. These champions were called judges (and later, kings). Some of these judges relied mostly on their own strength and as a result, they weren't very effective. Samson is a good case in point. But when these chosen people relied on God as their main source of strength, their personal victories led to a larger victory for the nation.

Of those four guys, Samuel and David best illustrated the secret strategy in action. They were actively yielded and obedient to God. They cultivated an intimate, friendship relationship with God. And when the Philistines attacked, they did two important things.

THE SECRET TO DEFEATING PHILISTINES:
1. They expressed faith, and
2. They did an act of courage.

When they did these two things, they won a small, personal victory. All God asked of these champions was that they courageously face the giant in front of them that day. David was already using this strategy when he tackled the bear and the lion, even before he faced Goliath. Over and over again, these four men were called on to face a big old enemy. If they expressed faith in God and faced their enemy with courage, they won their personal victory.

Let's look at some examples of this two-part strategy of faith and courage. It works with Philistines and you can also see the same principle at work against other enemies and obstacles.

	STATEMENT OF FAITH	ACT OF COURAGE
David vs. Goliath I Samuel 17	"You come against me with sword and spear and javelin, but I come against you in the name of the LORD Almighty, the God of the armies of Israel, whom you have defied. This day the LORD will hand you over to me, and I'll strike you down and cut off your head. Today I will give the carcasses of the Philistine army to the birds of the air and the beasts of the earth, and the whole world will know that there is a God in Israel. All those gathered here will know that it is not by sword or spear that the LORD saves; for the battle is the LORD's, and he will give all of you into our hands."	Armed with five stones and a slingshot, young David went out and faced Goliath, a huge battle-hardened warrior.
Jonathan I Sam. 14:1-14	"Perhaps the LORD will act in our behalf. Nothing can hinder the LORD from saving, whether by many or by few." "...if they say, `Come up to us,' we will climb up, because that will be our sign that the LORD has given them into our hands."	Vastly outnumbered, Jonathan and his armor bearer attacked a Philistine outpost.
Joshua & Caleb Num. 13 & 14	"The land we passed through and explored is exceedingly good. If the LORD is pleased with us, He will lead us into that land, a land flowing with milk and honey, and will give it to us. Only do not rebel against the LORD. And do not be afraid of the people of the land, because we will swallow them up. Their protection is gone, but the LORD is with us. Do not be afraid of them."	They tried to persuade the Israelites to go into the Promised Land even though the people threatened to stone them.
Shadrach, Meshach & Abednego Daniel 3	"O Nebuchadnezzar, we do not need to defend ourselves before you in this matter. If we are thrown into the blazing furnace, the God we serve is able to save us from it, and He will rescue us from your hand, O king. But even if He does not, we want you to know, O king, that we will not serve your gods or worship the image of gold you have set up."	They defied the king and refused to bow down before the statue even though it meant certain death in the fiery furnace.
Jesus Mark 14:36	"Abba, Father, everything is possible for You. Take this cup from Me. Yet not what I will, but what You will."	He went to the cross.

It may seem odd to talk about courage in a Bible study about trusting God. We've said that trust implies the feeling of safety. We trust God by running to Him for refuge. We trust God by letting Him help us to process our fears. None of that is an end in itself. You see, if we truly feel safe, if God truly delivers us from our fears, and if we know for sure that God will never abandon us, that assurance will fill us with courage. **Trust battles are inherently scary. But battles are meant to be won. And we win the trust part of the trust battle by sticking so close to God that His presence emboldens us to express faith and act courageously.**

(By the way, let's be clear how we define what we mean by "winning the victory." As you can see from the examples in this chart, all of them won the trust battle that day because they successfully trusted and obeyed God. That's what we mean when we say "winning the *trust* part of the trust battle." But not all of them escaped unscathed or got what they wanted.)

OK, remember when we talked about the difference between a pocket knife and a pair of scissors? We made the point that faith can stand alone, but trust in God is always linked to faith. Now, let's fine-tune what we aim for when we trust God. In listening prayer, awhile ago, I heard this.

> *The essence of trust is courage –*
> *courage to believe the Word*
> *in the midst of voices and circumstances to the contrary.*

The title of this book refers to *confident* trust in God. Everything we've learned so far has helped us to work through the wobbles in our trust, so we can have the courage to trust God.

We can do this two-step strategy in a variety of ways. In some trust battles, the circumstances crescendo into a decisive moment or turning point. That's the time to express our faith and do an act of courage. In other situations, we might need to do daily little exercises of faith and courage to meet the challenges of each day.

In offensive battles, when we step out in faith to do what God calls us to do, we use this two-part strategy. We can start our new project or ministry with lots of enthusiasm. At first it's easy to act courageously. It's just as important to express faith and do acts of courage when we hit obstacles, when the ministry gets tough or when the new job is harder than we anticipated.

In defensive battles, it may take the form of squarely facing the inevitable instead of denying reality. Courage means choosing to stay in a tough situation when the faint of heart would run away or become emotionally detached or irritable. It takes courage to set aside bitterness when others have hurt us and focus our energy on fixing the damage. Courage makes us crack jokes while we wait for our chemo treatment because we trust God – no matter the outcome. Courage speaks up for Jesus in front of a hostile crowd. Or just as courageously takes the high road in an argument by biting our tongue.

Jonathan's example can help us to avoid presumption or conceit. He gave God room to direct whether he should charge ahead or not. When the Philistines yelled for Jonathan to climb up, that was the sign Jonathan had asked for and he rightly concluded that God would "back up his act," so to speak if he attacked the Philistines. Jesus prayed for guidance in the Garden of Gethsemane. For Jesus, it took courage NOT to resist the people who arrested and crucified Him. We should also give God room to show us what courage will look like in our particular situation.

THE RESULTS

But, wait, there's more to this secret. Nobody was around when David wrestled the lion that threatened his flocks. He practiced faith and courage no matter what enemy came his way. But, eventually, for David, and for each of the people who faithfully and courageously met the enemies God directed them to face, an amazing thing would happen.

At least once in their lives, facing and defeating their personal giant would trigger a bunch of other activity. God would swoop into the picture and send panic on the enemy (per His promise in Exodus 23:27, 28). God would also energize the other Israelites to courageously fight the enemy. Because the champion won his personal victory, the nation would win a larger, national victory.

On the day David faced Goliath, he actually killed only one Philistine. But, by courageously defeating the one giant in front of him that day, his victory set the stage for the bigger, national victory. We see this in the other stories we mentioned. Jonathan and his armor bearer only killed twenty Philistines before God swept in, sent panic on the enemy and mobilized the Israelites to rout the Philistines that day. When Shadrach, Meshach and Abednego faced Nebuchadnezzar, their small, personal victory had a huge impact on the rest of the Jews in exile because the king changed his mind about forcing everyone to commit idolatry.

We need to be careful when we look at Christ's example because He is one of a kind. Theologically, *His* victory on the cross is also *our* victory. End of story. Having said that, it's always a good idea to look to Jesus so we can follow His example. And He perfectly modeled this principle of faith and courage, both on a personal scale, and as a catalyst for God's power to flow to others.

I used to think that trust battles were mainly an internal issue – our own personal struggle. It wasn't until I studied the Philistines that I noticed how often our personal trust battles are part of a larger problem, jointly experienced by many people. But think about the typical trust battles we've explored in this study. Financial crises, marital problems, work conflicts, decisions about whether to move or change jobs, serious illness, and ministry challenges all involve many people. Even purely internal trust battles like tackling a bad habit usually don't become a priority until we see how our habit hurts the people we love.

It's hard enough to win the trust battle inside our own hearts. It's even harder to win the larger trust battle going on within our family or our neighborhood or our church. What can one person do? We can't control the outcome. That lies in God's hands. And we can't control other people. God gives people freedom to make their own decisions and many people make poor choices, or at least choices we don't prefer.

So we can't control. But, the great news from the Philistines is that we have a crucial role to play. Hey, that sounds like Eldredge's *Third Eternal Truth*, doesn't it? **We may face many personal giants without it seeming to have much impact on anyone else. But, sooner or later, by winning our own trust battles, we can have a powerful and positive influence that helps to turn the tide for the larger community's trust battle.**

Faith and courage are contagious. We probably underestimate the degree to which we set the mood in our homes and influence the atmosphere at work and at church. Our children watch us. Our husbands can be either encouraged or discouraged by our reaction to situations. They often take it as a personal rebuke if we express worries, especially about finances. Courage neatly avoids that hazard and makes it easier to trust God as a couple. Other people watch how we handle life and the unsaved people around us are looking for someone who will inspire them.

I can't force anyone else to do anything. But it encourages me to see, in Scripture and in my own experiments, that winning my little victory blows the doors open and sets the stage for other people to win their battles. For instance, last year a young man in our church broke his leg. It was a nasty break and it wasn't healing properly, so he eventually ended up in the hospital. I felt God prompting me to go pray for him. Of course, I worried that I would look foolish. What if nothing happened?

My act of courage was to go to the hospital and say, out loud, that I felt God wanted to do something wonderful for him. His mom and dad were sitting by his bed, looking pretty dejected. But as soon as I spoke up, faith just burst forth within both of them. We all prayed in faith and his leg began to mend right away. I won my little battle against the fear that I would look foolish. But they got the bigger blessings of experiencing a big answer to prayer. It gives me such a kick when I see that young man walking around at church.

Faith and courage let God out of the box. God seems to enjoy responding lavishly when people express faith and act courageously. On the other hand, Jesus marveled at the unbelief expressed by people in His hometown. *"And he did not do many miracles there because of their lack of faith"* (Matthew 13:58). It's not that Jesus couldn't do many miracles. It's that He doesn't do many miracles when people don't expect them.

God has not given us the spirit of fear. When I was first learning how to practice listening prayer, God regularly led me into situations that required courage. And when I would obey His prompting, He would consistently do over and above what I could ask or even imagine. **God wants us to learn how to trust Him because He has things to do and people to bless through us.**

Faith and courage will be richly rewarded. Confident trust, that's what we want. Courageous trust helps us to hang in there until the battle is over. It makes us persevere. We endure. Listen to the promise in Hebrews 10:35, 36. *"So do not throw away your confidence; it will be richly rewarded. You need to persevere so that when you have done the will of God, you will receive what He has promised."*

God rewards us by giving us what He promised, back when we asked for a plan, back before the battle got into full swing. He rewards us by showing us more of His faithfulness and His utter reliability.

God rewards us even if the larger group chooses not to trust God. Joshua and Caleb illustrate this. The whole nation rejected God's promise and disobeyed Him, except for Joshua and Caleb. In the middle of judging all those other people, God rewarded Joshua by making him the next leader after Moses. God promised to give Caleb the land he had walked on when he first spied out the Promised Land, and when Joshua divided up the land, Caleb courageously asked for Hebron to claim that promise. It took courage to ask for Hebron because it was the hometown of Arba, the biggest giant of them all! And, by golly, he defeated Arba and settled into his brand new home.

I want to be like Caleb, don't you? I want to be full of faith and courage at the end of my life. I want to experience big answers to prayer and the blessing of a confident trust relationship with God. And I want to enjoy the whole territory God has promised to me. How about you?

FACE TIME WITH MY TRAINER

Read I Samuel 17:1–53 to answer the following questions.

What evidence suggests that Saul did not inquire of the Lord about how to handle Goliath? (vv. 1–11; 16, 25)

How did Saul and the Israelite army react to Goliath's threats? How did David react? (vv. 11, 16, 24)

What experiences had prepared David to trust God before he faced Goliath? (vv. 34–37)

What did David say to Saul and to Goliath that expressed his faith in God? (vv. 32, 45–47)

How did David show courage? (vv. 32; 38–40; 48, 49)

How did David's victory affect the Philistines and the other Israelite troops? (vv. 51–53)

PART 2: Questions & Reflection

1. As you read this bit of history about the Israelites, did their story remind you of any experiences in your own life? What lessons from their example can you apply to your own story?

2. Explain in your own words the two-part secret to defeating Philistines. Describe how you might do each one of these two steps in one of your current trust battles, and how you did it in at least one past trust battle.

3. We've talked a lot in this book about how it expresses trust in God to honestly take our fears and worries to God and to pray about our problems. So how does courage fit into this picture? Why will talking to God about our fears and our problems make it more likely that we will act with courage?

4. Why is it important for us to face and win our personal trust battles, even if it has no immediate effect on anyone else?

5. Jot down some of the trust battles you are dealing with right now. What other people are also affected by these trust battles? How has that frustrated you? How have you been able to influence others to trust God?

6. What did you find to be the most encouraging or intriguing idea in this chapter?

EXTRA CREDIT: *Is it about time for you to have a review day about the biggest trust battle you're going through right now? If so, maybe now would be a good time to do that. How did it go when you checked in with God about this trust battle? Had you strayed off track a bit? What new guidance did you receive? What date have you reserved on your schedule for your next review day?*

Angela's Story

When I graduated from law school, I was confused. At the time, I thought I was the only one who did not have a clue about how to practice law, but I was wrong. My classmates were also confused. I thought that life begins once I graduate, but I found out that life continues. I found myself completing one trust battle (law school) and immediately beginning another (the bar exam). After graduation, I felt just as stressed studying for the bar exam as I did when studying for finals. I thought I should be happy and celebrating. I was confused about my situation and did not trust God with my confusion. I just muddled around in it, continuing to be confused as I attended the bar exam prep course. Soon, I gave up hope while studying for the bar exam. I was just too confused and no one could help me.

I took my first bar exam in Missouri. I was so nervous that I spent most of the time in the bathroom. I felt sorry for the proctor who had to follow me to the bathroom several times that day. Needless to say, I did not finish the exam and so I failed the exam. Now what? I had a job waiting on me in Poplar Bluff, Missouri at the Public Defenders Office. Surely, they wanted a law graduate who could practice law. They invited me to come and defend indigent criminals while I studied for the exam. I accepted their offer. Some days, I just could not get out of the bed. I just knew that they were going to fire me. They did not. I was so depressed. I felt so lonely living in this small town and having to retake the bar exam.

I took the bar exam for a second time and failed again. I gave my notice to resign and left that small town. Now what? I stayed depressed and moved in with my parents while I studied for the bar exam that summer.

I took the bar exam for a third time. For a third time, I failed. Again, I asked myself, now what? I wondered if God had forsaken me. Did He even want me to be a lawyer?

Without any prayer and consultation, I joined the U.S. Army hoping to one day become a JAG Corps Officer. It was an awful experience. My platoon did not like females, let alone educated females. I did not become a JAG Corps Officer. I was living in a state of confusion. Out of desperation, I asked a minister at my last duty station how I could know if God wanted me to pass the bar exam. She did not answer my question or give me any direction. I was devastated. After all of these years, I still was confused and had no answers.

After being discharged, my husband and I moved to Miami. For the fourth time, I studied for the bar exam, but I changed what I did. I used a different bar prep course. This time I also prayed, held on to promises, fasted, worshipped Him daily, and studied my Bible. I had daily walks and talks with God while I exercised.

One day God spoke to me. He let me know that I would pass the Florida bar exam. I praised His name before I even took the exam. I thanked Him. I trusted Him. God successfully saw me through this trust battle. This time I could not wait to take the Florida bar exam. I knew the outcome before it had occurred. Finally, the day came when I took and passed the Florida Bar exam on the first try. Today, I tutor others for bar exams. God used my experiences to prepare me to give to others the help I wish someone could have given me.

CHAPTER 13

Power: Watching God Act

"Don't be afraid," the prophet answered.
"Those who are with us are more than those who are with them."
And Elisha prayed, "O LORD, open his eyes so he may see."
II Kings 6:16, 17a

I once spent a weekend with three ladies who could see angels. Judy sees angels mainly during those rare worship services when people make that intangible transition from just singing songs and begin to soar into heaven's praise. For her the fragrance of God's presence often signals the arrival of angels, in riotously spinning flashes of light, drawn like bees to honey.

Pat sees angels more as an invisible "substance" sensed by her spiritual eyes but not seen by her natural eye. The way she learned to see angels reminded her of those optical illusion art pieces composed of many little patches of color that appear to depict one thing unless you unfocus your eyes and squint until you can see the second thing superimposed over the first.

Apparently, RaJean has Elisha's ability to see angels at will. She also sees them most often in that space between the visible and the invisible, although she sees more clearly what they look like. She intrigued me. Other than this gift, she seemed like a down to earth, very sane and joyful Christian.

Our team spent the weekend doing a prayer assignment for San Diego that involved driving to various places in the county to pray. It was a holy time. Even I knew we would need the help of the angels to complete our assignment. So, suspending my natural skepticism toward someone I had just met, throughout the weekend I curiously asked RaJean what she saw. I wanted to learn what I could from her. How many angels did she see? What did they look like? What were they doing?

According to her, two gigantic angels assigned to our project followed us all weekend. Sometimes she saw one or two other angels, sometimes more. She commented that the owners of the restaurant where we ate lunch must know Christ because a large guardian angel stood on duty at the door.

All three women gave me suggestions about how to see angels. I began trying to spot angels before asking what RaJean saw. I was pretty hit or miss at first. And I had no way of knowing if RaJean was telling me the truth. Two things made me lean toward believing her.

The whole weekend felt like a divine appointment. We prayed specific requests asking for things that would be verifiable, even measurable by scientific instruments. God answered our exact prayers.

I was exhausted when I got home at the end of the weekend. There was not a breath of wind in our front yard that night. Suddenly the large fern in our flower bed caught my attention. Although the surrounding shrubbery and the azalea tree behind it remained motionless, the fern branches waved gently up and down for about a minute in a happy little welcome dance. I stood and watched with a big grin on my face until the fern became still again.

"I see you," I whispered and turned to unlock my front door.

I've only seen angels a few times, more in Pat's way than the others. Late one night I "saw" four young looking angels who guarded our Oceanside home. It was as if I saw where they occupied space, understood what they looked like and could sense that they lined up at attention before dispersing for duty. Occasionally I sense angels when people receive healing prayer. I saw angels in the hospital during my deepest pain. One day I asked for an angel to guard the door to my hospital room and later realized that God had also deployed other angels to keep people from entering the room until I was ready. I have a pretty good notion that the Kaiser electrician who fixed my call box was an angel, but that's another story.

That weekend with RaJean fed my yearning to see angels, not mainly to satisfy idle curiosity, but because angels hang out with God. I often pray that God will open my eyes to see what's going on in the supernatural dimension. I'm still such a novice and it frustrates me to feel so clueless much of the time. But I'm getting better at realizing that when I look at the church sanctuary or my living room, there's more to be seen than the furniture. I've learned to become still and to focus on praising God until I rest in His presence. Then I reach out with the eyes of my sprit, testing the atmosphere and asking God to show me whatever I need to see.

This chapter isn't about how to spot angels. For that, go to an expert like RaJean. However, **the mindset that looks past the surface picture to perceive angels in the unseen middle distance is an important asset in the school of trust training. During the battle, we trust God by looking past the battle we can see with our eyes so we can focus on the unseen.**

One of the deepest lessons of trust is to learn that, although the trust battle happens to us, we are support troops only. God and the angels bring the heavy artillery. Proverbs 21:31 says *"The horse is made ready for the day of battle, but victory rests with the Lord."*

Eldredge's *First Eternal Truth* states that *things are not what they appear.* That's a foundational truth for Christians. God gives every Christian the task of learning to live in the unseen. *"We live by faith, not by sight"* (II Cor. 5:7). Or listen to Paul's prayer in Ephesians

1:18 – 20. *"I pray also that **the eyes of your heart may be** enlightened in order that you may know the hope to which He has called you, the riches of His glorious inheritance in the saints, and His incomparably great power for us who believe. That power is like the working of His mighty strength, which He exerted in Christ when He raised Him from the dead and seated Him at His right hand in the heavenly realms..."* We see it all through the eyes of our hearts.

II Corinthians 4:17 – 18 applies most pointedly to this chapter. *"For our light and momentary troubles are achieving for us an eternal glory that far outweighs them all. So we fix our eyes not on what is seen, but on what is unseen. For what is seen is temporary, but what is unseen is eternal."*

In this chapter we will discuss what happens after we trust God for the trust battle. God help us to learn to fix our eyes on the unseen.

HOW DOES OUR TRUST BATTLE TURN OUT?

Trust battles make us nervous because God is so unpredictable. He's no Santa Claus or genie in a bottle. All of us know stories about strong Christians who lost their homes, whose children died, who went bankrupt, or who died for their faith. So, when we pray for God to deliver us, we have no guarantee that God will answer us a certain way. God's ways are mysterious. John Eldredge calls it "the wildness of God."

Who can trust such a God?

We can, that's who. It's in this very wildness of God that we learn His ways. God reveals Himself to us in the storm more than in the harbor. Our comfort zone teaches us nothing. The valley of the shadow of death is a master teacher. It shows us His glory.

It frustrates me when I see Christians hold on to the memory of one scary event or, worse yet, the report of what happened to someone else, and expect so little of God. Why do we fear our lives so much? We act like Gracie. Last summer Jim and I took Gracie, our golden retriever, for an evening walk by the Coronado ferry landing. She got spooked by some fireworks and ever since she acts skittish on that part of the strand.

Like Gracie, we act as if every trust battle will end in disaster because maybe one time something happened that spooked us. But the truth is, God has protected and delivered us "through many dangers, toils, and snares." The vast majority of all our trust battles end well whether or not we make any effort to trust God through it. God sends His rain on the just and on the unjust. He does good to us even when we gripe and worry. Thank goodness He doesn't measure out His answers based on our level of faith or trust. He pours out grace. Think about your trust battles. Isn't that true? "'Tis grace hath bro't me safe thus far, and grace will lead me home."

So, let's look at three typical outcomes. The first is the rarest and the second is by far the most common. We'll look at how to trust God in each scenario.

1. GOD FIGHTS THE BATTLE FOR US.

Hezekiah was one of the last good kings of Judah. He put into practice what we have discussed in this "during the battle" section. Sennacherib, king of Assyria, loomed on his horizon as his biggest trust issue. Sennacherib's enormous army had already defeated many nations much stronger than Judah, and had swallowed Israel whole, right next door.

Hezekiah responded by trusting God in many ways. He prepared Jerusalem for battle. He rerouted water to make Jerusalem less vulnerable to a siege. He repaired and reinforced the city walls. He built lookout towers and made plenty of weapons and shields. As the enemy armies approached, Hezekiah gave his people a pep talk.

> *Be strong and courageous. Do not be afraid or discouraged because of the king of Assyria and the vast army with him, for there is a greater power with us than with him. With him is only the arm of flesh, but with us is the LORD our God to help us and to fight our battles. II Chronicles 32:7, 8.*

Sennacherib sent couriers to ridicule their faith in God. Hezekiah cried out to God for help. Then the Assyrians set up the siege of Jerusalem. But when it came to a climax, God chose not to use Hezekiah's army. One morning the Judeans woke up and peeked over the city wall. It was unusually quiet. During the night God had sent an angel and 185,000 Assyrian soldiers died. Sennacherib packed up and went home, where his sons killed him a short time later.

Although Hezekiah's preparations prevented Sennacherib from immediately capturing the city, the reinforced city walls couldn't have withstood the Assyrian army forever. But God displayed His glory by fighting for Hezekiah.

Every once in a while God fights our battles for us. A church we know of was tormented by a power struggle. Even though pastors and elders are supposed to lead the church, in this dysfunctional church one wealthy church member actually ran the church. This carnal bully got angry when they tried to make some godly decisions and he began making wild threats. The leadership didn't know what to do other than pray. The man happened to work in a manufacturing plant and right in the middle of this crisis he went out to the warehouse and a whole stack of pallets fell on him crushing him to death. Everyone familiar with the situation saw it as a sobering example of God stepping in to fight the battle.

Sometimes God fights our battles for us in less dramatic ways. We may be embroiled in a bitter confrontation with someone and instead of resolving it by trying to reconcile, God may just give the person a change of heart.

Even though this scenario doesn't happen very often, I've learned to make room for God to act, if He chooses to do so, before I rush in to fix things myself. For instance, when we don't let anyone know that we need a particular thing, and just pray about it, it leaves room for God to meet our need more directly. It is so cool to need, say, $200, and have someone mail you that exact amount with a bemused comment that they just felt prompted to send it. I love having an inside joke with God!

2. GOD FIGHTS ON OUR SIDE, LEADING TO VICTORY.

Elisha's story is a good example of this scenario. God was already on the case while Elisha slept so he didn't need to ask for angels. It was enough that he saw them. Because he saw them, he wasn't afraid. His servant was afraid of the soldiers because that's all he could see.

Elisha realized that he didn't have to rely on his own strength to win the day. Elisha didn't pick up a weapon. He didn't try to reason with the enemy. He relied on God. When the enemy approached his door, all he did was to pray. Never before or after did Elisha pray to blind someone. It took an act of courage to pray as he did.

God answered his prayer and Elisha outwitted the enemy by leading them to the capital city. After a meal in their honor, they went home. Yet again, we see that when people yield themselves to God and live in harmony with Him, God rescues His own.

Though we may wish for God to help us in flashy ways like He did with Hezekiah and Elisha, it's better for us in the long run when we cultivate the ability to cooperate with God when He doesn't use miracles. In his book, *Disappointment with God*, Philip Yancey makes the excellent observation that the Israelites who left Egypt probably saw more miracles than any other generation of God's people in history yet they had the most anemic faith. They saw the ten plagues. They crossed the Red Sea on dry ground. They ate manna from heaven. They saw God's presence in the pillar of fire and cloud. Their shoes didn't wear out. They saw water gush from the rock. These miracles that they could see didn't help them to trust God. They grumbled about everything. Seeing miracles all the time made miracles a ho-hum kind of thing.

Jesus used miracles to make a point. When the Pharisees demanded that He prove His credentials by doing a miracle, He was suddenly fresh out. He graciously showed Thomas His scars because Thomas said he wouldn't believe until he had seen them. But Jesus told Thomas, *"Because you have seen Me, you have believed; blessed are those who have not seen and yet have believed"* (John. 20:29).

God trains us to trust Him by sending us a mix of a few obvious miracles and mostly subtle answers to prayer that we can miss if we aren't looking for them. That's why we need to ask God to open our eyes to see what He's doing.

Again, trust cultivates the mindset of seeing God as the main actor in solving our problems and viewing ourselves as support troops within that arena. We're not the general on the ground telling God what to do. God is the commander, telling us what to do, and deciding what outcome will best suit His purposes.

Trust also assumes God will deliver. Psalm 112 describes the person who fears the Lord. One of the qualities of such a person is found in verse 7. *"He will have no fear of bad news; his heart is steadfast, trusting in the Lord."* Trust views problems as a showcase for the display of God's glory. Dr. David Jeremiah puts it this way. "Could it be that one reason we have great problems is that God wants to show us great solutions? He longs to show us the riches of His grace and the poverty of our own resources."

3. GOD WORKS WITHIN US WHEN HE SAYS "NO."

Job described this scenario perfectly. *"What I feared has come upon me; what I dreaded has happened to me"* (Job 3:25). Some of you picked up this book because you are still struggling to make sense of a devastating blow. Most people have at least a few examples of these, some more than others. I've known my share. My worst childhood fears came true when I was abused. I've also known the grief of hope deferred that makes the heart sick, waiting for years and years and years for God to answer some of my most desperate prayers.

So what can we say? We feel like tongue-tied friends at a funeral. We don't want to say the wrong thing. But allow me to make some observations about what has helped me to make sense of these parts of my story. In these comments, I'm deliberately sticking to what I have learned for my situation. I'm heeding the advice of a lady I met who talked about how she came to terms with a painful eye ailment. She said that when she wrestled with God about her situation, she could receive what the Lord had to say to her but she resented it if someone else said the identical thing.

My story has taught me that it's unrealistic to expect that we'll never see trouble. The way we trust God must take that reality into account.

> Trusting in God does not, except in illusory religion, mean that He will ensure that none of the things you are afraid of will ever happen to you. On the contrary, it means that whatever you fear is quite likely to happen but that with God's help it will in the end turn out to be nothing to be afraid of. Jonathan Aitken, *Pride and Perjury*

A few years ago, I felt prompted to write about rebuilding trust in God. The biggest trust issue I had when I started to write about trust was that I was afraid if my mother found out what I was writing about, I'd lose my relationship with her. In her mind, writing represents a threat to the family secrets. Eventually, she did find out and the heated difference of opinion about whether I should write led to the breakdown I hoped to avoid. We haven't spoken for almost four years. That saddens me, but by the time our relationship crumbled, God had helped me to process that grief and yield it to Him. I hope someday we'll be able to reconnect. She's my mom and I love her. My trust in God has wrapped itself around the reality that what I feared the most came true. And it's okay.

When Jim and I planted churches we often ran into situations when the very thing we feared was what happened. Two churches died. God sent us to Iowa and nothing we expected to do there came to pass. Each time we moved, it represented a loss to me. It's hard for me to make friends and it broke my heart if I had found a friend. I'm lousy at maintaining long-distance relationships so my move usually signaled the end of that friendship. We bought a house for $30,000 when we planted our first church in Chino. Church members who still live in Chino paid off their tiny mortgages years ago. We turned our back on financial security each time we followed the Lord to a new place. That's why we've had more than our share of financial challenges.

Several things helped me to make my peace with the trauma of church planting. Jim and I both learned to focus more on obeying God to the best of our ability, and trusting the outcome to God. When we stand before God we want to hear Him say "Well done, good and *faithful* servant." God looks at our faithfulness. He doesn't insist on "good and *successful* servants."

I also learned to see those sacrifices as my participation in the suffering of Christ (I Peter 4:13). Jesus also left behind financial security and didn't have anywhere to lay His head. People rejected Him. His family misunderstood Him. Some revelations about Jesus can only come to us when we weep before Him and He says, "I know how you feel. It happened to Me, too."

Next to His suffering and compared to millions of other Christians who have suffered far more, my sufferings are pretty pathetic little scratches. But they are noble scars and I wear them with pride. *Henry V* is my favorite Shakespeare play. In the final battle, when the English were about to face the vastly larger French army, Henry gave his men this famous encouragement.

> He that shall live this day, and see old age,
> Will yearly on the vigil feast his neighbors,
> And say, tomorrow is Saint Crispin's Day.
> Then will he strip his sleeve and show his scars,
> And say, These wounds I had on Crispin's Day. (Act IV, Scene III)

The Apostle Paul would agree with Henry's sentiment. *"Finally, let no one cause me trouble, for I bear on my body the marks of Jesus"* (Gal. 6:17).

In the same speech, Henry V refers to his men as "we few, we happy few, we band of brothers." It is a privilege to serve Jesus. Nothing we sacrifice can ever compare to His sacrifice for us.

It brings me to tears to express the kindness of God. He doesn't forget our sacrifice. Jesus made us this promise. *"And everyone who has left houses or brothers or sisters or father or mother or children or fields for my sake will receive a hundred times as much and will inherit eternal life" (Matt. 19:29).* Jim and I have never gone hungry. God has always provided whatever we needed. I have a wealth of precious friends. I remember some guys from seminary days who felt called to the ministry but their wives held them back because they were afraid to give up financial security. Their foolishness makes me so sad. Look at all they missed!

Ironically, even though people who go through some horrible tragedy often feel as if God has forsaken them, it usually means that God has singled them out to do a much deeper work. For thirty years I struggled to know God. I feared Him. I thought He had abandoned me to my childhood abuser. During those same thirty years, God faithfully though silently prepared my heart.

When I look back on my entire life, one conclusion towers above the rest. God is the Redeemer. He has taken my worst experiences and shaped them into the containers that hold the best parts of my joy today. He truly has redeemed the years that the locusts have eaten. Everything I love to do, and most of the insights I have to share, come directly out of my deepest, but now redeemed, pain. He has bought back every sorrow and in the process of giving it back to me, He has turned water into wine. There's nothing He cannot redeem. He gives us beauty for ashes. He stands undaunted by a valley of dry bones or Lazarus four days dead in his grave.

A Redeemer such as that is worthy of our trust.

SOME CONCLUDING SUGGESTIONS

Ask God to open your eyes to see what He wants you to see. Ask to see angels or whatever else you need to see. Practice squinting into the middle distance in your living room or wherever your trust battle rages. What's at work that you haven't seen yet? Ask God to reveal His glory.

Watch. Look for angel sign. Before Jehoshaphat's battle in II Chronicles 20, they received this instruction. *"Take up your position; stand firm and see the deliverance the Lord will give you"* (v. 17). Watch for honey on the ground. *"O my Strength, I watch for You; You, O God, are my fortress"* (Psalm 59:9).

Praise God for what He will do. Praise in the middle of the battle, before you know the outcome, is the purest form of trust. Besides, praise attracts the angels.

Get out of the way. Yield to His will. Work the plan He's given, but quit trying to solve things yourself. Leave room for God to work. In most of my biggest trust battles, there has been a long waiting period. Then suddenly things heat up and I can sense from the crackle in the air that God is on the move. It's exhilarating to get into that zone of moving in step with God. It's worth waiting for, and you miss it altogether if you've run on ahead. I want you to experience that rush if you haven't already. You'll be hooked if you do.

FACE TIME WITH MY TRAINER

PART 1: Answer these Bible study questions BEFORE reading the chapter

Read II Kings 6:8 -- 23 to answer the following questions.

Why did the king of Aram decide to capture Elisha? (vv. 1 – 13)

What did the Elisha's servant see when he got up in the morning? (vv. 15 - 17)

Why didn't Elisha worry about the threat? What changed when Elisha asked God to open the eyes of his servant? (vv. 16 – 17)

How did God deliver Elisha and his servant from the enemy army? What tactic did Elisha use? (vv. 18 – 23)

Why do you suppose the bands from Aram stopped raiding Israel's territory? (v. 23)

PART 2: Questions & Reflection

1. Tell your favorite angel story. If you have more than one, tell one that happened to you or to someone close to you.

2. Go back to the lists of defensive and offensive trust battles you compiled at the end of Chapter Three. For each entry, think about how it turned out. Mark each one as follows:
Put a "1" if God fought the battle for you without significant involvement by you.
Put a "2" if God fought along side you and it ultimately turned out well.
Put a "3" if God worked within you when He said "no."

3. What did you notice when you reflected on those episodes of your life? How many 1's did you find? How many 2's? How many 3's?

4. Did you have many episodes marked with a "3?" Have you come to terms with them yet or do they still give you pain or skittishness toward God? If you feel comfortable doing so, share one of those stories. If you have made your peace regarding that story, please share what you learned.

5. This chapter talked about having noble scars, and about how God can redeem our suffering and our worst experiences. Do you have any noble scars? What are they? How have you begun to see God redeem one of your painful experiences?

6. What did you find to be the most encouraging or intriguing idea in this chapter?

EXTRA CREDIT: *When you have some time, go back and review all four of the chapters in this section, looking for the tips that you found most helpful to deal with this during the battle phase. Write a "Note to Self" checklist of things to remember or things to do the next time you find yourself in the middle of a trust battle. Include the four Trust Gate statements, found at the beginning of these four chapters.*

Marie's Story

A few years ago it was necessary for me to separate from my husband. His behavior had become unbearable from his drug abuse. My small children and I went to stay with a friend temporarily. I had no financial support or job. I couldn't return to my previous job because that whole industry was having major problems. All I could find was a part-time minimum wage job that was nowhere near enough to live on.

I had a close walk with the Lord and was trying to honor Him despite my situation. I prayed (really pleaded) for help and direction every day. It seemed impossible to find a better solution for us since my husband was not able to be reasoned with at that time.

My legal options were pretty scary. A legal separation would probably bring financial support and might even get us back into our home. But if the judge did not believe me about my husband's drug abuse he could award my husband joint custody and I wouldn't be able to protect our children. My husband was a master at hiding his addiction, and adamantly denied that he was using drugs.

I had heard of a drug test that was not possible to get around that can detect drug usage up to three months prior. It is called a hair follicle test. I asked my husband to prove he was not using drugs by taking the hair follicle test but he refused.

The scariest part of a legal separation (which is so close to a divorce) was the question "Am I stepping out of God's will?" I knew divorce was not God's desire for our lives, and if I acted in haste or anger it could easily become a divorce. With fear and trembling (and with approval from my church leadership) I prayerfully sought His will.

I retained an honorable Christian lawyer and began the legal separation process. Our lawyers arranged a date for family mediation and a court date. I felt so exposed to disaster and bathed the coming legal events in prayer with my prayer partners.

When the mediation appointment came, my husband was cool and calm. The mediator did not seem to believe my claims of my husband's drug use and I feared her recommendations to the judge. I had to resist the urge to disappear with my kids and chose to trust God in the legal process I felt He had me start.

On the day of court, God's loving care and protection showed through in such a glorious way! Things finally turned around for my whole family. The judge not only ordered my husband to vacate our house for the kids and me, and to pay child support, but my lawyer requested my husband take a hair follicle test and the judge agreed. My husband did not get joint custody and unsupervised visitation was very minimal until the test came back and until the next court date.

He failed the drug test. With his drug problem out in the open he was forced to either get help or lose his family. He chose help. It has been a long hard climb out of the pit but my husband is now drug free, going to church again and has submitted himself to our church leadership. He reads his Bible and is a good father to our kids. I dissolved the separation before the second court date. My husband is once again living with the kids and me.

I am now so confident in my caring Lord. No matter how rocky life gets, even if those in authority over me go terribly wayward, even when I don't know what to do, the Lord is able to protect and guide me through a maze of problems.

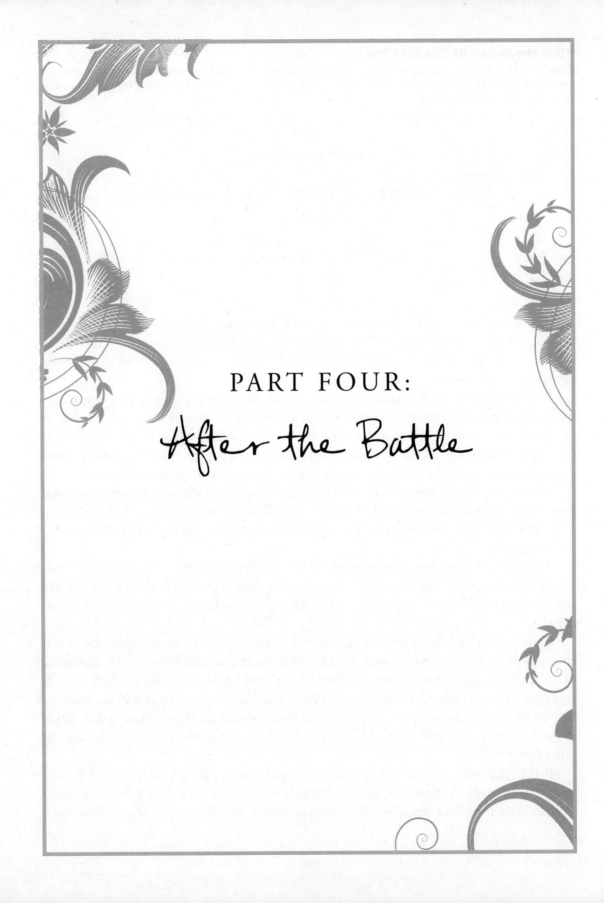

PART FOUR:

After the Battle

CHAPTER 14

The Safe Place to Recover

He makes me lie down in green pastures,
He leads me beside quiet waters, He restores my soul.
Psalm 23:2 – 3a

The season *after the battle* looks so radically different than the previous two seasons that many Christians go through this whole phase entirely unaware. For many people this season is a subtle no-man's land, an embarrassing parenthesis we try to ignore or an empty space between crises that we may not even notice.

If the latest trust battle took a lot out of us, *after the battle* begins when we desperately want to go crash somewhere. We long to just check out, to "veg" in front of the TV, or mindlessly eat ice cream. We want to clock out for awhile from being on duty as a strong Christian. "I'm tired, God. Just give me a break." That longing to crash, or at least to check out, feels pretty much the same whether the particular trust battle ended well or badly.

Trust battles aren't clear-cut like the boxes in a comic strip with clean starts and stops. One episode bleeds into another. Most of the time it dawns on us that, "Oh, I must be in after the battle," only because we begin to experience the signs of being in that phase.

So how do we know?

The clearest tip-off that we've entered the season after the battle is that something ends and we have an empty place in our heart. It may not seem like a big deal. So what that the school term ended, that we unpacked the last box at our new house, or that we're back from the trip?

Usually, there's a delayed reaction after a trust battle ends. We're only dimly aware of that empty place in our heart and at first we coast along on the leftover fumes of the adrenaline or the spiritual energy that sustained us through the trust battle. Many people rush to cover that empty space with busyness. Maybe we already scheduled new activities without realizing that we might need some recovery time. We suddenly notice the dirty dishes we left sitting in the sink when we ran off to sit with our friend at the hospital, the piles of laundry and the dusty furniture.

If the trust battle sidetracked us from our usual routine, it's perfectly normal for the things we set aside to clamor for our attention. We also often cover that hole in our heart with food or friends or noise or whatever will drown out that empty place. Why did I predictably gain ten pounds every time we moved? Now I know I was eating to settle down my heart that hadn't quite recovered from the last thing and that struggled to handle the new before it was ready.

Sometimes it takes a few weeks or months before the letdown and unprocessed emotions overtake us and we slip into the crash or the blahs. However long delayed, we hit *after the battle* when we find ourselves spiraling down into depression or exhaustion. Our emotions go blank. We feel nothing but numbness or "blah-ness" even about the Lord. Those great Bible promises that kept us chugging along through the last big trust battle like the little engine that could, seem to sputter and lurch to a stop. Now we couldn't pray our way out of a paper bag.

Most of us already know much about how to trust God when fears and worries loom over our future. And many of us have gotten great practice tackling our giants with faith and courage. Now we will explore how to trust God when we feel most exhausted and spent, when we feel least spiritual, and when all we desperately want to do is crash.

WHY WE'RE SO VULNERABLE AFTER THE BATTLE

Many Christians tend to be **performance oriented** and feel vaguely uncomfortable when they aren't performing. Even though we would never say that God loves us for what we do, it's difficult not to act as if we believed that. It feels more comfortable to "work hard" to trust God during the battle and we don't exactly know what to do with ourselves afterwards.

We also assume that God values our works more than He values us, that no matter how we feel, we need to suck it up and go do great things for God. We sometimes minimize our feelings as if they shouldn't matter to us or that they don't matter to God. Particularly when grief or sorrow paralyzes us (because, let's face it, that's what sorrow does), we can make matters worse beating ourselves up for our paralysis and flogging our beleaguered heart with wildly unrealistic expectations of what we should be doing if only we could "snap out of it."

Also, *we often interpret our normal fatigue and flatness as sin.* This stems from a faulty notion about verses such as Romans 12:11. *"Never be lacking in zeal, but keep your spiritual fervor, serving the Lord."* For years that verse haunted me. I wrongly assumed that God demands non-stop fever pitched enthusiasm. So when I wore myself out doing ministry, or even when I was going through my monthly period and felt awful, I tended to withdraw from God in shame while I tip-toed away to recover strength. Then I'd drag my feet, dreading the thought that I had to confess my supposed sin (of being a frail human) before God would accept me again.

Regardless of the circumstances, *Satan often concentrates his main attack on spiritual warriors before and after the battle to catch us off guard.* It's just like Satan to kick us when we're down. As the glow fades we tend to second-guess ourselves and little doubts creep in.

We congratulate ourselves if we win a victory in one of our little trust battles and forget that our enemy has his eye on winning a war. After the battle, he's busy whispering that God won't accept us when we have nothing to offer Him, that it's okay to take a vacation from trusting God, or that God is such a demanding taskmaster He would never let us rest and recover. If our enemy can get us to snag one little bit of baggage from each trust battle, sooner or later maybe he can get us to take a real tumble.

So what's our game plan after the battle? In this chapter we will introduce five steps in a process to recover after a trust battle. It mirrors the strategy military officers use to help their soldiers recover after an actual battle. Military commanders first move their soldiers back to a secure location (1. run for shelter). They allow them to (2. rest) and get their wounds bandaged up (3. rejuvenate). Then they give their soldiers an opportunity to debrief about the recent battle (4. reflect), before giving them new instructions (5. rejoice and get a new assignment).

I've found these five steps helpful no matter what happened in the trust battle. It's especially helpful for processing grief or loss. I go through all five steps to recover after big things and pick and choose whatever helps me bounce back from less draining situations. We will concentrate on the first three steps in this chapter and devote separate chapters to explore the last two steps in more detail. In Chapter 16 we will offer a perspective on those painful trust issues that remain unresolved.

OUR GOAL AFTER THE BATTLE is to let God help us to recover fully – by resting, and by dealing with any hurtful baggage we picked up during the last battle – so that we move forward with childlike trust in God.

Our Heavenly Father knows us well. He knows how to defeat every scheme of the enemy and He always knows exactly what we need, especially when all we want to do is crash.

RUN FOR SHELTER: RUNNING IN THROUGH THE CASTLE GATES

"Be my rock of refuge, to which I can always go." (Ps. 71:3)

One of my biggest Aha! moments of all time came when I figured out that it was okay to crash in God's presence. I didn't have to run away from God to recover. God gladly welcomes me all the time. In fact, when He first began to teach me to trust Him, He was the One who pushed me to rest. He focused all my early trust training lessons on this phase after the battle.

After He had walked with me through a few *after the battle* seasons I became more sobered about this phase. I finally realized the extent of my vulnerability and knew that it would probably include stretches of feeling totally numb. So when I had the thought that, "Oh, I must be in after the battle," it became a bigger deal to entrust myself to God. I don't know about you, but when I crash, I crash.

So how do we crash in God's presence? It all goes back to what we already know. The *hasa* form of trust means running for refuge. Before the battle we ran to God to help us evaluate our problem. During the battle we ran to God for help during the action. Now, once again we run to God, this time to protect us while we recover, knowing that we will probably feel blah and lifeless for awhile.

This moment, on the brink of this phase, reminds me of times back in the hospital when I lay on the gurney before they wheeled me into surgery. Jim would sit by the gurney holding my hand and Dr. Bartos would drop by the pre-op wearing his green surgical scrubs and Harley-Davidson dew-rag. I couldn't control the outcome in any way. At my weakest, I had to entrust myself into the care of another to do for me what I couldn't do for myself. I wasn't even going to be conscious during surgery. Some fearful patients in pre-op thrashed around before they got their sedative. I didn't. I knew Jim would never leave me and by then I trusted Dr. Bartos to do a good job and bring me back alive. Most importantly, at that most vulnerable time, I entrusted myself into God's care.

On the cross Jesus perfectly exemplified this kind of trust when he faced death itself: *"Father, into Your hands I commit my spirit"* (Luke 23:46).

When we feel ourselves slipping into a crash, take a moment to pray. *"Father, I'm really tired now and vulnerable after this battle. Into Your hands I commit my spirit. Thank You for letting me crash in the shelter of Your presence. Please keep me safe and be my strength when I have no strength. Guide me through this season and restore my soul as only You can. In Jesus' name, Amen."*

Depending on the severity of the battle it might be a good idea to **ask a friend or two to keep us in prayer as we recover.** That extra layer of protection helps keep us safe.

Let's spend a few minutes on **Elijah's story.** He served as a prophet to the northern kingdom of Israel during the reign of Ahab the king. About sixty years before Ahab's time, Israel split off from the southern kingdom of Judah, and immediately fell into dreadful idolatry. Any northerners that wanted to worship the true God had migrated to Judah long before. So Elijah had a lonely and difficult calling. In I Kings 18 Elijah did three very demanding tasks in a row. He single-handedly challenged the prophets of Baal on Mt. Carmel. Then he prayed intensely in seven rounds of travail prayer to end the 3½ year drought. Finally, he ran the equivalent of a marathon race from Mt. Carmel to Jezreel.

Afterwards, Ahab's wife, Jezebel, threatened to kill him and this time he ran in terror. I Kings 19:4 records that, after a day's journey into the desert, *"he came to a broom tree, sat under it and prayed that he might die. 'I have had enough, Lord,' he said. 'Take my life; I am no better than my ancestors.'"* Later, he traveled for forty days until he reached Mt. Horeb. He felt fear, depression and exhaustion. But his instinct to run was a good one because he ran <u>to</u> Mt. Horeb, also known as Mt. Sinai, the holy mountain, the mountain of God. He ran to God.

REST: CURLING UP IN ONE OF THE BEDROOMS

"My soul finds rest in God alone; my salvation comes from Him." (Psalm 62:1)

Isn't it amazing that God provides rest? The same God who inspired Paul to write Romans 12:11 (quoted earlier), also set up Sabbath rest. Jesus said that the Sabbath was made for man – to help us! God created us with a built-in need for sleep. He insisted that farm land lie fallow every seventh year. Sometimes the most spiritual thing we can do is to go take a nap!

God commands us to keep the Sabbath holy. It requires trust to obey that commandment. The Israelite farmer worked hard for six days. Each night he saw a dozen things to do the next day. Yet on the seventh day, as an act of trust, he set aside his chores and celebrated the Sabbath instead. We can get so full of ourselves and begin to think that everything depends on us. How foolish! I didn't fully realize how exhausted I was until God took me in hand and insisted that I rest. But even if we aren't exhausted, the Sabbath principle says that we should take a break, if only to say, *"I know it doesn't all depend on me. God, it's on Your shoulders, not mine."*

Besides, rest has great health benefits. Firefighters, police officers and soldiers have some unusual health challenges. During emergencies their bodies get a surge of adrenaline that helps them to handle the crisis. But they can develop various health problems like ulcers or heart disease if they don't rest between crises and allow the adrenaline time to drain away. Workaholic Christians can get into the same unhealthy pattern. Our spirit also needs rest between trust battles to maintain spiritual health over the long haul. We don't have to apologize for seeking Sabbath rest for our spirit at such times. It's a holy activity.

After the battle it's perfectly normal for our devotional times to be dry and lifeless. Our prayers will tend to lack pizzazz and Scripture may seem pretty boring. Don't worry about that. It's nothing more than emotional and spiritual flatness. It isn't sin. And by resting in the Lord, we're doing the most constructive thing possible for our walk with God. Carefully taking these steps of renewal will rekindle our enthusiasm and bring new zest to our prayer and Bible study.

When I'm processing a deep sorrow, this stage always scares me the most. The tree analogy we've talked about before (Ps. 92:12, 13) gives me hope at these times. This rest stage is like that tree in the dead of winter. It has lost all its leaves. It's bare and lifeless. Numb. It seems as if winter will never end. This is the one time when I'm always forced to rely on the passive trust (see Chapter 1) because, no matter how hard I try, I can't climb out by myself. Usually, I can't even cry out. I'm just too tired. But I'm here to say that it is enough to know – not even to verbalize – just to know that God is faithful. He will send the spring into my heart someday.

How do we rest?

Get some sleep and try to free up your schedule for rest. Even if you maintain your normal schedule, try to fill your first day or so with non-stressful tasks. Also, try to avoid scheduling two intense activities back to back.

Do activities that feed your spirit. I've asked many Christians what they do to nourish their spirit. Their lists vary but here are some typical suggestions.

- GO TO CHURCH. Duh! That's what God means by keeping the Sabbath. Fit other activities in after that one. Let the music and the sermon minister to your spirit. Reconnect with fellow believers as soon as possible.

- Listen to Christian music. Play the piano or guitar.

- Take a walk in the woods or sit at the beach and watch the waves.

- Attend a symphony or stroll through an art museum. Seek out beauty.

- Putter around. Organize your sock drawer. Pull a few weeds.

- Work on a creative project like painting or scrap booking.

- Find something light but encouraging to read.

- Visit with good friends.

Figure out what nourishes your spirit and make time to do that. None of these activities is very intense. We can do them in God's presence, but we're more passive than active. I call it "the passive practice of the presence of God."

Now that we've run into the castle of God our Refuge, let's find a bedroom and snuggle under the blankets. When we wake, we can rest in His presence calmly and enjoy the peace. Again, at this stage we're pretty numb. We're taking a mental break, trusting God to protect us until we're ready to move on to the next step.

Elijah's story illustrates this step so well. He plopped down under the broom tree and fell asleep. After the angel gave him food and drink he slept again. Then he traveled forty days to Mt. Horeb. Hiking is good for the soul. It could be that he began walking without consciously picking a direction. But the walking itself, day after day, renewed his spirit because it was such an elemental activity.

REJUVENATE: GETTING OUR WOUNDS HEALED AT THE INFIRMARY

"Trust in Him at all times, O people; pour out your hearts to Him, for God is our refuge." (Psalm 62:8)

For me, healing comes after rest because at first I'm just too tired to say much to God. I've learned not to rush from stage to stage of recovery but allow time for each. Elijah prayed out of exhaustion. The angel gave him bread and water several times and helped him to sleep. That must have touched this lonely prophet at a deep level.

How do we do this?

Tell God how you feel. Elijah told God he wanted to die. Usually if the battle has been tough, we don't feel particularly spiritual. We feel tired and grouchy or angry or discouraged or conceited or all of the above. But it helps so much to say it out loud to God. He knows we are just dust. When I'm exhausted, I can tell Jim how I feel knowing he'll forget the actual words and receive my pain. My husband is so kind to me, but God is even kinder.

Let God comfort you. In this phase we go to the castle infirmary. God bandages up our wounds and listens to us. Did you notice how kind God was to Elijah? He never once scolded Elijah in this whole story. He sent an angel with comfort food. This is a blessing far too many strong Christians miss out on because they mistakenly think they must always be "on duty" with God. God ministers to me in these times by reminding me of who I am in Christ, of how much He loves me, that He's on the case even when I'm tired, and He will see me through. *"Indeed, He who watches over Israel [and me] will neither slumber nor sleep"* (Psalm 121:4).

Sadly, sometimes we get hurt by other people during the battle – or realize we need to make amends for some hurtful thing we did. If we gloss over the process of forgiveness, true healing can't take place. When I've suffered a deep injury, I usually don't begin to address it until after the initial rest period. When you first become aware that you need to forgive someone, commit it to God and ask Him to help you to deal with it thoroughly. Then in this phase, begin by telling God how you feel about the injury and allow Him to minister to you. True forgiveness in which your spirit is healed will take place over time as you walk through it with God's help.

After the dust settles a bit, we may realize that we also need to mend some fences. It's a good idea to handle this is as soon as possible. I try to confess my sins right away, but I've found that if the reconciliation process might be somewhat touchy, it's best to have that heart to heart talk after all parties feel fresher and more rested, but quickly enough so that events are fresh in everyone's memory.

REFLECT: SPENDING TIME
DEBRIEFING IN THE TRAINING CENTER

"You guide me with your counsel, and afterward you will take me into glory." (Ps. 73:24)

In Chapter 16 we'll explore this stage in detail. After we've rested and received healing for our wounds, we head to the training center. By now we have regained some objectivity but the battle is still fresh in our minds. This is prime time for God to help us reflect on what happened in the trust battle. What went well? What gave us trouble? Who do we need to finish forgiving? What can we do better next time? Most Christians have not learned how to get the most from their trust battles because they don't do this step. But, it's a great step to learn for anyone serious about learning to trust God.

REJOICE & GET A NEW ASSIGNMENT:
CHECKING OUT THE VIEW FROM THE RAMPARTS

"But my eyes are fixed on You, O Sovereign Lord; in You I take refuge." (Ps. 141:8a)

At this stage God takes us to the top of the castle and together we look over the castle walls while He gives us our new assignment. Active Christians usually love this stage best because they can get back to work. But our future effectiveness will depend on how well we processed the other four stages. We can see this stage in Elijah's life in I Kings 19:11-18. God revealed Himself in the still small voice and then gave Elijah new instructions.

How do we do this step?

Keep your focus on God Himself. The defining characteristic of this step is that we receive a fresh vision of God. Elijah had never seen God this way before. Our greatest source of strength comes from seeing God high and lifted up. The whole point of this five-step process has been to strengthen ourselves in the Lord and this is the pinnacle of that process.

God often reveals Himself as a **contrast** to what we struggled with in the most recent battle. What lesser refuge gave us pain? Did our friends disappoint us? God is the friend who never disappoints. Did someone betray or forsake us? God will never leave us or forsake us. Did our own sins, weaknesses or failures trip us up? God is not like us. He shows us His perfect goodness, power and wisdom and generously shares it with us. In each case, true healing comes when we turn away from the lesser refuge and rely more completely on God our Great Refuge.

Right after the battle we often feel tired and flat, and God seems silent. But there always comes a time, especially if we persevere through the stages of recovery, when God reveals Himself to us. Like a good dad playing hide and seek with his toddler God lets us find Him (Jeremiah 29:12-14, Matthew 7:7, 8). And then we see that the apparent silence has been His gracious gift to whet our appetite for a new vision of God's glory.

Wait patiently for God to reveal our new assignment. Active Christians can't wait to get back in action. However, we can mistakenly assume that means doing exactly what we did before. If we led a Bible study yesterday, recovery must mean that we'll lead a Bible study tomorrow. If we planned vacation Bible School last year, we should automatically volunteer to plan this next one.

But notice that didn't happen to Elijah. In fact, this marked a major transition in Elijah's ministry. In the next chapter (20:13), God sent a different prophet to hassle Ahab. Later on, the Bible mentions 400 other prophets of Baal. But God never asked Elijah to repeat the Mt. Carmel challenge. Nevertheless, Elijah left Mt. Horeb with a bounce in his step. He was at peace with God and ready to complete the tasks God gave him as king maker and as Elisha's mentor. He did both jobs well. If we keep our eyes on God alone, then we will be flexible to go wherever God leads.

FINAL THOUGHTS

How long is this likely to take?

It totally depends on our situation. Elijah checked out of regular ministry for six weeks. It may take one day to recover from a one-day battle. If our battle has been long and hard, the recovery might take weeks or months, sometimes years.

It also depends on whether we need to go through every phase of recovery or just a few. When I have a single day of battle, it might be enough just to pray for protection, take a nap and then return to active duty. Longer battles might require more stages. The more stages we need, the more time it will take.

How can I apply this in my busy life?

By Each Situation: When you find yourself in need of extended recovery, take time to take stock. After some grueling experiences, it might be well worth the time to spend a month or two at a Christian retreat or counseling center.

Most of you can't take off from work when you need to recover. Even so, try to free up your schedule to rest the first day or two. Then fit the remaining stages into morning quiet times and how you spend discretionary time.

As a Lifestyle: If you regularly do activities that strengthen your spirit, it's easier to recover after a particular trust battle. Here are some suggestions:

- **Use your day off wisely.** Actually take the day off. Don't load it with lots of stressful errands if you can squeeze them in elsewhere. Some people return to work exhausted. That wasn't why God instituted the concept of the day of rest. Go to church.

- **Use your vacation time wisely.** Ditto what I said above. Actually rest. Get out and enjoy God's creation. Let it refresh your spirit. I know that family obligations call, but don't let them monopolize all your time.

- **Develop the habit of taking prayer retreats.** A lot of healing and refocusing can happen when you get away to spend time alone with God. My husband and I try to take two to four prayer retreats a year. They can be one to three days long and bring tremendous renewal.

- **Regularly do activities that strengthen your spirit.** Does painting renew your spirit? Take an art class. Find room for at least one regular activity that renews your spirit. We hesitate to make time for these things because it seems as if "committed" Christians should spend every waking minute doing the Lord's work. And you certainly shouldn't cram your schedule with arts and crafts. But not only does such activity renew your spirit, it also makes you a more balanced (not to mention, more interesting) Christian.

- **Develop supportive relationships with people who understand how to recover after the battle.** I have several of these friendships and they are such a blessing. They can often see better than I can what I need to do next; whether to slow down to allow more healing time or to jump back into the fray. Often, when I have trouble pouring out my heart to God, they act as God's gracious stand in, to hear me with compassion.

- **Be careful not to over-commit your schedule.** Some folks use busyness to anesthetize their emotions. Jesus was always busy but never rushed or frantic. This might require a major lifestyle change.

When we crash in God's presence He gently and wisely fills us up again to serve others out of that overflow of blessing. Paul mentions this benefit in II Corinthians 1:3-4. *"Praise be to the God and Father of our Lord Jesus Christ, the Father of compassion and the God of all comfort, Who comforts us in all our troubles, so that we can comfort those in any trouble with the comfort we ourselves have received from God."* When we run to God for rest and renewal, the comfort He gives to us becomes comfort we can pass on to others. The sweetness of His acceptance when we were most weak becomes a foundational touchstone of our child-like trust. The fresh vision of God's glory reflects off our shining face as we tackle a new day.

FACE TIME WITH MY TRAINER

PART 1: Answer these Bible study questions BEFORE reading the chapter

Quickly skim I Kings 18:16 – 46 just to get a feel for the background of this story. What three incredibly intense things did Elijah do within one day's time?

1. (Verses 16 – 40)
2. (Verses 41 – 45)
3. (Verse 46)

Read I Kings 19:1 – 18 to answer these questions.

RUN: After Elijah ran to the broom tree where else did he run? (v. 8)

REST: By the time Elijah got to the broom tree, how was he feeling and why? (vv. 1 – 5)

REJUVENATE: How did the angel minister to Elijah? (vv. 5 – 8)

REFLECT: Describe Elijah's encounter with God in vv. 9 – 13. What do you think Elijah learned about God from that experience?

What complaint did Elijah discuss with God? (vv. 14 -18)

REJOICE & RE-ASSIGN: What new assignments did God give to Elijah? (vv. 15 – 18)

1. What are some of the tip-offs that you might be entering after the battle? Why do many Christians go through this season entirely unaware? Has that ever happened to you?

2. What are three reasons why people may be vulnerable after the battle? What's your reaction to those three points? Do you agree or disagree, or was it just a new thought? Explain.

3. Describe how to "crash in God's presence." How does it express *hasa* trust in God to do this?

4. What is our goal after the battle? How would reaching this goal avoid the pitfalls that hit firefighters and others who jump from crisis to crisis without a break? How would it avoid the opposite pitfall of becoming trapped, wallowing in the grievances and hurts of the past?

5. Have you experienced that urge to "check out" to go crash somewhere away from God? What do you tend to want to turn to when you want to fill up the empty place in your heart?

6. Describe a time when you recovered well after a trust battle. How many of these steps did you go through in some way? How comfortable are you with taking time off to rest?

7. What activities refresh your spirit? When was the last time you did one of these things? Is there something you could begin to do to develop more of a lifestyle that strengthens your spirit?

8. What did you find to be the most encouraging or intriguing idea in this chapter?

Catherine's Story: Part One

I loved my job teaching at a Christian elementary school. So I was shocked when the principal asked for my resignation in January. I met with him several times from January to June, each time really thinking he would reconsider. My husband and I also met with deacons, school board members, and the pastor. Most of the time, I truly felt hope, but kept praying in earnest, including times of fasting.

In June, I was diagnosed with cancer and had surgery. This was not emotionally traumatic but was perhaps more physically traumatic than I've realized. The real day of lost hope came August 1 when the teachers returned to orientation, and I was not there. As late as two weeks earlier, the school didn't have a 4th grade teacher so I was sure they would call me in desperation. Instead, they gave the job to the pastor's wife.

It was also my first day of radiation. The radiation personnel swore up and down radiation would do nothing more than burn my skin and make me feel physically tired. Perhaps so, but my spirit about went to Hades that day.

Many, many times in my past, good seemed to come fairly soon after bad. It also seemed to come fairly quickly after I "got serious with God" and all that that involves: making sure I've forgiven everyone, truly recommitting my life and future to Him, asking Him to search me thoroughly and help me find and give up any iniquity.

This time I wasn't recovering -- and still haven't. I have confessed, forgiven, thanked God for the trials, etc. I truly thought I'd be back in ministry -- or at least a job -- by mid to late August. Of course, everyone and their brother told me God had something better in store or He wouldn't have let this happen. Nothing better has happened, and that hurts. That caused me to doubt Christianity, God, prayer, Christian ministry, myself, and especially God's leading – because I felt strongly that He was leading and would restore my teaching position.

RUNNING - I feel like I ran to God immediately, though more from fear than help. Quite honestly, I don't often feel His comfort, and I've talked with Him about it.

REST - I came across your article [in a prayer magazine] at the beginning of October and e-mailed you about that time. I evaluated all the doubts and realizedthat I was still tired and beaten down and still needed emotional and physical rest. I didn't feel the physical fatigue the radiologists said I would but I think it tired my spirit.

My rest included the following: Reading and Christian radio blessed me. I also enjoyed participating in some online religious forums and did some journaling.

Subbing restored my self-worth and gave me interaction with children and co-workers. Some days I'd walk down the hall and a whole class of kids I had subbed for the day before would wave and ask if I was coming to their class. I also sat in on several teachers and watched them in action. I would follow up with questions as to why they did or didn't do something. I am still amazed at how many of the same things I had been criticized for doing in my own classes were practiced with good results by these good teachers. Subbing has also restored my desire to teach.

HEALING: I don't know that I'm healed. Physically, I am better. The cancer is gone but emotionally I still hurt. I do have more good days than bad days. I think I turned a corner this past January when we decided to start having company again. I guess I quit crying every day about that time, too. So depending on when you mark the start of my battle, it has taken 4-12 months to get this far.

CHAPTER 15

Debriefing the Plan

Since You are my rock and my fortress,
For the sake of Your name lead me and guide me.
Psalm 31:3

One evening I felt prompted to pray for a friend whom we'll call Patty. I let Jim know I'd be busy for awhile and went to the guest room. I prayed up one side and down the other, worshipped with gusto, listened for instructions and did battle in the Spirit. Once when I checked in with the Lord for the next thing to pray, I heard a clear command,

"Put on your shoes."

What?

Now, if you know me at all, you know that I hate shoes. I never wear them at home. I dutifully slipped on my shoes and went back to prayer. But those darned shoes kept distracting me. Why did God tell me to put them on? I asked. No answer. Hours went by. Somehow I got the idea I was going to win a big prayer victory. I pictured Patty calling, inviting me to come right over to celebrate. And, hey, I'd be ready because I already had on my shoes.

Midnight came and went. No phone call. My prayers became frantic. I convinced myself that I had failed. I hadn't heard right. Who was I kidding? Me, hear from God? I'm nobody. God must be so angry and disappointed with me. Listening prayer was just a crock. And I am an idiot.

Jim finally put me out of my misery about 2 am.

"Honey, come to bed. It's OK."

I cried myself to sleep. The next morning every muscle ached. I felt exhausted and numb. By afternoon I braced myself for the critique I dreaded. I hung my head in shame and begged God to help me figure out where I went wrong.

Suddenly my prayer room filled with wave upon wave of God's pleasure and approval.

"My precious Dionne, I am SO proud of you!"

A snatch of verse went through my mind: *"to obey is better than sacrifice."* I was so taken aback by this unexpected turn of events that I fumbled with my Bible, hunting for the rest of the verse in I Samuel 15:22. *"But Samuel replied, 'Does the Lord delight in burnt offerings and sacrifices as much as in obeying the voice of the Lord? To obey is better than sacrifice, and to heed is better than the fat of rams.'"*

"Yes, Dionne, that's what you did. You obeyed My voice even though it made no sense to you. I DELIGHT in people who obey My voice. I love that you value My voice."

Together we dismantled those wrong conclusions I had drawn. I didn't fail because Patty never called. That was my own assumption. God received my intercession on her behalf and He would guard His mystery by answering in ways I wouldn't see or understand. I came out of that debriefing time with a bolder confidence that I was on the right track to pursue listening prayer and a deeper trust that God loved me and knew what He was about. He picked shoes on purpose, because, well, He knows me.

I have been eagerly anticipating this opportunity to share the material in this chapter. People don't talk much about this privilege God grants to those of us who follow Him to draw near and let Him make sense of our story. It's one of the best parts of that *"goodness… stored up"* that David mentioned in Psalm 31. And it breaks my heart that so few Christians take advantage of this blessing.

Back in Chapter 1 we made the comment that the battles of our lives can either shake or strengthen our trust in God. Some people can experience a spectacular answer to prayer at the climax of a trust battle and still walk away without making the connections that stabilize and grow their trust in God. This step of debriefing cements the lesson and ensures that the lesson we take away from our trust battle is the one God wanted to teach us, and not our misunderstanding.

Jesus often debriefed with His disciples. Mark 4:34 points out that *"He did not say anything to them [the crowds] without using a parable. But when He was alone with His own disciples, He explained everything."* I think that the episodes in our own biography are like a series of parables. We sort of get the plot and maybe a general idea about what it might mean. The vast majority of us look back at our life story scratching our heads muttering,

"Beats me why that happened."

But we are children of the King, students in the school of trust training. God has more for us. He can explain the parables that make up our life story. After Jesus sent the 72 disciples on a preaching assignment they all returned and gave their report. It was a rollicking meeting. Jesus shared amazing insights with them and then, *"full of joy through the Holy Spirit,"* He burst into praise.

> *I praise You, Father, Lord of heaven and earth, because You have hidden these things from the wise and learned, and revealed them to little children. Yes, Father, for this was Your good pleasure. (Luke 10:21)*

Nobody would ever mistake those burly fishermen and bureaucrats and zealots for little children. But they had that healthy childlikeness that marks genuine trust in God. And what

He did for them, face to face, He stands ready to do for us through the Holy Spirit who lives within us. In fact, it fills Him with joy to reveal these precious secrets to us.

By the way, Bible scholars have a rule of thumb for interpreting parables. Each parable illustrates one main point. It's not wise to make every twig and bird mean something. Likewise, as we faithfully debrief with Jesus after each battle, look for one main "take away" idea, one new insight or one tweak of the way we do things.

In this chapter we'll explore a laundry list compiled from dozens of my own debriefing sessions. Think of them as seed thoughts if debriefing is new to you. **Remember, we can expect God to give us insight and perspective, not the ultimate answer to why something happened to us.** The list below covers three broad categories: a review of the battle, getting rid of baggage, and figuring out what to do differently next time around.

THE AFTER ACTION REVIEW

This is the simplest type of debrief. The U.S. Army does this AAR (they love referring to everything by its initials) in a group meeting after a training exercise or a battle. An officer helps the soldiers to discuss three questions:

1. What was supposed to happen? (What was the stated objective?)
2. What actually happened?
3. What lessons can we learn so we'll do better next time?

During basic training and at the duty stations, the folks in charge schedule regular training exercises that deliberately create harsh conditions and then expect soldiers to do their job under those conditions. Our son, Zach, trained with the Army Signal Corp. It usually took his squad about two hours to run all the cables and connect the phone lines. Zach described training exercises in which they set up and dismantled their equipment once every six hours, day and night, for three days in different types of terrain.

Back at base camp, the AAR cemented the lessons they learned and gave them ideas for next time. People nailed down their individual assignments within the team task.

Another type of training exercise prepares for an anticipated problem. It reminds me of a recent Super Bowl game. Devin Hester was the fantastic kick return guy for the Chicago Bears. So the Indianapolis Colts scheduled extra training exercises just to handle Hester. On the first play of the game, Hester caught the ball and ran 92 yards for a touch down. But then the Colts remembered their training. The Colts kept his hands off the ball for the most of the game, and when he got the ball they didn't let him make any yardage. Indianapolis won the game.

How does that apply to us? God knows ahead of time exactly what we need to learn so we'll be ready for what's ahead. Those AAR questions are great ones to take to Jesus, our commander. Now would be a good time to pull out that dog-eared 3 x 5 card we wrote up back in Chapter 8. Psalm 18:34 promises that *"He trains my hands for battle."* This is where

He does much of that training. Take advantage of it. Other questions to ask at this time might include:

- What "Aha" moments did I have during this trust battle? What did I figure out?
- What Bible verses did I find helpful? Should I memorize any of them?
- What part(s) of my existing trust network did this trust battle shake? How much more willing am I to put my primary trust in You for this area?
- How well did I put into practice the guidance I received on my 3 x 5 card?
- How did my Christian friends help me? Could I have been wiser about working together with them?
- What did I learn about You during this battle? How did this trust battle affect my relationship with You?
- What do I need to do now so I'll be more prepared the next time around?

I spend a lot of time in listening prayer during this phase looking for answers to these questions. Many Christians seem to think we should never question God. Of course, we aren't supposed to test Him. But He's been quite patient and forthcoming when I ask Him questions like these.

This may seem silly, but I actually take notes about these debriefing sessions and log some of them in database form. Just the process of writing it down helps me to remember what I'm learning. Also, when I add the latest entry, sometimes I notice patterns that I haven't seen before. For instance, I noticed that I often got depressed when I became overtired. That may seem obvious. But sometimes I would launch into a full-blown trust battle against depression when I should have just bowed out of the whole thing and taken a nap instead.

Now let's turn our attention to getting rid of some unwanted baggage.

CHECK FOR ARROWS IN YOUR SHIELD OF FAITH

We already know from Paul's discussion of the armor of God that we should *"take up the shield of faith, with which you can extinguish all the flaming arrows of the evil one"* (Eph. 6:16). One day while studying Elijah's story I ran across Psalm 76:1 – 3. *"In Judah God is known; His name is great in Israel. His tent is in Salem, His dwelling place in Zion.* **There He broke the flashing arrows, the shields and swords, the weapons of war."** (My highlight) Those three things connected in my mind in an "Aha!" moment that has been a huge blessing.

Paul refers to Satan sending flaming arrows but the Psalmist talks about God breaking the flashing enemy arrows. It dawned on me that Satan's flaming arrows act like a bee stinger, which can still hurt us after the bee dies. God can break Satan's arrows so they don't continue to hurt us. Let me show you how this worked in Elijah's story.

The arrow Satan shot at Elijah was an arrow of self-pity and doubt called "You're the only one." In I Kings 18:21, Elijah challenged the crowd on Mt. Carmel to stand up for God. No one budged. At that exact moment, Satan shot his arrow at Elijah, "You're the only one." Zing! Elijah chose to hold up his shield of faith but even his statement of faith showed that he had absorbed the impact of this arrow. Look at verse 22. *"Then Elijah said to them, 'I am the only one of the Lord's prophets left, but....'"*

Like most of the arrows Satan shoots at us, this one was partly true and partly false. It was true that no one stepped forward on Mt. Carmel. But when Elijah ran into Obadiah, a few days before, Obadiah told him about a hundred prophets he had hidden from Jezebel. Although apparently they didn't go to Mt. Carmel, Elijah knew of at least 101 other true believers in Israel. Yet he really believed the arrow of doubt called "I'm the only one." By the time Elijah got to Mt. Horeb, he had become infected by this flaming arrow. Both times that he addressed God, he complained that he was the only one left.

However, he did the best thing possible by bringing this arrow to God because God broke it decisively. He did this by letting Elijah know that there were actually 7,000 believers in Israel. So he was not the only one, but one of 7,000. Also, God told him to anoint Elisha to succeed him. For the rest of Elijah's time on earth, Elisha traveled with him as his disciple and companion. So Elijah was not the only one; he was one of two.

Satan sends us three types of doubt:

- Doubts about God *(If God really loved me, He wouldn't let this happen.)*
- Doubts about ourselves *(I'm no good with money. I'm worthless. I have no faith.)*
- Doubts about people *(I'm the only one. People let you down. Men are stupid.)*

All three types of doubt challenge God's trustworthiness, either directly or indirectly. Notice how God phrased His reply. *"Yet I reserve seven thousand in Israel...."* When we give in to self-doubt, we question God's ability to finish the work He started in us even though He promises over and over again that He will. Do we think we are too hard a case for God?

Peter absorbed an arrow of self-doubt when he betrayed Jesus three times. Let's call his arrow, "When the chips are down, I will betray my Lord." Watch how Jesus handled it. He met privately with Peter and forgave him. (By the way, that's under the "Healing" phase of our "after the battle" recovery time.) Jesus did his debrief with Peter at the beach over breakfast fish. He asked Peter three times, "Do you love Me?" and gave him a threefold commissioning to ministry. But then Jesus told Peter that one day he would die a martyr's death. That broke the arrow of self-doubt, replacing it with this truth, "Peter, when the chips are down, you will die for Me." I suspect breaking that arrow helps to explain Peter's boldness in the Book of Acts.

Doubts about people, especially other Christians, are just as destructive. Never forget that Satan is called *"the accuser of our brothers"* (Rev. 12:10). Some of our doubts are poisonously false. These nagging doubts undermine our relationships. Sure, nobody's perfect. Christians can hurt us badly. I'm not suggesting naivety. But, like it or not, God channels most of what we need to grow in Christ through imperfect Christians in imperfect churches. If we walk away with a chip on our shoulder we mainly hurt ourselves.

Plus, it makes us a pain in the neck. Doesn't it make you want to scream when you faithfully stick with people through their troubles while they endlessly whine about how

Christians can't be trusted? You want to shake them and say, "Dude, what am I, chopped liver?"

But, wait a minute, you might be thinking. Isn't it a key premise of this book that God uses conflicts and crises to wean us away from trusting people unthinkingly, so that we'll trust God instead as our great refuge? Well, yes and no. God trains us to trust Him by showing us *the truth* about our trust network. He shows us actual inadequacy that we didn't see before. Then He steers us toward a deeper trust in Him and a clear-eyed forgiveness toward those who wronged us. By contrast, Satan tries to fill our minds with lies. If we fall for his *lies*, then he tries to seduce us into reaching over-broad conclusions that write off whole groups just because of a few bad apples.

During this debrief, check for any nagging doubt. If you find one, bring it to Jesus and ask Him to break its power in your life. The first arrow God broke for me was one called, "I am unworthy." Actually, I'll bet you recognized that one, and also Elijah's arrow: "I'm the only one." I did. Satan shoots it against many active Christians, especially intercessors and Sunday School teachers. That's a great arrow to break!

Roman soldiers finished repairing their shields by oiling them. After God breaks these arrows ask the Holy Spirit to consecrate your shield once again with His healing presence so that you return to battle with an unencumbered simplicity of faith in Christ.

LET GO OF THE "GOOD WORK"— WHETHER IT WAS A SUCCESS OR A FAILURE.

This comes out of Hebrews 13:15, 16, which says, *"Through Jesus, therefore, let us continually offer to God a sacrifice of praise – the fruit of lips that confess His name. And do not forget to <u>do good</u> and to share with others, for with such sacrifices God is pleased."* I learned this lesson when I was asked to speak to a women's group in another church. I prepared well after making every aspect of the presentation a matter of prayer.

Nobody bothered to mention that the ladies were all quite elderly. They grazed from a full buffet and then settled in for my talk. Most of them fell sound asleep! I was devastated. Why had that happened? Hadn't I heard the Lord correctly on what to say or how to present it?

In response, the Lord commented on Hebrews 13:16, saying, **"The sacrifice of good works can be given twice."** The first time we give this sacrifice by working hard to be as obedient and prepared as possible. The sacrifice becomes the good deed, done well. Sometimes that's the end of it.

But if our thoughts return to that good work, either to dwell on how well we did, or to second-guess all the mistakes we made, then it's time to give it a second time. I gave that "good work" again when I prayed like this. *"Father, I have no idea why You led me to give a talk to a room full of snoring ladies. But I give You that presentation again. Please use it, or **don't use it,** however You choose. I leave the results to You. Help me to forget about it, one way or the other, and move on in simple obedience to You."*

We make a liberating statement of trust the second time we give God our good deeds. If Christians do not regularly dump the baggage of past ministry we get weighed down. Over time, we can lose effectiveness because of this constant habit of second-guessing. The safest place to keep these memories is under the blanket of God's sovereignty.

FINISH THE WORK OF FORGIVENESS.

If people injured us, we must forgive them as soon as possible. I don't mean to imply that we can dilly-dally on this important matter. However, if it's a deep injury, it's unrealistic to think that forgiveness will take place in a moment. During this phase of recovery, ask God to show you any unresolved forgiveness issue. Discuss it with a counselor if necessary.

It helps me to imagine myself at the foot of the cross and to deal with that person, and with my own lack of forgiveness, in the light of the death of Jesus. If it seems appropriate to speak to that person about the issue, follow the steps of Matthew 18:15-17. How they respond is their business. If they don't choose to receive forgiveness or if they rebuff efforts to reconcile, that's their loss. It's our responsibility to extend forgiveness to them.

Sometimes at this stage of recovery, we might remember something which happened long ago, that has nothing to do with this particular situation. Whatever God brings to mind needs to be dealt with now. Trust Him to walk you through it.

Our effectiveness in ministry and in prayer depends on having an unbroken channel to receive God's forgiveness. We maintain that channel by regularly clearing our hearts of any unforgiving attitude toward anyone. Trust in God flourishes in an atmosphere of openness and forgiveness, so we need to take care not to allow a root of bitterness (Heb. 12:15) toward others to interfere. Whatever the grievance, dump it. Nothing that anyone ever did to us is worth holding on to if it shuts us off from an unbroken trust relationship with Christ.

Now let's look at how to avoid some unnecessary future battles.

WHAT EXACTLY DID WE REAP,
AND SHOULD WE START SOWING SOMETHING ELSE?

The divine moral law of harvest is as real as the law of gravity. *"Do not be deceived: God cannot be mocked. A man reaps what he sows. The one who sows to please his sinful nature, from that nature will reap destruction; the one who sows to please the Spirit, from the Spirit will reap eternal life"* (Gal. 6:7, 8).

If we got fired for drug abuse, it's all well and good to trust God to help us find a new job. However, maybe we should dig deeper in this debrief and ask a few more basic questions. Maybe we should ask God to help us tackle whatever pain has motivated us to make such unhealthy choices.

If we had an unpleasant confrontation with a work mate or a friend, did we do mean or thoughtless things that hurt them? If we had a health scare, did our careless eating habits, haphazard exercise or our habits of worry or impatience contribute to the problem?

This debrief is the time for problem-solving, not a new opportunity to beat ourselves up. Sure, all of us can do better. Confess sin and repent. But remember that we're talking this over with Jesus who loves us and died for those sins. We can trust Him not to kick us when we're down. (The more we learn to trust God, the more He helps us to quit beating ourselves up. We're in this together.)

Instead, let's start thinking constructively. What can we start sowing so we'll reap a better crop next time? Let God help you pick one constructive thing to do. In between trust battles, maybe work on learning how to listen better. The best investment I ever made in my spiritual walk was the two years I devoted to learning to distinguish God's voice.

Maybe cut out sweets or join a gym. Or maybe look for ways to sow grace and mercy into the lives of people around you. Random acts of senseless kindness. Anyway, I'd much rather reap a harvest from seeds like grace, mercy and kindness. Wouldn't you?

HAVE WE LEARNED OUR LESSON YET?

Sometimes God allows the same scenario to play itself out several times just so that we'll finally get sick of it and look for a better solution. That's how I found Psalm 18. If our trust battles give us déjà vu, maybe it's time to ask the Lord if He has a larger lesson to teach us.

Two examples. First, enabling behavior. When we jump in to rescue our floundering family member, it can hurt us. Maybe we loan money we can ill afford to someone, and then have a trust battle regarding our own financial hardship.

Enabling doesn't make people love us. In the debrief, let's ask what woundedness made us incapable of a wiser decision. When we enable, we volunteer to become a lesser refuge for that person. Wouldn't it be better for everyone if we stepped back and let God be their Refuge? Next time around, refuse our usual trust battle, financial struggle or whatever. We already know that one well. Instead, focus on trusting God to keep our loved one safe while they thrash around. Resign from the job of being their lesser refuge. It gives God a chance to fill that vacancy.

Or, second, let's look at unhealthy friendships. God pays attention to the alliances we make. Nations make alliances so that, if they get attacked, other nations will help them fight their battles. We can also make unspoken alliances when we agree to side with our friend or family member, no matter what. Of course, we should help each other. But be careful if they expect us to regularly get embroiled in their interpersonal conflicts. Children can get caught between bickering divorced parents. Or we can land in the middle of church squabbles because our friends got upset, not us. The resulting turmoil feels like a defensive trust battle over which we have no control.

Sometimes we have to go through several cycles before we're willing to take a look at this. God may well want us to break or renegotiate that alliance. We'll be in for a huge trust challenge trying to weather our friend's wrath and sense of betrayal the next time they assume we'll hop on board, and we don't. But that's the smarter trust battle to fight. We need to reframe that scenario into an offensive trust battle in which we make the choice, not them.

Proverbs 22:3 says this. *"A prudent man sees danger and takes refuge, but the simple keep going and suffer for it."* Let's learn how to take refuge in God for the wisely unfought trust battle.

This chapter concludes the discussion, begun in Chapter 14, of the process to recover "after the battle." It's a helpful and practical way to renew our strength and, if done well, it restores balance and takes us to new dimensions of wholeness.

- Rest restores our body.
- Healing restores our emotions.
- Debriefing restores our mind.
- Celebration and worship restores our spirit.

Our goal is healthy childlikeness, our inner little child walking happily with our heavenly Daddy, unburdened by any baggage of woundedness or bitterness, more confident than ever of God's reliability and curious to discover what lies around the next bend in the story of our life.

FACE TIME WITH MY TRAINER

PART 1: Answer these Bible study questions BEFORE reading the chapter

Read I Kings 18:7 – 15 to answer the following questions.
How had Obadiah helped the prophets survive during Jezebel's purge? (v. 13)

How many righteous prophets did Obadiah mention to Elijah? (v. 13)

Read I Kings 18:20 – 22. When Elijah challenged the people at Mt. Carmel, how many people came forward to stand with him? (vv. 21 – 22)

Read I Kings 19:10 – 18. Twice in this section Elijah made the same complaint to God. What was it? Was his complaint true? Explain your answer. (vv. 10, 14)

Read Mark 6:7 – 13; 30, 31. When the disciples returned, what did they do and what did Jesus say they should do next? (vv. 30 – 31)

Skim Luke 10:1 – 16 and read 17 – 24 to answer these questions. What was the mood of the 72 when they returned to report to Jesus? Talk about one new thing they learned during this debriefing session.

PART 2: Questions & Reflection

1. Describe one practical lesson you learned as a result of one of your trust battles.

2. When you read the section about breaking arrows of doubt, did it remind you of a doubt that you would like God to break for you? What would you call the doubt? Spend time in prayer asking God to break that arrow.

3. Did you remember a past doubt that God has already broken? Describe the doubt and how God helped break its power in your life.

4. Do you find yourself dwelling on a good deed you did, either with pride or with regret? What is it? If you do, lay it before the Lord to give it to Him a second time.

5. Does one of your trust battle scenarios give you déjà vu? If so, ask God to show you how you could jump off that merry-go-round and fight a different trust battle next time around.

6. What did you find to be the most encouraging or intriguing idea in this chapter?

AN ONGOING RESOURCE: *Check out the Debriefing Prayer Guide starting on the next page, which you can use whenever you would like to reflect on a recent trust battle. Why not pick one of your latest trust battles to try it out and give it a test run? Share whatever you feel comfortable sharing. Did you find this debriefing process helpful? Why or why not?*

Prayer Guide: Reflecting and Debriefing

"He trains my hands for battle..." Psalm 18:34

Begin with prayer asking God to help you to debrief. Start by doing any applicable part of the *After Action Review*. Then do as much or as little as you feel led to do in the next three sections. FEEL FREE TO MAKE THIS AS SIMPLE AS POSSIBLE. Look for ONE take away lesson from this trust battle.

#1 AFTER ACTION REVIEW

1. **What was supposed to happen? (What was the stated objective?)**
   [Refer to that 3 x 5 card of guidance and jot down the plan, any promises and any strategies God gave in the "before the battle" phase.]

2. **What actually happened?**
   a. Jot a few notes about what happened during each phase of this trust battle, just to remember the highlights of this episode.
   b. **Take special care to record any "Aha" moments that I had during this battle.** (This is the most important part of this entire debriefing time.)

3. **What lessons can I learn so I'll do better next time?**
   - Complete this sentence: "As I went through this trust battle, I began to realize that You were trying to teach me more about...." What did I learn?
   - Think of something that I tried out that worked well or pretty well. What was it?
   - Think of something that I may not have done this time around but that I see now might be a good strategy next time around.
   - How well did I put into practice the guidance I received on my 3 x 5 card?
   - Did something happen that put me on alert to a strategy that Satan used or might use against me or others? Did I get an idea about how to combat his scheme?
   - What Bible verses did I find helpful? Should I memorize any of them?
   - What part(s) of my existing trust network did this trust battle shake? How much more willing am I to put my primary trust in You for this area?
   - How did my Christian friends help me? Could I have been wiser about working together with them?
   - What did I learn about You during this battle? Most especially, how did this trust battle affect my relationship with You?
   - What do I need to do now so I'll be more prepared the next time around?

The next two parts help us to check to see if we are still carrying around some unwanted emotional baggage.

#2 IS THERE ANYONE I NEED TO FORGIVE?

This is the first type of baggage that we need to investigate and handle. During this trust battle, did anyone hurt my feelings, act badly or unkindly to me, insult or belittle me, or let me down?

This section can help to analyze this a little more to see if I just need to practice forbearance, forgive them, or chalk it up as an opportunity to suffer for Christ.

Do I need to show forbearance or is this a matter that requires forgiveness?

Forbearance: Did this person hurt me unintentionally? Did they react out of character because they were under stress? Should I just cut them some slack because they're human, made a human mistake, and I'd want them to cut me slack if our positions were reversed? If I let it go, would they likely never or rarely do it again? Can I just extend mercy, and let them off the hook as an act of love? *"Above all, love each other deeply, because love covers over a multitude of sins"* (I Peter 4:8).

> **If the answer is yes** to these questions, pray to release any left over animosity toward this person. Pray to bless them. Ask God to show me how to make a kind gesture toward them that will get me back to thinking about them in a loving way.

Forgiveness: Did this person do something malicious and intentional? Did they harm me or my loved one? Will what they did leave lasting damage that I'll need to work on repairing? Do I feel they should have apologized for what they did? Did their words or actions show a pattern of thoughtless or sinful behavior? Do I feel that they sinned against me?

> **If the answer is yes,** then work on forgiving them and try to reconcile with them, if possible. Use the guidelines of Matthew 18 if the person is a Christian. Seek counseling, if necessary, to sort out my feelings and to forgive them.

Suffering for Jesus: Did this person punish me or treat me badly simply because I took a stand for Jesus by witnessing to them or by standing up for righteousness? Did this person retaliate against me or someone I love simply because my godly witness annoyed or convicted them of sin? Did they withhold some benefit from me solely because of a prejudice against Christians?

> **If the answer is yes,** (and I didn't act in an obnoxious or prideful way), then rejoice and be glad that Jesus has granted me the privilege of sharing in His suffering. Freely forgive the person, make no attempt to reconcile with them or to get them to apologize, and entrust myself to God to be my avenger. Pray to bless this person. (Matthew 5:11, 12 and Romans 12:19, 20 will help if this is the situation.)

> **If I suffered or endured hardship in order to serve Christ,** lay that suffering at His feet and thank Him for His promises and for the privilege of suffering for His sake. (Matthew 19:29 and Philippians 1:29 will be helpful if this is the situation.)

Lastly, is there anything for which I need to forgive myself? Just checking.

#3 CHECKLIST OF OTHER POSSIBLE BAGGAGE

If you answer yes to any of the questions in this chart, then spend some time taking care of it. (The right hand column refers you to the section in Chapter 16, if you would like to refresh your memory on that topic.) Please, don't go overboard. Do only what God seems to nudge you to do.

QUESTION	REFER TO:
• Did I start to doubt (or did I become aware of a doubt) about God or myself? • I know that God uses trust battles to wean me from trusting other people inappropriately. But did this trust battle make me cynical about people or bring to light a deep-seated doubt about people or groups that went beyond that?	Check for arrows in your shield of faith
• Do I find myself obsessing or dwelling on what happened, either in a prideful way or with regret or second-guessing?	Let go of the good work
• Did I run into trouble because of my own thoughtlessness, bad habit or foolishness?	What exactly did we reap?
• Did I get a sense of déjà vu during this trust battle? • Could I have done things differently that would have allowed me to skip this trust battle altogether? • Did I get into trouble because I enabled or supported someone else's bad behavior?	Have we learned our lesson yet?

#4 FEEDBACK

After you finish your debriefing time, ask one of your prayer partners to help you to get another perspective on this trust battle. Be sure to pick someone who loves you, preferably one of your trusted prayer partners or a companion on your journey. Whatever you do, don't go to someone who will just nitpick!

Share with them whatever you feel like sharing with them about what you figured out during this debriefing time. Ask them for their perspective. Most especially, ask them to tell you what they see that you did well (or that you made progress in) that you haven't noticed yet. My guess is that they will remember things that you forgot all about, and that you have been too hard on yourself, noticing all the things you did wrong and forgetting your progress. So give your friend a chance to encourage you.

Spend some time rejoicing with them about all the good things that came out of this trust battle, even if the only thing that came out of it was that you survived it! If you get to laughing, or if you break into praise and thanks to God for all His goodness, hey, that's even better. Enjoy!

Catherine's Story: Part Two

DEBRIEFING: I think I am still in this stage, and I think it will take a while, perhaps another year.

Staying at the church was probably a good move because we found more people supported us than we had realized. Several times a month people came up and told us they had heard what happened, said it had happened to many others, and that WE had shown Christ-likeness through the whole ordeal. (I didn't expect that we were perceived in such a positive light after what the principal had said to me.) I definitely want to take responsibility where I need to, but it was good to hear that it wasn't all my fault. That is part of the overcoming half-truths debriefing that you mention in your chapter.

Again, we didn't stay to be bragged on; we stayed because we didn't have anywhere else we were comfortable going. We didn't want to appear that we had been run off. God wasn't leading us to leave, and I thought we shouldn't make a decision in the first year, like after a death or divorce.

I have had time to reflect on my two years of teaching, and definitely know things I would do differently if I were to return. I have also been studying and reading about conflict resolution and have tried to put that into practice wherever possible.

It has been hard to do, but I have also gone to some parents of former students, co-workers (not the supervisor, pastor, or principal, though), and friends I've known for a while and asked them to give me feedback on my personality and interactions with people. I've asked them to be very honest and tell me what I can improve on, and how I can keep this from happening again. I've asked if they think I'm teacher material or if I should look for another career. I have received good feedback that makes me think people are being honest with me and not holding back. I have some things I can change. Subbing, to mention it again, gives me opportunity to work on these things, too.

(I mention this last paragraph to explain why debriefing is taking me so long. I only get up enough nerve to talk with people every so often.)

You have a good point about leaving the good work. I went into teaching 4th grade at that school planning to be there 10-12 years, until my daughter graduated. Therefore, I took extra time to make and file lessons, transparencies, etc., that I could use year after year. I had detailed notes so I wouldn't have to spend the hours I did the first year learning the material. I have probably 40-50 notebooks of transparencies that are only good for that particular 4th grade curriculum; I can't use them anywhere else!

I left what I could for the new teacher but have since found out that she does not use them; in fact, they are not even in her classroom, which is my daughter's church classroom. This "wastefulness" grieves me so deeply. But, like you say in this chapter, I keep giving it to the Lord as a sacrifice. My husband also reminds me that the 34 kids over the two years that I taught probably don't think of it as wastefulness at all.

CHAPTER 16

Wrestling with God

Then the man said, "Let Me go for it is daybreak."
But Jacob replied, "I will not let You go unless You bless me."
Genesis 32:26

After months on the sidelines, watching the love story unfold between Jacob and her beautiful little sister, Rachel, Leah knew in her bones that her father's devious plot against Jacob would hurt her most of all. While servants dressed her in bridal clothing, she fought the claustrophobic premonition that her life was over. Heart pounding, she squinted through the veil that hid her plain face, and slowly walked toward the music and the merry-makers, trying not to think about what it could have been like to marry a husband who wanted her.

Her wedding night was magical. Leah fell hopelessly in love. In the dark she gave herself with maidenly enthusiasm, caught up in the spell of Jacob's passionate embrace. For one night of wistful hope she imagined Jacob seeing the gift of love she freely gave to him, and loving her back.

Morning dawned. Jacob's drowsy good humor vanished in blistering wrath and revulsion. There was Leah! Arguments, cold shoulders and cutting snipes settled into an unhappy new routine. Jacob's scathing rejection haunted her solitary nights and nauseous mornings. It poured salt on her wounds to hear them giggle and whisper in the nearby tent. She turned to Jacob's God out of loneliness, and when her baby was born, she named him Reuben, *"because God has seen my misery."*

She prayed every night for Jacob to love her a little. He should love me, if only for the baby. Nothing changed. Why didn't God do anything? She felt pretty dejected when she gave birth to Simeon two years later. *"The Lord heard the news that I am unloved."* Sniff! Maybe He heard it through the grapevine.

Three more years of unanswered prayer left Leah depressed and cynical. Why hadn't God helped her? She gave up her little fantasy that Jacob would ever love her, and named her third boy Levi, reflecting that *"now at last my husband will become attached to me."* Her forlorn realism tasted bitter on her tongue.

Leah was sitting by herself on the hillside the first time she sensed the Presence. Her weeping gave way to peace. She savored the sensation of being deeply known by God and opened her heart to listen. Slowly her self-protective layers of cynicism and reserve melted away and she began to see herself through His eyes – not as a flawed reject, but as one chosen and blessed. More than ten years after her traumatic wedding, she gave birth to her fourth child and called him Judah. *"This time I will praise the Lord."*

Leah's bratty little sister lost her power to disturb Leah's peace, even when Rachel manipulated Jacob into bedding her maid and picked competitive baby names: Dan – *"God has vindicated me and given me a son,"* and Naphtali – *"I have had a great struggle with my sister and I have prevailed."*

With some trepidation, Leah gave her own maid to Jacob, but resisted the temptation to one-up her sister, calling Zilpah's first baby, Gad, *"What good fortune."* Gradually her positive attitude and calm good humor won her the respect and friendship of women in the camp, which she celebrated when naming Asher. *"How happy I am. The women will call me happy."*

Although, admittedly, we've made a few guesses about Leah's story, there's no denying that Leah's life features a lovely story arc of character transformation, spanning the years between her first baby and her last. The insecure unhappy girl – who desperately sought acceptance and love from people who didn't have it in them to give – matured and became a beautiful soul. Anchored within God's blessing, she made a life for herself in the place where God put her. She found satisfying relationships and enjoyed the blessings of sons growing up all around her. She never escaped; she transcended.

She received with gratitude the gifts God gave her. With Issachar, her fifth son, she affirmed that *"God has rewarded me for giving my maidservant to my husband."* And with the self-confidence of a truly contented woman, she called her sixth son, Zebulun, *"God has presented me with a precious gift. This time my husband will treat me with honor."*

And he did just that. Though Jacob carried a torch for Rachel long after her premature death in childbirth, he still buried Leah – not Rachel – in the family tomb which held the bones of Abraham, Sarah, Isaac and Rebekah. Honoring his last wishes, his sons carried his bones from Egypt, bypassing Rachel's tomb to bury him with Leah, the unloved wife who slowly but surely carved out a good life for herself as the primary caregiver and mother for all his sons.

In this chapter we plunge into the deep end of the pool and tackle long-term trust issues that defy simple solutions. We've been discussing how to recover after the battle. If the outcome of a trust battle reflected an especially painful 'no' answer from God, the last two chapters have suggested ways to process our grief and disappointment. This may take awhile and include some degree of wrestling with God before we find peace.

However, this chapter is mainly for people who see this book coming to an end and it still hasn't solved your most frustrating issue. Yes, you have some trust battles that fall into a neat little before, during, and after model. But you've been stuck in the "during" phase of your core trust battle for years, with no end in sight. Or disaster struck and the life you loved got yanked right out from under you. Maybe you twiddle on a shelf waiting endlessly for your dream to come true. Or maybe, like me, you started out with two strikes against you.

How do we handle the feelings stirred by such stubborn problems? Back in Chapter 7, we made the point that we trust God by taking our feelings to God, allowing Him to sort them out for us and help us to receive His peace. II Thessalonians 3:16 says, *"May the Lord of peace Himself continually grant you peace in every circumstance"* (NASB), holding out the theoretical possibility that we can find genuine contentment in every situation.

Hopefully, by now we know how to trust God in *the small moment* – by turning to God in whatever way connects us to His presence and power. The simplest breath prayer or yielded Godward glance can well and truly express our trust and bring our hearts to peace.

We've also spent many chapters exploring ways to trust God through the twists and turns of a particular trust battle. We usually juggle several battles at any one time, picking up new ones like cards in a game, and laying down others as they draw to a close. For these individual trust battles, we learned to take our feelings to God, because so often, the battle over our emotions is the focal point of God's activity to train us to trust Him.

In this chapter we will focus on the trust battle "cards" that stay in our hand for years. Most of us, if we're honest, have at least one area that torments us. Sometimes it's on the front burner of our attention and sometimes on the back burner, but it's always there, painful and discouraging and puzzling. Sometimes we're more emotionally equipped to deal with it. Just when we think we're making progress in our walk with God or this "trust business," it rears its ugly head, and our best intentions fly out the window. We dejectedly sigh that it would be so much easier to trust God if we didn't have to put up with *that* person, or deal with *that* problem or struggle with *that* liability. Or star in our particular life story.

These cards harbor our deepest feelings of hopelessness, skepticism and pain. Many of us suppress our pain with a pat answer that keeps us shallow but in control: "Forgive and forget!" "Don't question God!" "It's all my fault – or all his fault!" Many of us head for the comfort of food or various addictions or busyness to mask the pain even from ourselves, which only complicates and more deeply ensnares us instead of solving anything.

Remembering that unexamined emotions have enormous power, and that they tend to degenerate if left to themselves, in this chapter we'll make the case for bringing our questions and struggles out into the open, even if it means wrestling with God over our big unsolved issues. We exercise active trust in God when we bring our subterranean pockets of doubt and discouragement into the light of God's presence, instead of allowing them to bear their poisonous fruit unchallenged.

This may mean admitting to God that we're angry with Him or frustrated or full of questions. We walk a tightrope here trying to avoid falling into unbelief or rebellion, and that's why this trust gate is a tight fit and not for the faint of heart. And, mind you, we have no excuse ever to sass or disrespect God. So, please let's not do that. Deal?

The Bible sometimes refers to our relationship with God using the analogy of marriage. Even though God is always totally right, and any misunderstanding is always completely ours, it's undeniable that God sometimes baffles and exasperates us in a men-are-from-Mars-women-are-from-Venus sort of way. He is infinitely "Other." For some of us, the only pathway toward a truly satisfying love relationship with God takes us through territory where we need to grapple with Him about our seemingly irreconcilable differences.

This chapter is maybe my most autobiographical. Like it or not, my story is one of profound brokenness and painfully slow progress, a thousand scattered puzzle pieces without the picture on a box. Brennan Manning admitted in his book *Ruthless Trust* that "the biggest obstacle on my journey of trust has been an oppressive sense of insecurity, inadequacy, inferiority and low self-esteem." To people like us it seems daunting to voice the questions that torment us, because we dread finding out that our life story is all a monstrous, unfixable mistake. Because God's ways are unseen and so *Other*, and we are so broken and have such thoroughly heathen hearts, we can find many excuses to resent God, but not talk to Him about it.

Against that backdrop, I submit that it takes courage and faith to rise up to engage in the struggle for wholeness and to bring this most messy of all our trust battles to Jesus. In this chapter we'll look at our story as a whole, especially those aggravating areas in which we wait and wait. We'll make four observations about God that may encourage us to reconcile with God over our whole life story and those running themes that linger unresolved. Then, we'll share four suggestions for how to wrestle with God in a constructive and productive way.

FOUR ENCOURAGING OBSERVATIONS ABOUT GOD

God has a completely different orientation toward time. One of the hardest adjustments that Jim and I had to make when we first got married was in our opposite time orientation, so I know a bit about this. Jim wants to be everywhere ten minutes early. He always knows what time it is. I get lost in projects and forget what day it is. We see this internal time orientation in restaurants and foreign cultures. Some places are Johnny-on-the-spot and others are slow as molasses. We can get all upset about it, or open ourselves to another point of view and settle in to enjoy a different cadence.

A lot of what we call "waiting for God" is simply that we haven't synchronized ourselves to God's timetable. God thinks in terms of lifetimes and multigenerational plans. God took a leisurely decade or so to answer Leah's wedding night prayer.

And she never saw most of the honor God heaped upon her. Before time began, God had already chosen Leah (not Rachel) to be the woman through whose generational line He gave us His precious Son, Jesus, 1900 years later. That attention to detail on God's part boggles the mind.

At the other extreme, God is always in the eternal Now. C. S. Lewis said this in *Letters to Malcolm:* "To be God is to enjoy an infinite present where nothing has yet passed away and nothing is still to come." You've heard before that, if all human history is the line drawn on a piece of paper, God is the paper. God has already actually witnessed every moment of our life in this world – and the next one (!) – and already knows exactly how He will help us each step along the way. When we run to Him in a panic, He already knows how it'll turn out.

It's no coincidence that the theme of waiting runs through this book about trusting God, because waiting supremely tests our capacity to trust God. **As a veteran of many long waits, I've come to value these waiting times because the most significant transformational stuff happens during the wait, precisely when we think nothing is happening.**

I used to focus on *my* feeling of impatience, drumming my fingers, waiting for God to show up. But *God* is the patient one, waiting for me and for us to quit thrashing around, and quit insisting on microwave minute answers when He's made it clear He prefers slow-cooking.

Generally, it takes time to exhaust the alternatives before we settle down and turn to Him. So, let's try to get in step with His timetable as soon as possible. Sorry, that doesn't make it end more quickly. It just gets us on the same page as God so we cooperate instead of working at cross-purposes. Plus, it's easier to be patient if we know God's really up to something.

The biggest upside of waiting is that it triggers some fabulous promises about waiting on God. That morphs our delay into a holy time, jam-packed with promised blessings (For instance, Psalm 37:34; Prov. 20:22; Isa. 64:4; and Micah 7:7). Whenever we find ourselves waiting, we can practice waiting on God. Over time, our shaky efforts can turn into the confidence of expectancy and hope.

> *Therefore the Lord waits to be gracious to you, and therefore He exalts Himself to show mercy to you. For the Lord is a God of justice. Blessed are all those who wait for Him! Isaiah 30:18 (ESV)*

Long waiting periods polish off the rough edges of our carnal nature and kill our pride more effectively than any other tool. So, explore those promises and grapple with God if you must. It's worth it. People who truly trust God have mastered the skill of how to wait on Him.

God doesn't write formula stories. You know how you can often predict the ending of many television shows by the first commercial break? That's because hack writers use formula plotlines and cookie cutter characters. Comedies look pretty much alike, as do detective stories, love stories and mysteries.

The best writers don't rely on formulas, even when they write stories that fit within a genre of storytelling. They create original characters and deftly take them through plot twists that often only make sense in retrospect.

Well, God is a great writer!

However, that may frustrate us because we'd like to star in the formula story of being born wealthy, popular, smart and beautiful, marrying a great guy, raising perfect children, and living happily ever after until we die in our sleep of extreme old age and satisfaction. Oh, and experiencing nothing but victory and ecstasy in our walk with Christ.

But then, Dadgummit, God puts us into our story.

In I Corinthians 7, the Apostle Paul repeatedly makes the astounding point that God personally assigns our life story to us. *"Only let each person lead <u>the life that the Lord has</u>*

assigned to him, and to which God has called him....*Were you a slave when called? Do not be concerned about it. But if you can gain your freedom, avail yourself of the opportunity. For he who was called in the Lord as a slave is a freedman of the Lord. Likewise he who was free when called is a slave of Christ*" (I Cor. 7:17, 21, 22 ESV).

Whether talking about our marital status, our economic status, or the mistakes we made to mess up our lives, Paul says that we can rest assured that God has sovereignly overseen our life circumstances, and that, because we belong to Jesus, He can help us to live *that* situation to its fullest.

That doesn't mean we're doomed to our fate, or that we shouldn't seize opportunities to improve our situation. But, we aren't held hostage until our circumstances change. By God's power we can transcend them and live well wherever God plants us.

It took me years to come to terms with what I've just said. I've done a lot of wrestling with God trying to make sense of why God put me in the family He did and why I had to struggle where I did. So, I'm not Pollyanna here. Life is tough. But our God is good, and He knows how to write great stories, even when they open with an "Act I" like yours or mine.

God doesn't waste pain. Hebrews 12:10, 11 says it this way. *"Our fathers disciplined us for a little while as they thought best; but God disciplines us for our good, that we may share in His holiness. No discipline seems pleasant at the time, but painful. Later on, however, it produces a harvest of righteousness and peace for those who have been trained by it."* We get skittish around the word *discipline*, but Paul used a pretty generic word referring to the regular education of children. This comes full circle from what we said in Chapter One about God training our arms for battle. God is a great teacher. He carefully prepares personalized lesson plans as a sure sign of His love and commitment to us (see Heb. 12:5 – 9). He unerringly knows what will do us the most good.

In *Story*, Robert McKee's textbook on story writing, he makes the point that "human nature is fundamentally conservative. We never do more than we have to, expend any energy we don't have to, take any risks we don't have to, change *if we don't have to*. Why should we? Why do anything the hard way if we can get what we want the easy way" – however we define that term? McKee observes that usually, people only change because some seemingly insurmountable obstacle or opposition forces them to make changes. He calls it the Principle of Antagonism, and comments that "the more powerful and complex the forces of antagonism opposing the character, the more completely realized character and story *must* become."

We can certainly waste pain by not immediately running to God for help and by not rising to the occasion to face the challenge before us. In the words of the old hymn, "Oh, what needless pain we bear all because we do not carry everything to God in prayer." But let's remember that God is bigger than us, and He does not waste pain. He knows how to move our story along from Point A to Point B. He knows when we need rest and when we need to take our next step. The only situations that force us to grow are ones we can't easily escape or manipulate. Knowing that, He lovingly puts tailor made, unavoidable obstacles across our path.

Jesus is a friend of sinners like you and me. He is on our side. He understands that we are but dust. Some struggles take us a long time to resolve. And that's not a bad thing. It took Leah four babies to come to some kind of peace. We're talking four years at least, and more likely, ten or twelve. God really did see her misery. He noticed her, the invisible, unloved sister, and loved her through her journey into wholeness.

We struggle because we want to solve everything now, and fix everything now. But God knows that we can usually only handle one increment of change at a time. He doesn't dump the truck on us. He also knows that it often takes us a long time to come to the end of ourselves, and that we learn by failing again and again before we're willing to entertain the possibility of trying a new approach.

Mind you, He is <u>not</u> on our side to rubber stamp any sense of entitlement, that somehow He owes us the baby we long for, or the husband we dream of, or the job we think would be perfect or the story line we think would suit us best. Sooner or later, we have to get off our high horse and humble ourselves before God. But even when we're at our most selfish and self-absorbed, He never leaves us (Heb. 13:5).

Although our dim-witted, deluded hearts must grieve Him quite often, apparently, God sees something to value and redeem. His compassion is easily aroused, His commitment never wavers. He doesn't hold His nose. *"If God is for us, who is against us? He who did not spare His own Son, but delivered Him up for us all, how will He not also with Him freely give us all things"* (Rom. 8:31b, 32 NASB).

FOUR SUGGESTIONS TO WRESTLE WITH GOD MOST PRODUCTIVELY

Embrace the struggle that doesn't seem to go away. Instead of taking the easy way out, or sinking into hopelessness, try looking squarely at your core trust issues. Make one more attempt to whittle away at the challenge. If you've prayed in vain for God to rescue you from this struggle, begin to regard your struggle as a gift from God, designed to help you to grow.

I don't know if you're this way, but I tend to regard any delay as either my failure or someone else's meanness. I'm learning that, if I've tried my best to move forward, if I've tackled every obstacle and I'm still stuck, then maybe I should relax and yield to God's agenda and His timetable. **Above all, trust the process.** Yes, Jesus healed the deaf and the lame in an instant. But the business of transforming our minds is a life-long process with no shortcuts.

I've also noticed that, when it comes to spiritual and emotional growth, we can see much further ahead than what we can incorporate. So, for instance, we pray like mad to be patient (right now), but don't see that to become patient would mean learning a dozen little intermediate "patience lessons," finding healing for various childhood wounds, and spending tons of time in the presence of our patient Savior who supplies patience as fruit, not as a deed.

We embrace the struggle by looking courageously for the one next thing to tackle. We eat our elephant one bite at a time. Does that mean going to a counselor and staring into the abyss of our own angry hearts? Do it. Does it mean reading some books to educate ourselves? Do it. Does it mean getting serious about that support group? Do it. Do the next thing. Fight the good fight.

Sometimes the peace we find is not a solution, but rather just the assurance that this is the right arena in which to struggle. This is the life God has assigned to us and the obstacles lovingly chosen to make us like Christ.

Stand in your honest pain. While it may be fairly simple to tell God how we feel when we get that unexpected bill in the mail, or when someone cuts us off on the freeway, it's no small matter to get real before God about our core issues. Usually we have to dig through layers of self-delusion and despair, yank our brains out of the well-worn ruts of our mental riffs, turn away from the blame game, and face some pretty devastating insecurity. It is not for the faint of heart.

Psalm 51:6 says *"Surely You desire truth in the inner parts; You teach me wisdom in the inmost place."* That guiding verse stood me in good stead on my long journey because the unflinching quest for the truth heals us. It really does set us free, at least it does when we say it to Jesus and hear it from Him.

I've seen it over and over again in healing prayer. The pray-ee begins with anguish and turmoil, asking for the moon, scared that God won't help and afraid to tell the truth. We pray and listen and help them to dig down to that pain that has torn them up inside these many years.

And then the small miracle happens. Jesus meets them in their pain and tells them exactly what they most need to hear. Suddenly, angry accusations fall away and we all stand amazed when He speaks the good word, which touches and heals and restores courage. And somehow it doesn't matter so much that we didn't get all the answers, because we see once again how well God knows us and how unerringly He knows the one thing we most need next.

Question your assumptions. That small miracle only happens if we're willing to let go of our presuppositions and lay down our riff when Jesus offers us the next step out. That's hard. We invest a lot of energy in our riffs. Our mental ruts can get so deep that it's hard to switch direction. A guy I know has come several times to a crossroad moment where he could have chosen the path to wholeness. Each time he turns his back on it and picks up the rags of his grudges and grievances. And he stays stuck. A few times in healing prayer I've seen someone momentarily grasp a healing truth, and for a few minutes see clearly how they could walk with new insight, only to have them sink back into reconstructing their old enslaving complaints, as if they hadn't heard a thing. Maybe next time they'll be ready.

Transformation is unpredictable. The invitation can come as a jolt or as a whisper on the wind. Take Leah's story. It's easy for us to connect the dots of her emotional journey between her wedding and her third baby. She had low self-esteem and thought she could only feel better if Jacob loved her. Since he didn't, she felt frustrated and trapped. In her worldview,

God was good or not good depending on whether He answered her prayer to change Jacob.

What happened? What changed Leah's mind? We'll never know. Somehow, she made an about face. She saw God, really saw Him, not as someone who had to answer her prayer in a certain way, but as Himself. When she saw God this new way, it changed how she saw herself. That's always the way it goes. We are made in God's image and when we finally see Him we remember who we are. Genuine worship will heal our hearts and satisfy our deepest need. It appears that Leah shed her neediness regarding Jacob, opening her heart to find satisfaction elsewhere – with God, with good friends, and with her children. By the end, she honestly didn't view it as a personal defeat, or as lowered expectations to feel certain and satisfied that Jacob would honor her.

That's the weird thing about change. We want the situation *out there* to change and we want to see prompt and total internal change. When we don't see change, it can drive us to despair. In their book *The Sacred Romance,* Brent Curtis and John Eldredge make the excellent observation that "one of the most poisonous of all Satan's whispers is simply, 'Things will never change.'" Satan is a big fat liar. Don't believe him. *"All things are possible with God"* (Mark 10:27).

Having said that, change almost always comes after we stop insisting it come to us on our terms. At some point we have to challenge our assumption that God owes us anything, or that those bad people out there control our lives, or that God will love us and accept us only after we get our act together.

Leah found contentment and made profound changes only after she made peace with the fact that her outward circumstances would never change. Her sister never got over being bratty and spoiled rotten, and Jacob always loved Rachel best.

Seek out the joys to be found in the messy meantime. I hope you've found encouragement for your long-term struggles and some fresh strategies for those obstacles that hang on year after year.

But, hey, we can get overwhelmed by our troubles, and that's unnecessary. There's more to life than the struggle, and a sense of perspective and proportion can make our hardships easier to handle. I like what it says in Proverbs 15:15. *"All the days of the oppressed are wretched, but the cheerful heart has a continual feast."* It took me years to realize that every morning I can choose either the feast or the wretchedness. The more I view my struggles as a good gift from God, lovingly designed to help me grow in grace, the more my eyes open to the feast around me every day.

I love the story of Leah and her courage to wrestle with God until she found joy and contentment. It has delighted me to see women in our Bible study grapple with God in recent years and find the hope that anchors their soul in spite of difficult outward circumstances. It's always such a kick to witness the joy that comes after the long night of weeping.

But most of us live out our lives in the messy meantime, before the breakthroughs and the Aha! moments. We can see our struggles as an agony, or trust God by beginning to see it as choreography. Contentment and joy can be ours in the meantime. It reminds me of one of my favorite Hillel quotations. "I get up. I walk. I fall down. Meanwhile, I keep dancing."

FACE TIME WITH MY TRAINER

Skim Genesis 29:14 – 30 and put yourself in Leah's shoes.
What are some reasons why Leah might have been unhappy with her life?

Skim Genesis 29:31 – 30:20 just for context. Note the names of Leah's six sons and Zilpah's two sons, and the reason Leah gave for naming each one. (Don't worry about Rachel's or Bilhah's sons.)

PART 2: QUESTIONS & REFLECTION

1. How does the story of Leah illustrate what it means to wrestle with God?

2. Why can it express trust to wrestle with God? What are the risks of wrestling with God?

3. How would you describe your biggest ongoing trust battle, the "card" you've held in your hand the longest? What part of that issue is still unresolved? What progress have you made?

4. What makes you feel most discontented with your life story? Read I Corinthians 7. What would you say is *"the life that the Lord has assigned"* to you? How would you look at your life story differently if you viewed it as a calling from God?

5. Review Hebrews 12:5 – 11 and think about the pain you've experienced. How would it change your perspective to see that God does not waste pain?

6. As you read through the suggestions, what did it encourage you to start doing or to continue doing?

7. What did you find to be the most encouraging or intriguing idea in this chapter?

Ruby's Story

I had a happy life. I worked for the county during the week. My weekends and evenings were devoted to my family, church and a Christian renewal organization. My four adult children were all Christians, and it gave us great joy to know that they were all involved in ministries in their own churches.

One Saturday in the fall of the year, our second son called us from the hospital where he was waiting for surgery. We rushed to the hospital. We had no idea he was even sick! That day, he told us that he was a homosexual and that he had contracted AIDS from his homosexual involvement. He told us he was having a catheter put into his heart so that he could have daily chemo treatment for AIDS.

We were stunned. We didn't have a clue that he was homosexual. Greg had so many friends, from newborns to the elderly, some of whom were homosexual. How could this happen? What did I do wrong?

I couldn't understand how Greg could get involved in this lifestyle. After all, although he was not deaf himself, in college he had learned sign language so that he could have a ministry to deaf people, and by then he was active in the deaf community. He taught sign language, headed up the deaf ministry in a large church, and was even discipling a deaf young man.

He also had a great job with the county, where he used his talents in training others and he represented the county in state seminars, winning several awards at work. How could God let this happen, even letting this terrible disease destroy his brain?

I was very angry with God, crying and yelling out at Him. I struggled daily for weeks. Yet I knew in my very being that God loved me. I knew I could not get through this on my own. I felt totally helpless in dealing with my anger and the fact that I could do nothing to fix the problem. Where could I turn for peace to weather the storms of life?

As Greg's health deteriorated, we moved him into our home to care for him. Some of Greg's homosexual friends could see the love and care we provided for Greg and we were able to share the gospel with many of them.

One day, when I asked Greg what he wanted for Christmas, he looked me in the eyes and said, "A new body." I told him he would get one soon.

It took me a long, long time to come to terms with his death. Eventually, I got involved in a support group called Spatula that helps other Christian parents who are also dealing with this situation. Helping those parents cope helped me to make my peace with what happened to me. I find comfort in knowing I will see my son again as I know He is safe in the arms of Jesus.

CHAPTER 17

Praise: Thanking God for Acting

I will extol the Lord at all times;
His praise will always be on my lips.
Psalm 34:1

I just finished weaving a baby blanket for our first grandchild on my 42" floor loom. I love when the weaving settles into that Zen zone of automatic motion, the shuttles flying back and forth across the warp. I love the interplay of color and pattern and the miraculous way that hundreds of separate threads come together to create a new fabric or a tapestry.

Weaving connects me with women clear back to the dawn of time. For instance, the theme of spinning and weaving runs through the account of the excellent wife in Proverbs 31. *"She selects wool and flax and works with eager hands.... She makes coverings for her bed; she is clothed in fine linen and purple."* She spins, holding the distaff, and sells linen and sashes in the marketplace. I may not be in her league, but I know this woman.

Sadly, although I loved it, weaving used to bring out the more painful aspects of my perfectionistic heart. I would pour myself into a weaving project, weave it to the best of my ability and then turn right around to criticize it mercilessly.

I rarely run into a weaver or even someone who knows much about weaving. But if people commented on one of my woven wall hangings, or noticed that I wore a woven vest, I felt driven to point out all the flaws. Most people didn't have a clue what I was talking about when I referred to my uneven selvedge edges or the mistakes in the twill or the overshot. They would squint at the piece and nod sagely, as if they saw it too. And even untrained eyes could spot some of my more glaring errors if they started to look.

The curse of perfectionism is that it demands 100% perfection and rejects whatever falls short of that unattainable standard. Perfectionists tend to be very unhappy people. I know I was.

I had been weaving for a few years when one of our son's elementary school teachers asked me to do a weaving demonstration for her study unit on Navajo Indians. I wasn't as familiar with this type of weaving, so I checked out some library books, including a fascinating book about *The Weaver's Pathway* by Noel Bennett.

Navajo artisans have a curious habit of inserting what they call *the weaver's path* into each woven blanket or pottery piece. For instance, if a rug has an inside color surrounded by an outside border color, the weaver will weave one strand of the inside color out to the edge in the upper right hand corner. It looks like a mistake. Navajo potters decorate their pottery with distinctive zigzag motifs. These motifs might circle the rim or dot the body of the pot. But one of the design motifs will have one less zag than all the rest. (You might not find this in mass produced rugs and pots at tourist traps, but it's a distinguishing feature of Navajo art.)

Why did they do that? At first, Navajo weavers said simply that *the weaver's path* provided an escape route for evil spirits. Later, when their work received respect, the weavers shared that there was more to the tradition. They included *a weaver's path,* not merely to provide an escape route for any stray evil spirit, but to give their own creative spirit a way to escape from a project that might have taken them months to complete. *The weaver's path* was their way of thanking the Great Spirit for allowing them to create the piece and for letting them borrow those motifs and colors. Furthermore, they left something deliberately incomplete, out of gratitude for being able to use those motifs, and as an act of faith that they would have other opportunities to create beautiful things.

Isn't that a lovely idea? The wisdom of *the weaver's path* took root in my heart. On my next weaving project I deliberately left one minor mistake uncorrected and called it my weaver's path. My whole attitude changed when I took the option of 100% perfection out of the equation. I began to enjoy my weavings and my attitude shifted from self-condemnation to gratitude. *Thank You, God, for allowing me to create something beautiful. And thank You, Holy Spirit, for the lovely weavings I will enjoy making another day, here on earth and up in heaven.*

The principle of the weaver's path even found its way into other areas of my life. It helped me to escape the tyranny and joylessness of the 100% standard. Jesus died on a cross because we can't attain 100% perfection in most areas of our lives except for math tests. We all fall short of perfection, both morally and in our relationships.

And that brings me back to trust, the topic of this book. The truth is that we often fall short of perfect trust. Sometimes we run elsewhere. Sometimes we stubbornly hoard our worries or anger because we don't want God to mess with them. Maybe we aren't ready to let go of our rage or we haven't finished our pity party. We feel sort of obligated to worry about our children.

Yet, God is good.

God spent years gently teaching me how to trust Him. Time after time I failed miserably to muster up any semblance of trust in God. I would talk about my doubts and worries and obsess about my fears. But God showed mercy and delivered me from my troubles anyway. God's relentless goodness eventually won my heart. I stopped blaming Him for my trials and started to trust Him earlier on in each trust battle.

We won't trust perfectly until we see Jesus face to face. Yet God covers all, and sustains and sanctifies us. Sure, we can kick ourselves around the room for the times we felt overwhelmed instead of serenely sailing through our latest trust battle. Or we can lift our eyes and begin to thank God for His inexhaustible faithfulness.

- Thank You for letting me run to You and for welcoming me every time.
- Thank You for letting me bring my little heart to You, filled with fears, worries and resentment, and for patiently helping me to sort out my feelings.
- Thank You for giving me a plan of action and a promise to claim.
- Thank You for friends who come alongside to pray for me and who bring me honey when I need it the most.
- Thank You for all the things You do over and under, around me and within me that bring me through each battle.
- Thank You for giving me rest and renewed strength after the battle.
- And thank You for bridging the huge gaps in my trust with Your grace and mercy.

We end this study of trust training with an exploration of praise and gratitude. You'd think this would be easy. Obviously, we should praise God. But this topic is full of pitfalls. If we celebrate well, it gives us a solid exclamation point at the end of our trust battle. It lets us savor the moment and sets us up in a beautiful way to face the start of our next trust battle. If we slide by this phase – and the vast majority of Christians do exactly that – it robs us of tremendous treasure we could have gained from the trust battle we just finished.

We will discuss three big ideas in this chapter that will help us to end a trust battle on the right note and set the stage for our next trust battle.

We already talked about the first big idea in the introduction. Gratitude helps us to escape from our last trust battle, just like *the weaver's path* helped Navaho weavers to escape from their creative endeavors. This isn't a new idea to us. We spent two chapters learning how to rest and recover after the battle so we could move on to the next challenge without any baggage. We can be so hard on ourselves. So the first big idea is to let go of any lingering regret about how we did in this trust battle and shift our focus to gratitude. Maybe like this.

> **#1 Gratitude** – The weaver's path: Father, thank You for letting me learn more about how to trust You, and thank You for not insisting on 100% perfection. I look forward to rising to new challenges in the days ahead, knowing You'll continue to help me.

CELEBRATION: WHY IT'S HARD TO PRAISE GOD

Let me share a story and then let's unpack it. It illustrates some reasons why we might have trouble praising God. A few years ago I helped start a short-term prayer group to pray for a national election. We met for two months before the election, and one time afterward.

As a group we prayerfully discussed what to ask of God and came up with twelve God-sized, God-honoring prayer requests. My prayer partners were seasoned prayer warriors who knew how to pray up a storm. I admired them a lot and still do.

Unfortunately, they were of the old school that zooms right to requests and doesn't spend much time on worship. I tried to encourage us to praise God for at least five minutes before we launched into our prayer requests. A few times they lasted a whole five minutes, but usually they would forget themselves within a minute or two. Oh, well.

On Election Day, I watched with delight as God answered all of our requests. It was a huge prayer victory. I couldn't wait to meet again and have a fabulous time praising God for going far above and beyond what we had even requested. We gathered in high spirits. I suggested that we praise God and thank Him for each answer to prayer.

A few people thanked God. And then things stalled. Someone mentioned some bad news they heard on a news program. Instantly, the group shifted away from praise and thanks. People started to gripe about the most frustrating and daunting aspects of the political process. The whole idea of praising God fizzled. People left that meeting feeling like underdogs in a never-ending losing struggle. Oddly enough, they seemed much more comfortable in that underdog, defeated position than when I was trying to get them to thank God for answering our prayers.

I pondered that meeting for many months. What had happened? Why did they find it so hard to praise God? Why did they feel more comfortable in an underdog, losing position? What could I have done differently? What could I learn from that story?

That story showed me that Christians have, by and large, not learned how to celebrate the victories at the end of trust battles. Many of those precious people had served as missionaries in difficult mission fields where the successes were few and far between. They spent most of their time in that powerless role as lone voices in the wilderness. So it made total sense that they had grown comfortable in that role. They didn't know how to handle victory.

However, we aren't always slogging it out in the middle of a trust battle. Every once in awhile, we win. And clearly, we have not learned how to celebrate those victories. **I began to see that an essential skill to cultivate in the school of trust training is this skill of celebration.**

In the U.S.A., we celebrate Thanksgiving one day a year. We associate it most closely with the pilgrim's first winter. We tend to toss in all of our reflection and gratitude on that same day. But many families go through the motions of thanksgiving in a pretty half-hearted way. If we even remember to do it, maybe we go around the table and say one thing we're thankful for, while the rest of the family continues to munch on turkey and green bean casserole. Then we go back to the real business of the day – football.

By contrast, the Jewish calendar had far more celebration days and encouraged much more individual participation. They had a feast for celebrating the Passover. The meal itself reenacted the story, salt water for the tears, the bitter herbs for sorrow, the unleavened bread for the haste of the journey and four different cups each recalling something else.

They spent a whole week camping in booths to remember God's faithfulness during their wilderness wanderings. They exchanged gifts on Purim to recall Esther's bravery and Haman's defeat. During Hanukah, Jews light candles to remember the miracle of the oil that didn't run out for eight days.

By contrast, other than communion and baptism, Christians celebrate mainly by attending a church service. We sing songs about Jesus' birth at Christmas and about the resurrection on Easter Sunday. And we have no concept of reenacting or celebrating great personal victories.

Our church started a ministry to skaters. Recently, God poured out blessing in the form of unexpected and positive publicity and several business endorsements. We had a great day. Over a hundred skaters showed up and four skaters accepted Christ. How much did the whole church celebrate? Someone announced the results in church and we broke into spontaneous applause that lasted maybe ten seconds. That's it. That was the extent of the church-wide celebration. Then we moved on to the next item on the program.

Ten seconds of celebration can't possibly balance the memory of months of back-breaking work and thousands of invested dollars. If we don't adequately celebrate our trust battle victories we will look back and remember only the struggle. We'll think of ministry as hard, not as rewarding. We'll remember waiting and waiting for our answer to prayer – but not the answer.

It's even more dismal when we think about our personal trust battles. When was the last time that we spent even one day devoted to celebrating a huge victory in one of our trust battles?

When we go through a crisis we beat the bushes to add our prayer request to prayer chains from here to China. But how many of us go back to those same prayer chains to report the answer to prayer? The answer: not many.

I'm not suggesting that we belabor things. In many ways a trust battle is like a love story. Usually the hero and heroine must overcome many hardships and obstacles to get together. We're willing to sit through two hours of a movie or read four hundred pages because we're waiting for that payoff scene when they finally run into each other's arms and have that big kiss. It doesn't have to be a long scene. But if it isn't there, we feel cheated.

In the same way, a good solid celebration gives the perfect closure to all the hardships and obstacles we trudged through in our trust battle. If we skip over celebration we cheat ourselves and the people who prayed for us. Let's consider three ways to celebrate.

Stop and savor the victory. Don't let the moment slide by. Healing prayer taught me this principle. In healing prayer sessions, people often start out in deep pain. Then Jesus shows up in His wonderful way. Sometimes a person will hear that He forgives them. Or He speaks a truth that shatters the pain of a lie that has enslaved them. I've learned to stop and let them sit in that moment and enjoy the presence of Jesus. They need to savor that sensation of knowing that Jesus has forgiven that heavy sin that shamed and tormented them. It helps to savor the freedom, the peace, and the sweetness of His presence. We may go on to other areas in that prayer time, but savoring the moment seals that piece.

I've also gotten into the habit of making time afterwards to relive the prayer time with Jesus. I can't talk to other people about what happened. It's confidential. But I revisit it with Jesus, savoring the blessing. *I love what You did. I love watching You work. I never would have guessed You would go in that direction. Thank You for showing up when I cried out for help and direction.* It's a sweet quiet moment between fellow-laborers. Sometimes He applies things He spoke to them into my life as well. Abba Father takes pleasure in His children and enjoys bringing us into a deeper intimacy. *"The joy of the LORD is your strength"* (Neh. 8:10). I savor His joy. He gets such a kick out of setting the captives free!

Share the good news. A good rule of thumb here is to go back to everyone you asked to pray. Send out a follow-up praise report to those prayer chains. Whose shoulder did you cry on when you went through the battle? Let them know what happened. If the whole church prayed for you, ask to give a short praise report. If the non-Christians at work know what you went through, let them know how God worked things out.

After God lifted David out of the slimy pit in Psalm 40, and set his feet on a rock, that victory overflowed into praise and testimony. *"He put a new song in my mouth, a hymn of praise to our God. Many will see and fear and put their trust in the LORD"* (Ps. 40:3). *"Come and see what God has done, how awesome His works in man's behalf! …. Come and listen, all you who fear God; let me tell you what He has done for me"* (Ps. 66:5, 16).

Celebrate praise anniversaries. I think those Israelites were on to something when they sprinkled so many celebrations throughout their calendar year. Why can't we do the same? I regretted not knowing my spiritual birthday. So we paid attention to the date each of our sons accepted Christ. We celebrated their spiritual birthday with a birthday cake, a gift and a retelling of the story of how they accepted Jesus. It was a fun way to build faith.

Back in Chapter 9, I mentioned that painful church crisis. For several years, Jim and I marked the anniversary of that church discipline meeting by treating the elders and their wives to an evening out. We remembered God's faithfulness to our church and expressed our appreciation to each other once again.

I'm still in a trust battle regarding the surgery last year. My surgical incision hasn't healed in one spot. It's easy to mark the month anniversaries – nine months and counting. But the Lord cautioned me to take care which date I celebrate and why. I could remember August 25th, the date of my first surgery, or September 1, the day I almost died before my big surgery. It's okay to mark those days so long as I mainly remember them as the times God saved my life.

But the date I really need to watch for hasn't come yet, and if I'm not careful, I could miss it. The best date to celebrate will be the first day I don't have to change the dressing on my incision because it has completely healed. On the anniversary of that date I want to throw a party and invite all the friends who prayed for me and helped me during this long recovery. If you're around, you can come. We'll eat cake and share glory stories about God's goodness.

Celebration needs to be the capstone, the final scene, the closure to our trust battle. We need to celebrate our trust battle victories intentionally and publicly. Don't let the moment pass without stopping to thank God. And put on your thinking cap to figure out a fitting way to remember the anniversary of an especially huge victory.

#2 Celebration: Thank You for working wonders in my life. Help me to notice and to savor today's victories. I love watching You work. Show me how to celebrate this victory and how I can brag on You to others.

FAITH REMINDERS

I made my first faith reminder after studying the story of Joshua leading the Israelites across the Jordan River. The twelve stones seemed like such a simple idea. Anybody can pile up some rocks. Yet I saw their value to stimulate faith. That rock pile reminded them of a major offensive trust battle that their generation won, unlike their parents who failed the same test. It started a conversation. *What do these stones mean?* The question stirred up faith in the Israelites when they retold the story and in their children as they heard the answer.

I studied that story soon after that traumatic church discipline meeting. I felt so grateful to God, and I could tell that if I didn't set up some kind of twelve-stone reminder I might easily forget. So I wove a simple tapestry showing twelve stones on a hillside. It hangs above our kitchen table. It reminds me of the "Wilson* Crisis." (* In my head I say their real name.)

That began my collection of two kinds of faith reminders. One kind reminded me of times I saw God do something wonderful in our family story. The other kind made some kind of statement of faith. In these reminders, I showed two things side by side: what I felt to be true (usually something sad or discouraging) and what I affirmed by faith to be true.

My first statement of faith used the promise in Psalm One, that the righteous is like a tree planted by water. I did a double-weave tapestry that interwove a layer of red fabric with a layer of rainbow stripes. On one side, I showed what I felt to be true, that I was a red tree (full of pain). I felt like God was fulfilling His promises all around me but not in my life. On the faith side I showed God fulfilling His promises in me, even though I couldn't see it at the time. On that side the tree is rainbow stripes against a red background.

That rainbow tree hung on my wall for fifteen years before what I felt to be true merged with what I affirmed. Meanwhile I chose to believe God in spite of all evidence to the contrary.

Someone gave me a blue ceramic angel just before Zach deployed to Afghanistan. It sat on the fireplace mantle as my statement of faith that God would protect our son. Now that Zach has returned, it sits there as a faith reminder that God answered thousands of prayers for our son.

I counted seventeen of these faith reminders scattered throughout my house in various stages of fulfillment. Honestly, sometimes I forget they're there. You know how it goes with stuff you see everyday. But there is a cumulative effect of five woven statements of faith, three woven praise reminders, one pile of river rock, the obsidian, the ceramic angel and the bear in the car, one plaque of my life verse, three paintings that remind me of God's faithfulness even during my turbulent childhood, and my floor loom. They remind me that gradually over the years God has fulfilled every one of His promises. God has been relentlessly good to me.

When I started writing this book I thought it would be nice to include stories from other people about how God had helped them through their own trust battles. It mystified me when so many mature Christians drew a blank. If they could remember anything, they usually remembered crisis stories that happened long ago. Why couldn't they remember any day-to-day trust battles? We all go through dozens of them.

How come I was full of stories? You know by now I struggled a lot learning how to trust God. For years, trusting God was a topic of bafflement for me, not expertise. So, why could I remember God's faithfulness to me? A big clue comes from these faith reminders. I remember my own stories because something on the wall or on the mantle reminds me. I am surrounded by a great cloud of witnesses.[2]

I encourage you to begin this habit. Your faith reminders don't have to be any more complicated than piling up twelve stones. Buy a knickknack that captures what you want to remember. Let it flow out of your personality. Write a song or a story. Frame the safety pin that your baby swallowed or a sliver of windshield from that accident you survived. Create a statement of faith that juxtaposes what you feel and what you believe, and watch God turn it into a trust triumph. Make it odd, so someone will ask what it means. And remember. Remember.

> **#3 Faith Reminders:** Father, help me think of ways to remember what You've done for me. Give me creative ideas to keep the evidence of Your trustworthiness always before my eyes. Show me how to make reminders that prompt conversation, so I can tell my story again.

COMMENCEMENT DAY

Well, fellow students in the school of trust training, here we are at the end of this study. I hope you have learned how to bend the bow of bronze that David talked about in Psalm 18. And that you have seen God begin to train your arm for battle so you can scale a wall and stand on the heights. We've introduced some new tools to help you to analyze your trust battle and to know what to do next. I hope this study has given you new insight into your own life story and that you have been able to see God at work even in your more painful episodes.

We can always trust our heavenly Father. I hope you have begun to see more clearly that in every way our Abba is the best of fathers. Let the following words of encouragement go deep into your spirit.

Abba consistently does what He says He will do. He always keeps His promises (II Cor. 1:20). He loves you unconditionally. He has loved you since before the beginning of time and He will never stop loving you (Jer. 31:3).

He sees you as a unique person. He knows what you will say before the thought enters your head and He understands all your little quirks and habits (Ps. 139:3, 4). Yet He completely accepts you (Rom. 15:7). He knows you and takes delight in the "you" He has created you to be. He knows your life story and He always knows what needs to happen

---

[2] Most of the stories that found their way into this book have come from brave women in the three Bible study groups that studied early versions of this material. Thank you, my friends! It has given me great joy to help people to remember their own wonderful stories.

next. His plans always have your best interests at heart (Jer. 29:11). He weaves together every part of your story, the happy days and the sad ones, and works everything together for good (Rom. 8:28).

Perhaps some of the people who should have loved and protected you didn't keep you safe. But you are always safe with Him. *"The eternal God is your refuge, and underneath are the everlasting arms"* (Deut. 33:27). He always takes good care of His own (Ps. 23) and He will make it His business to meet every need you will every have (Phil. 4:19).

You may have run into people who condemned you and set a standard you could never reach. But, even though God is perfectly holy, and He sets the highest standard of all, yet He has made a way for you to please Him. He has torn down the barriers that keep you from enjoying His presence. He paid the costliest price, the death of His dear Son, so you could have peace with Him. He gives you the righteousness of Jesus and the empowerment of the Holy Spirit so that you can truly please Him. And when you mess up, He gives you a way to make things right. When you confess your sins, He freely and fully forgives you (I Jn. 1:9) and forgets your sin (Jer. 31:34).

When you come before Him bruised and battered, He never condemns you (Rom. 8:1). Instead, He will always sit with you and listen to your grief and give you new hope. He'll never walk away (Heb. 13:5). He'll never give up on you. You can always trust Him. Always.

This is the God I have tried to share with you in this book. Isn't He wonderful? Doesn't He just take your breath away?

I debated about whether to talk about what to do between battles. It's true that sometimes we find ourselves in those dull days when nothing much is going on. But I decided against it because I remembered that picture of trust we explored in Chapter 5, the picture of that little girl walking hand in hand with her daddy. In this book we have tried to tear down the defense mechanisms and wrong conclusions that keep us from being that happy little girl.

What I pray for you is that your trust in God will become more confident and more childlike. And whether your day is calm and boring, or whether your walk takes you through the valley of the shadow of death, that you will gladly place your chubby little hand in His and let Him lead you home.

FACE TIME WITH MY TRAINER

The Bible is full of examples of faith reminders or memorials. These took many forms. For each of the following passages, skim the background story to summarize what the people were supposed to remember. What faith reminder was set up in each story or passage?

#1 The faith reminder: (Joshua 4:20)
Was to remind people about… (Josh. 3:14 – 4:24)

#2 The faith reminder: (Gen. 9:13)
Was to remind people and _____ about… (Gen. 9:8 - 16)

#3 The faith reminder: (Gen. 28:18, 22)
Was to remind people about… (Gen. 28:10 – 22)

#4 The faith reminder: (Exodus 28:9, 10) [on the High Priest's ephod/vest]
Was to remind people and _____ about… (Exodus 28:9 – 12, 29)

#5 The faith reminder: (Exodus 15:1 - 18)
Was to remind people about… (Exodus 14:19 – 31)

#6 The faith reminder: (Esther 9:17 - 19)
Was to remind people about… (Esther 8:11 – 9:1)

#7 The faith reminder: (Gen. 32:32)
Was to remind people about… (Gen. 32:22 – 32)

PART 2: Questions & Reflection

1. When you read about *the weaver's path,* did it remind you of any tendency within yourself to be critical of your efforts to trust God instead of encouraged by progress you have made learning to trust God? If it did, would you be willing to lay down that sense of self-condemnation?

2. Write down one new idea about how to trust God that you tried out because you read this book. Thank God that He will give you new opportunities to practice that idea in future trust battles.

3. Have you learned this "essential skill of celebrating?" What have you already learned to do? What ideas would you like to try out?

4. Think back to your most dramatic or most recent completed trust battle. What is it? Do you think you have celebrated it enough? Spend a few moments savoring that victory before the Lord. Can you think of a way to celebrate it more fully or more intentionally? What ideas did you get?

5. Does your family have any personal celebrations that reenact some answer to prayer or memory of God's faithfulness? If so, what do you do? Did this chapter give you any ideas of things you would like to celebrate together more intentionally? If so, what?

6. Walk around your house and look for faith reminders. What did you find? If you found a lot, good for you! Keep doing what you're doing. If not, think of one faith reminder you could put together to remember some significant answer to prayer. If possible, bring one of your faith reminders to Bible study. Be prepared to share the story behind it.

7. What did you find to be the most encouraging or intriguing idea in this chapter?

EXTRA CREDIT: *When you have some time, go back and review all four of the chapters in this section, looking for the tips that you found most helpful to deal with this after the battle phase. Write a **"Note to Self"** checklist of things to remember or things to do the next time you find yourself in this season **after the battle**. Include the four **Trust Gate** statements, found at the beginning of these four chapters.*

God is most glorified in us when we are most satisfied in Him. ~ John Piper

Karen's Story

Fifteen years ago my only daughter, the youngest of six children, developed some health issues that hinted of leukemia. Of course this was a terrifying possibility that would bring any parent to their knees. It did. Renee was only a year old at the time. She had five older brothers, ages 6 to 9, still innocent and impressionable, a perfect time for God to work and He did.

We have a little cedar box that sits on top of our fireplace mantle. We picked it up in a souvenir shop during a family vacation to Las Vegas, of all places. The box is just big enough to hold a small stack of 3 x 5 note cards. Made of red cedar, fitted with a hinged lid adorned by two small gold praying hands, it contains several pieces of paper with prayers of thanksgiving and petition that my young sons scribbled out during that time. As young adults my sons are not walking with the Lord.

I reviewed the items in that prayer box recently. Back then our oldest son, who has given us the most heartbreak, wrote some really great requests that have since been answered. He asked for God's guidance regarding some work decisions, health for my mother-in-law who had two bouts with breast cancer, healing for Tommy's wrist, Dad's hand, infection in his leg, about Grandpa's job, and one praise "that my sister didn't have leukemia."

Even though I had not used the box in many years I decided to reinstate it. Now, fifteen years later, I have added some of my own little pieces of paper that hold my current and nagging requests. Having this little cedar box with the praying hands in my home is my faith reminder that God answers prayer, and that in time He will answer my prayers for my adult children that they will once again make Jesus Lord of their lives.